Playing with Water

Playing with Water

Passion and Solitude
on a Philippine Island

James Hamilton-Paterson

NEW AMSTERDAM
New York

Copyright © James Hamilton-Paterson 1987.

First published in 1987 by
NEW AMSTERDAM BOOKS
101 Main Street
Franklin, NY 13775

Twentieth-Century Lives paperback published in 1994.

Library of Congress Cataloging-in-Publication Data

Hamilton-Paterson, James.
  Playing with water.

  Bibliography: p. 281
  1. Philippines—Description and travel—1975
2. Hamilton-Paterson, James—Journeys—Philippines.
I. Title.
DS660. H36   1987   959. 9'046   87 -21993
ISBN 0-941533-10-7 (cloth)
ISBN 0-941533-82-4 (paper)

This book is printed on acid-free paper.

Printed in the United States of America.

for
Jane Stephens

Armour, poison, camouflage and a hidden way of life are very common in reef dwellers. In the labyrinthine world of tunnels and crevices, where soft-bodied and vulnerable creatures hide, specialised carnivores amongst the crustaceans, worms and molluscs roam as well, living their whole adult lives there and continually stalking their prey. This largely concealed world within the reef is an extensive, vital and thriving one.

Charles R. C. Sheppard
A Natural History of the Coral Reef

It is a convention of Western thought to believe all cultures are compelled to explore, that human beings seek new land because their economies drive them onward. Lost in this valid but nevertheless impersonal observation is the notion of a simpler longing, of a human desire for a less complicated life, for fresh intimacy and renewal. These, too, draw us into new landscapes. And desire causes imagination to misconstrue what it finds.

Barry Lopez
Arctic Dreams

I am a man of curious temperament who prefers on most occasions to be dumb. It is a selfish trait in my character which I try to master. Whenever I walk or travel I am generally silent; I like to observe the scenery closely, and sometimes I lose all consciousness of myself in it. The old proverb 'Two's company . . .' does not hold true in my case; it would be difficult for me to find any second person who could walk with me and would be happy if I did not talk.

Chiang Yee
The Silent Traveller

Contents

Acknowledgements

My debt to the people of *baranggays* Kansulay and Sabay is boundless. This book stands as only a small piece of evidence of their affection and disclosure over the last seven years, their generosity of spirit which to a large extent has reshaped my life.

The convention holds that in such circumstances it would be invidious to single out individuals for special mention. Of course this is true. Of course, also, there have been certain people with whom I have spent appreciably more time, people who have withstood for far longer the foreign habits and linguistic fumblings of an alien who is also a writer. I should like to think that if ever I had adopted an interrogative mode with any of them I had not done so for anything so unmannerly and banal as mere information.

This being said I would like to extend all love and thanks to Noel Historillo and his family, to Siyo and Josefina Mabato and their family, to 'Ding' Pampola and his family. For their help at *baranggay* council level as well as for their friendship I thank Clodualdo and Julie Lauresta and also Nick Malvar. Finally I owe an especial debt of gratitude to Maria Historillo whose late husband Embing I, too, affectionately mourn.

A word of warning to them all: 'Kansulay' and 'Sabay' are real places only in the sense that 'Akenfield' was real. Neither they nor the people in them are imaginary, but all have been passed through an imagination. Locations, characters and events are often composites. The originals of the 'Sorianos', for example, live in another province altogether and have no connection with Kansulay. So those who think they infallibly recognise people, places or even the author in this book will be mistaken. On the other hand there is nothing in these pages which is not as true as I am able to make it.

Introduction

In the middle Sixties I lived for a year in Libya during which time I made several friends among the personnel of the huge American air base outside Tripoli, Wheelus Field AFB. Two of these were a couple in their late twenties. He was an engineer from Dayton, a large gentle fellow besotted with fast cars. His wife was a Filipina whom I first met when I stopped to help her change a wheel. From that incident a friendship grew which effectively ended, as such things often do, with the expiry of our respective contracts. One night we were sitting in a car I had bought with her husband's help, a 1956 Ford Fairlane with tinted windscreen and automatic transmission. We were not far from Base, on the edge of semi-desert across which drifted the scent of orange groves from some Italian's plantation. She looked up at the silhouette of a date palm and said: 'We have coconuts at home, not dates. Every day my father makes beer from coconut sap.'

The wistfulness, the 'we' told me she was not talking as a naturalised American. The way she spoke hinted at an unknown rurality, a place of great difference whose language I had heard her use to her children but which I knew annoyed her husband because it sounded 'native' and excluded him. With that interest which exiles often feel for each other I wanted to see her real homeland, wherever it was her father made coconut beer. While we were talking the F-4 Phantoms were taking off thunderously in pairs, their afterburners and navigation lights floating up over the boundary fence into the soft North African night. They were bound for bombing ranges and training grounds deep in the desert, for they were practising war. The great build-up had come: everyone was going to Vietnam. *Re-Up Now!* was the slogan printed on the inside cover of the book matches sold on Base. Re-Enlist! Don't be left out! Don't miss victory! Think of your career! I owed my Fairlane to this injunction which had been obeyed so briskly by the car's previous owner he had let me have it for $100 the day before he was posted back to the States.

A few years later I finally made it to South-East Asia myself. I was a journalist, a freelance writer, a drifter. In the grip of that monstrous magic war I visited nearly all the principal countries of the area, certainly those in some way actively drawn into the Vietnam conflict. The notable exception was the Philippines. I knew that President Magsaysay had committed the Philippines to the covert war in Vietnam; I knew that President Marcos had reneged on his own campaign promise and had committed the two thousand-strong Philcag. I knew about the US bases in the Philippines, about fabled Manila and R&R, and I knew about a girl's father who made coconut beer. Yet I never went there. Always something cropped up.

Ever since then that country has had for me something of an air of unfinished business: unfinished in 1979 when I finally went for the first time and unfinished today in my regular commutings, my residences which now take up more than a third of each year.

PART ONE

Tiwarik and Kansulay

1

The places a writer writes are always somewhere else. He may describe a journey, a foreign land; but no matter how faithfully he disposes his rocks and trees, his tokens of difference and the humdrum exotica he comes to love, certain delinquent breezes drift through landscape and writer alike dishevelling things at their root. One of those breezes is no doubt what John Clare overheard beneath Salters Tree:

> The wind in that eternal ditty sings
> Humming of future things that burns the mind
> To leave some fragment of itself behind

while another, less mystical but no less mysterious, blows up from the writer's own past and causes everything in his eye to lean imperceptibly in a peculiar direction. A third breeze is the one which in a sense blew this book into being by carrying me unerringly if wanderingly on a journey which began at a scarred school desk and ended thirty-three years later on the island of Tiwarik.

One June day in 1953 aged twelve I sat in a classroom and drew a map. I deduce this because by some fluke a single exercise book of mine survived all the burnings and sheddings of clutter and turned up last year. It is full of references to the Coronation of that month as well as badly done French exercises and pencil drawings of aeroplanes and islands. When it so unexpectedly came to light I turned it in my hands as if it were a teacup dredged from the *Titanic*: a trivial object made weighty by the mere fact of having survived a long-ago disaster, the very implausibility of its physical presence having me turn its pages with a disbelief almost bordering on reverence. On the

penultimate page I found a sketch which made me sit
straight down on the floor and stare and stare. For there on
the ruled paper was a drawing of Tiwarik, an island in the
Philippines I had first set eyes on only two years before.
True, the map was not correct in every detail, but in its
main features – outline, peak, a grassfield – it was probably
as good a map as I could have produced at that age had I
been drawing it from actual memory.

This discovery made a silent concussion in my life. For a
week I was bemused. It was like a twist in the plot halfway
through a novel which suddenly makes new sense of events
and at once invalidates one's presumed understanding of
the narrative. What had happened? Had I had some
psychic prefiguring of a place I was destined to visit? Or
once having invented somewhere had I doomed thirty years
of my life to discovering its analogue?

There is a third possibility which I now think is the most
likely explanation. The shape I drew was not dreamed up
that far-off June day but had existed for me since infancy in
a rudimentary way. Maybe if I had been asked to draw a
picture of my own mind I might have imagined it looking
something like that – a damaged poached egg with uplands
and downlands and immense bluish distances. From that
earliest moment when its outlines wavered and turned
milky and became firm I was not in search of a physical
counterpart for it, not even unconsciously. But when I
stumbled on one called Tiwarik Island there was an instant
of profound recognition. Later the chance finding of my
boyhood doodle showed me a shape I had once seen so
clearly and had later forgotten.

The effect of finding this sketch has not been to make the
intervening years an irrelevance or a pilgrimage, a waste of
time or a purposeful trek. All that has happened is that
everything I have done, all the countries I have lived in and
passed through, now seem congruous and coherent. That is
all. There is no meaning to it but it is consistent in some
way. I could not have planned it or done differently. It was
neither willed nor unintended. To have discovered that, at
least, produces from nowhere a billowy sense of freedom. It
is as if until that day came when I was to crouch alone on

Tiwarik with monsoon rains drumming on my back and deliver myself of a great dying worm I could never have been truly carefree.

I first set foot on Tiwarik during a mis-timed fishing trip in 1983 when a friend and I pitched a wind-whipped tarpaulin on the beach and huddled beneath it for two days and nights. The island was for us merely a blob of land amid a churn of waters, our view of it occluded by grey squalls of rain – actually the tail-end of Typhoon Litang – and reduced to the stretch of coral shingle on which we crouched. Behind us amorphous shrubbery rose steeply to unseeable heights. We were wet through and cold, for the tropics can be cold in a way which has little connection with thermometers. The temperature does drop, of course, but the perceived cold is as much the effect on the spirits of being denied the usual blaze of noon, the languid air drifting through the walls of one's wicker hut and up between the bamboo slats of its floor.

We would leave our tarpaulin to haul the boat higher up the coral strand until the tips of its outriggers nosed into the thorns at the cliffs' foot. Then we hurried back to shelter and threw ourselves face down once more, scrabbling absently into the coral fragments, sifting branches, twigs, chips of sponge and brain from the millions of infant conchs no bigger than mauve seeds whose inhabitants had long since predeceased us. We passed many listless hours examining this graveyard by day; by night the incessant clicking of hermit crabs and their plucking at our toes and hair reminded us there was no flesh which this shore might not absorb. A moment's inattention and it could digest us too.

On the second occasion I arrived alone and for months, during which Tiwarik Island was reborn and became alive for me. The day was blue as I crossed the strait, the water blue and purple beneath the keel. Clear under the silent glass into which my paddle dipped as into lacquer lay the squares and minarets, arcades and loggias of the sea floor

which linked Tiwarik with the mainland. Had I known it
then I would have been terrified, enchanted, that one night
in the future I would make a reverse crossing down there,
working amongst its spires and crags and over its plains
and stinging pastures by the light of a torch and with a thin
polythene air-hose stuck in my mouth.

Of course the island could not assume an identity before
it had acquired a position. My memory of that first visit was
of a lost and roaring beach nowhere in particular. The view
then had been what any stranded tourist might have seen.
But a traveller works to let a place into his imagination (or
maybe to chip it free) else he becomes weary and discour-
aged by an endlessness of mere location. Even on that first
unpromising landfall something of Tiwarik's significance
must have struck me. It was after all an inveterate childhood sketcher of imaginary islands who had watched the
South China Sea fling tons of coral chips into the air and
tried to light driftwood fires in the lee of the boat to cook
rice. Even that partial view from beneath the flapping
eyelid of a tarpaulin had been enough for the boy within: he
had recognised from a series of glimpses an entire terrain
and the man without had had no choice but to return. The
jungle, the cave, the pathways later to be dotted by his feet
across the grassfield, all were already there in his head.
Conventional child, though, he had once pencilled bea-
cons on all his islands' high points to light when the speck
of a schooner appeared at the universe's rim. He could not
have guessed that in later life rescue was the very last thing
he would want; that on the contrary in his desire to be lost
he would long to light an anti-beacon of enchanted kindling
whose invisible smoke would envelop his world and render
it transparent. The island's image would waver and be gone,
leaving the captain of the distant schooner thoughtfully to
push together his telescope and enter 'mirage' in the ship's
log.

Tiwarik lies little more than a mile off the coast, immediately opposite the fishing village of Sabay which from the
seaward side appears as a straggle of huts on stilts half lost
among the coconut groves. In front of them on the stony
beach boats are drawn up, each of which in time becomes

identifiable so it is possible on any particular day to read the beach and know who is doing what. The island is uninhabited (uninhabitable, practically, since there is no water) and tiny, being about a quarter of a mile across. But its size on a map – and I have never seen a map large-scale enough to mark it – would be deceptive, for it rises to a peak off in one corner which cannot be less than four hundred feet above the sea. There are no beaches, merely that one shifting coral strand on which we camped, maybe a hundred yards long and facing the mainland. The rest of Tiwarik rises from gurgling boulders more or less vertically up volcanic cliffs of black rock. From one quarter there is a steep sweep of coarse tall *cogon** grass up to the forest which caps the peak. Seen from the strait on a breezy day the sunlight goes running up and up through this wild grassfield. It is the same effect as with young hair and similarly afflicts me with deepest melancholy, affection and pleasure.

The island is normally used by fishermen in transit. The locals from Sabay and from Sirao and Malubog a few miles up the coast stop there and cook their lunch over driftwood fires lit between lumps of coral. They sit and repair their spear guns and lie up under the thin shade of the thorn bushes to snooze away the noon. Some of Tiwarik's transients are from much farther afield, coming from provinces and islands in the south, Visayans speaking motley dialects and burnt black by the sun, journeying for weeks on end through the archipelago and selling their catches as they go. These are nomads whose boats have a subtly different cut and the left-over scraps of whose food are red with chili. They may sit out a storm on Tiwarik or appear at dusk to drape their nets among the corals. By dawn they have gone, leaving only the long scars of their keels.

At any time a pair of dots might appear in the middle of the empty glitter, insectival as the minute twitch of paddles becomes visible. They land for a while then depart leaving blackened stones and several fish-spines. It comes to seem less volitional on their part than that the sea which sweeps through the strait has carried them here and borne

*See Glossary, p. 267.

them off again; that Tiwarik stands like a rock in a stream past which the water scurries, depositing small flotsams which eddy momentarily in freak pockets of calm before being carried away. This is not entirely fanciful; it is tempting to gaze across at Sabay only a mile or so away and think how swimmable it looks. In fact it is, but you must choose the moment. The current becomes very fast when the tide is going out. It is one of the place's minor deceptions. When the sea is flat calm and the sun seems to hold everything in slow motion you can identify the distant figures on the beach opposite – Arman's red T-shirt as he carries a pail from water's edge to his beached boat *Jhon-Jhon* – and the sense of being able to talk to him is so strong it suggests that a mere few minutes' pleasurable exertion could annul that small gap which separates you. As you were swept off down the coast for the thirty-hour drift through the archipelago to Luzon or – missing that – the rather longer trip to Taiwan you would have ample time to reflect on the un-novel idea that calm tropical surfaces can conceal fatal business.

As I prepared to become a resident of this beautiful and significant rock, this divider of a current, a sense of austerity and impermanence exhilarated me. I knew I had reached somewhere, while of course reserving the right at a later date to deny ever having felt anything so portentous. After all I was already accustomed to the living conditions I would find there: I could hardly expect to learn anything new about leaky grass roofs and driftwood fires, the mildew and charcoal which bit by bit give all one's few possessions a familiar and uniform colour. But to live alone in the middle of the sea would be something different. Hitherto I had always had a great bulk of interior at my back, mountains and forest patched with the orange scars of primitive agriculture receding into hazy distances with the sea comfortably confined behind a ruled margin of coastline. From now on the terms of living were to be drawn by water.

That first sunlit morning of my return to Tiwarik, instead of doing the useful and practical things I had intended I simply climbed up above the beach to the grassfield and lay there looking down at the map of my new world the corals drew beneath the blue water. In the drowse, the half-shut eyes against the glare, the mind deceives itself. It sets itself adrift and feels the island move. The current coursing past Sabay towards Malubog and far Kansulay is no current but a wake. The sea is still; it is the island bearing the mind off on a voyage of its own with its sole inhabitant, its Crusoe.

Because I have never seen Tiwarik on a map I do not know if the island has an official name. Presumably it must, for the American Navy charted these waters most thoroughly when they supplanted the Spanish in 1898 as the Philippines' occupying colonial power. Then in 1942 the Japanese took over forcibly, occasioning General MacArthur's famous promise to return which he made as he stepped off Corregidor Island in Manila Bay into the light surface craft which carried him away to another theatre of war. Maybe the Japanese forces gave Tiwarik a name of their own during the three years of their occupation. Yet it seems unlikely they would have bothered with so insignificant a blob of land: there was much else to do besides work out Japanese name-equivalents for all seven thousand one hundred-odd islands in the archipelago. In fact I do not wish to know the official name of this place. I am afraid that discovering it would damage its identity. It would be like trying to adjust to an old friend who had suddenly changed his name by Deed Poll.

It is the locals who call the island 'Tiwarik', which in Tagalog is 'upside down'. The reason for this is not clear unless it is that from its seaward aspect the lump of hill with its awry cap of jungle appears oddly top-heavy and might fancifully be imagined turning turtle one stormy night, trapping its undetermined load of snakes, insects, tree-lizards and single majestic pair of sea-eagles among brush and branch under tangled foam. This apart, 'Tiwarik' might have been some long-dead fisherman's nickname or a corruption of a forgotten original word not necessarily even Tagalog, since the influence of Visayan dialects is everywhere in the language the locals speak.

Tiwarik is, come to that, the name they give to the razor
fish, *Aeoliscus strigatus*, which can be seen in small groups
among the corals, its delicate snout pointing down and the
three-inch blade of its translucent body with single dark
streak switching and tilting in the drifts of current. The
balletic precision with which all members of the group act
as one is remarkable, as is their agility for fish holding their
bodies vertically in the water. Only if really chased or
threatened does their angle change, heads coming up a few
degrees for short evasive bursts. This *tiwarik* is not eaten
except in a special circumstance. Dried and then powdered it is slipped into someone's drink and becomes a
potion guaranteed to make the drinker fall in love.
Everybody smiles but knows it works, so its potency is
much feared and *tiwarik* is resorted to only by the most
desperately unrequited: as with all spells one can never be
absolutely sure that the fulfilment of a dream will in the
long run turn out to have been wholly a good thing.
Certainly it does seem to potentiate the effects of alcohol. I
once saw a girl become stertorously drunk after (allegedly)
only two small glasses of *tuba*. After a night's vomiting she
awoke next morning with a headache and said dolefully she
had been magicked with *tiwarik* and that she knew who had
done it. She was inconsolable: the man in question was not
her fiancé, whom she would now have to renounce in favour
of the lout who had long pursued her and had now won her
by underhand means.

Surely the upside-down fish is powerful. With a flimsy
body quite possibly toxic and quite possibly not, maybe its
posture invests it with a sympathetic magic to express a
condition which crosses a large cultural barrier: that of
being head over heels in love.[1]

For five years, on and off, I had been living up in the hills
behind Kansulay, another tiny village some thirty miles
along the coast from Sabay and Tiwarik Island. It is yet
another oddity in my relationship with the island that I
should have been living so near it for so long without

suspecting its existence. But thirty miles is very far in a province which has yet to build a tarmac road around its coast.

As is the way in the Philippine provinces, where everyone seems to know everybody else, I already had an introduction to the *baranggay* Captain at Sabay. It turned out he had long known of me since until a year ago one of his daughters had taught at the elementary school in whose catchment area Kansulay lay. The presence of a strange *'kano* living on his own in the woods was much gossiped about and in consequence Sabay knew of me before I knew of it. One day I walked down to the village and caught the first of a series of battered jeepneys which took me along the rutted coastal road for hours past anonymous villages among the palms, *barrios* and *baranggays* whose names I never learned, to ever-smaller provincial townships where I changed jeeps: Bulangan, Malubog, Sirao. After Sirao the road vanished into a track ridged with grey–black lava, on the left the slopes of the massif rising above the groves and bearing its rain-forests into cloud, on the right the mobile blue of water. And there suddenly Tiwarik, placed just so on the other side of its strait the better to be seen entire.

I was received in Sabay with caution and some astonishment. The smaller children ran away and hid behind their mothers' legs or under the huts. Everyone smiled with unease. This changed to warmth and interest as soon as I had named names, spoken the magic syllables and identified myself as one encompassed – no matter how peripherally – by the huge and complex circle of family, friends and acquaintances spreading outward from Sabay. So this was the *'kano* from Kansulay? And he wanted to live on Tiwarik? Well, why not? But on the other hand, why? There was nothing there, no hotels or discos, no white beach, not even fresh water. Captain Sanso was baffled, not unreasonably, since I could give no explanation he would find plausible, especially not when I told him of the miserable and involuntary two days I had already spent there. I just thought I'd go back for a bit, I said, and did he have any objection to my putting up a temporary hut in which to live?

Captain Sanso did not own Tiwarik but he thought this a
fine idea. Already, I knew, he was working out the spin-offs
of my presence for his impoverished village. I in turn had
decided how much in default of rent I should contribute to
the local economy. For the equivalent of twenty pounds he
would provide me with materials and labour with which to
build my house. Until its completion I was, of course, to
stay with him. I was deeply grateful and observed that the
village pump needed renewing, something which I was sure
would happen in the near future if things worked out well.
So a deal was struck inside his own sitting-room on whose
naked cement-block wall was nailed a Lions International
plaque reminding the reader of the Captain's subscription
to the principle of mutual help. He sent his bodyguard/
factotum off to the village shop for a bottle of ESQ rum with
which to toast ourselves. Within an hour of arriving in
Sabay I was in the middle of a drinking session.

Filipino drinking habits have a strange, intense air to
them. In Europe, even when the drinking is done by the
round as in an English pub, people do it mostly at their own
rate and from their own glass. In the Philippines a single
glass circulates, refilled as each drinker downs it at a gulp.
When a spirit like rum is drunk a glass of water is on hand to
act as a 'chaser'. To see a table of people knocking back
slugs of spirit with a shudder and at once follow it with a
slaking gulp of water makes one think of an ordeal rather
than a convivial custom. The drinking takes on an insistent,
almost brutal rhythm. It is as if people were drinking to
become drunk, as they usually end by becoming. What
makes the custom more bearable is the code which insists
on a plate of *pulutan* on the table: any kind of food which
people can pick at with a communal fork or spoon. This
may be no more than salted peanuts or it may be a stew of
chicken or dog, vegetables done in coconut milk, fried fish.
There is also a formula with which a timid or queasy
drinker may skip a round by nominating a *sakop* or proxy. I
have frequent recourse to this system; remarkably few
nominees ever decline the extra burden.

Captain Sanso introduces me to his youngest brother
Arman, to Totoy and Danding and Silo and Jhoby and

Bokbok. The names, at once familiar and unmemorable, slide through my rum-fumed brain. I smile until my face aches answering question after question. How old am I? Where is my companion? Why am I not married? Why do I want to live on Tiwarik? Is there treasure there? Where did I learn Tagalog? I answer some of the questions, duck others. The affability is tangible but under it curiosity runs with a hard and knowing edge: nobody does anything or is anything without good reason. From long experience I am conscious that these strangers are likely to become daily colleagues and friends. I try to make a dignified impression but merely look stupid because I keep forgetting who is who. Occasionally when I glance up from the arena of the table, now covered in puddles of rum, water and stew at which flies are sipping, I notice faces pressing in at the doorway, children's curious faces, an old man with a stick. A group of girls bursts into giggles behind me so I turn and to their embarrassment ask them what they are *really* laughing at. Eventually one of them covers her mouth with a hand, a girl of saintly beauty who asks nearly inaudibly if I am related to the actor George Hamilton. I tell her that I expect I am if one were to go back several centuries. For some reason this excites the girls still further.

In the late afternoon I strike a drunken deal with Arman to hire a small *bangka* from him, something in which I can paddle back and forth between Tiwarik and Sabay and the next morning, clear-headed and seen off from the beach by children, I head towards the island with the early sun rushing down on all sides. I bound over the wavelets; my arms seem tireless with excitement and well-being. I am filled with the overwhelming desire to do something, there is no telling what.

That was the day I never did do anything but climb up to the grassfield and daydream. It was not until the following day I made a serious effort to acquire Tiwarik's geography. Until I knew what the island contained and how it lay I could not begin to build my house. Site is everything, of course; I had freedom of choice since I had no claim on the land and the hut I was going to put up would probably not outlive the first serious typhoon.

A position at the foot of the cliffs near where my companion and I had taken shelter had always been a possibility but I now found that the coral strand had changed its shape and position. Before, there had been a steep bank of shingle with a declivity which filled with water at high tide and became a hot lagoon before draining away at low tide. This bank had now vanished and with it the recurrent lagoon. Instead there was a spit of shingle jutting from an altogether narrower beach like a miniature port with its jetty. I soon realised that the whole coral bank shifted constantly, changing its shape with nearly every tide and during severe storms practically disappearing for a while as violent currents swirled it away. Yet it always returned. Consequently landing on Tiwarik was seldom the same twice running. I took pleasure in this feature. No sooner had the blackened corals, clumped together as supports for fishermen's cooking pots, become familiar in their disposition than the sea scoured the beach clean of all sites taking with it the carefully-collected piles of fish spines (otherwise a menace to bare feet), cigarette packets, frayed ends of nylon twine and crisp curls of abrasive skin torn off a species of trigger-fish known locally and mystifyingly as *bagets* or 'teenager'. All in all, then, this strand was clearly no place for a house.

The ideal site, of course, was somewhere on the uplands where with the sea-eagles I could command the bright gulfs to every horizon. However, my scrambles up the cliffs had made it clear that convenience would have to take priority over enchantment: the thought of carrying water daily up to the top of the island was too forbidding. It was going to be enough to fetch it from the mainland in the first place. Eventually I compromised and chose a spot above one end of the strand where a prehistoric fall of Tiwarik's black igneous rock had left a ledge, roughly level and some twenty feet deep, covered in shingle and a scatter of topsoil on which grew a succulent mat of vines. From here I could gaze across the strait to Sabay, watch the comings and goings on its beach or let my eyes travel up the great slopes of the cordillera behind it, past the tilted prairies of *cogon* to the gorges of scree and observe the veilings and vanishings of cloud about the peaks. Even the most unsatisfied eye might not grow restless at such an outlook.

I gave Captain Sanso money, he gave orders. Soon *bang-kas* laden with helpers landed on Tiwarik's strand and the cliffs echoed to the sound of bamboos being split. Several sorties to the top of the island were organised and various stout timbers borne back from the forest, dripping with sap which dangled snot-like from their cut ends. Apart from nails, tools and nylon line little had to be brought from the mainland. The one exception was palm fronds for weaving the panels of *sulirap* with which to cover the bare bones of roof and walls. The lack of a single palm tree on Tiwarik was fairly conclusive proof that the island had never been inhabited. There was not even a wild papaya tree, which surprised me for I had already noticed the steady traffic of birds across the strait and would have imagined they had long since brought in their gut the seeds of this ubiquitous tree. The papaya, like the dragonfly, is unchanged from its fossil predecessors: a survivor which seems to suggest it is perfect in some way not immediately apparent (certainly not in the boringly-flavoured, cheesy-textured fruit it bears like skin tags round its bole).

At the end of three days I have a simple house and several new friends. Arman, perhaps by virtue of being the Captain's brother, has about him an ease and openness which makes him accessible. He is immediately recognisable as a fisherman for instead of the uniform Asian black his hair is a strange layered thatch of brown with auburn tints and streaks of authentic dark blond. Only the fisher-boys' hair goes this colour, and only if their fishing is full-time and involves diving. Ordinary fishermen – generally the older ones – who sit in boats for hours with a hook and line remain largely unaffected. Arman also has a diver's physique: deep chest and shoulders, slender waist, powerful thighs. At twenty-seven he must be past his physical peak but is still probably the fittest of all Sabay's fishermen because – as I discover later – he alone does not smoke.

Arman has brought with him his young cousin Intoy, a boy in his earliest teens whose hair is also tawny. Intoy is unabashed by my foreignness, is openly curious about the whim which has brought me here, wants to know if I have any *komiks* with me. He laughs a good deal and leaps about like a sprite. Once he discovers I am a spear-fisherman we have an earnest discussion about techniques and trigger design which brings Arman and the others over. This of all subjects seems to be the great ice-breaker. We might have had one of those knowing, raunchy conversations about sex which occasionally serve but I would not have been treated as seriously as I now am when I describe my own method of waterproofing a cheap Chinese flashlight for night diving. Intoy asks about the commonest species of fish 'where you come from'. He means Kansulay and makes it sound as remote and vague as England (which everyone in the provinces here thinks is one of the states of the Union).

When finally my house is complete Intoy walks all round it appraisingly and announces he will live here. Arman promotes this idea.

'You can't live without a companion,' he says.

I tell him I am quite used to it. Everyone is aghast so it is clear they had none of them believed me at the drinking session that first afternoon.

'At least you must have a *bantay*,' somebody suggests.

I don't think I will need a guard, there being no-one else on Tiwarik.

'Ruffians come here,' says Arman darkly. 'All sorts of criminals from the Visayas. They may land one night, creep up and cut your throat.'

I say I think I am more likely to die several fathoms down than have my throat cut.

'Well then, you must have a servant. Intoy here will keep you in firewood and bring your water across each day. He's a good boy, quite strong.'

'About as strong as boiled seaweed,' agrees another boy whose job has been to cook rice for the construction team. Amid laughter he and Intoy tussle and roll down the shingle spit into the shallows where they thrash like porpoises. I know why Arman is insisting. It is partly that my payment of his cousin for houseboy duties would bring some money into the child's family but also it is a matter of propriety. That a visitor – especially a *'kano* – should live nearby unaided is not correct. I recognise this; it has taken me several years to establish my independence at Kansulay in a way which merely makes people rueful and indulgent rather than giving offence.

I explain I am a writer who needs time and space to himself. Intoy comes up and dumps himself down, dripping and panting, and says I can send him away whenever I wish. And in fact at that moment I want them all to go away and leave me alone with my new house.

After a bit they do and I lie on my stomach on the floor and watch from the open doorway their little flotilla nearing Sabay. The bamboo strips beneath me smell sweetly of sap, their curved surfaces still green. It will be some weeks before they turn to blond and the nail heads to black.

Later that same evening after eating fish and rice by firelight I go back down to the shore to clean the dishes in the lapsing wavelets, scrubbing them round with handfuls of gravel. They remain coated with a film of cooking oil which will stay constant day after day. The moon is dazzling, awesome, full this very night. A drift of silver molecules washes away from the dishes; it will be broken down by marine organisms within the hour.

First nights in strange places can determine how one sees them for ever after. This is my second first night on Tiwarik and it is determined not to efface itself into just another tropic nocturnal. The puddled mercury which is the sea, the wheeling galaxies above and the island at my back full of the metallic sheen of leaves give off the strangest light. It is as if everything generated its own luminescence which the moon then gathers into its brilliant lens. Tonight the moon stimulates the secretion of light from things much as the regular use of a well encourages the flow of its own waters. The whole of Tiwarik, that irregular bulk of rock and soil jutting from the ocean, must be veined with capillaries along which this light leaks and gathers and overflows from cliff face and grass blade and forest canopy. The serenity and clearness seem a good omen and I go back up to my hut with the dishes, content to be here.

But the omens are not yet finished. I blow out the lamp

and lie on the floor listening to the slow breathing of the sea below, the crickets in the grass around the house. From nearby a gnarled rattling prefaces a tree-lizard's loud repeated call as it names itself in Tagalog: *tu-ko, tu-ko, tu-ko* ... American troops in Vietnam knew it as the *fuck-you* lizard but the sound of these syllables is less close, maybe saying more about the namer than about the named. As I lie pleasurably adrift I become aware of change. The noises are fewer, the chirpings and chitterings are stilled, the harsher cries from up in the island's cap of jungle die away. Even the sea sounds muffled. I open my eyes. Instead of brilliant chinks of moonlight in walls and roof there is nothing but dark. I get up, open the door and fumble down the bamboo steps into a weird landscape.

The moon is still there but it has nearly gone out. Its flawless disc is still flawless but now dulled to a deep amber as if seen through a piece of broken beer bottle. A primaeval shiver runs over me, a sense of having been transported a million years forward to the Earth's end. It would be more bearable if the insect noises were still confidently asserting independence of such cosmic trivia. But nothing moves. It is as if all living creatures together with the sea and the wind were silenced by the desolation of total eclipse.

As the minutes go by and the Earth is held motionless I recover sufficiently to reflect on my amazing good fortune. At school there had occasionally been announcements that everyone could skip the class immediately following Break in order to watch a partial eclipse of the sun, and we had dutifully gathered outside with pieces of smoked glass. But it had always been cloudy, that grey overcast which conspires to shield Britain from the universe. After half an hour we all trooped in again, not even particularly disappointed and with our faces smeared with lamp-black. Yet here, my second first night on Tiwarik, there is a total eclipse of a full moon in a cloudless sky which lasts for nearly two hours. It is astounding.

Certainly it is easy to understand people's terror of eclipses, even of the moon. When on my ninth birthday I was given an Army signal lamp I was enraptured by it and its accessories but became wary of one particular piece of equipment. This was a pair of rubber goggles with deep red lenses for use when a red glass cap was fitted over the lamp, enabling the signaller to send without the beam giving away his position. The first time I went out into the garden on a sunny day wearing them I was seized with a complete terror of the apocalypse. The world had turned to blood. The tennis lawn and the cherry trees were an alien landscape, as it were Mars at war. Above it flamed a terrifying sky, raging with billows of incandescent gases. I was suddenly the last person alive anywhere, my parents and sister and dog a million years dead on another world and I condemned to witness the destruction by fire of the universe before myself being consumed. I tore the goggles from my face and surfaced into warm June sunlight. Beneath its reassuring lambency the lawn was now a luscious green while in the sky overhead the boiling smoke had changed to mild heaps of drifting cumulus. Thereafter whenever I wished to frighten myself I would walk about wearing the goggles, sweat pooling in the rubber eyecups, partially emboldened by the spicules of white light leaking in at the side of the lenses through ventilation holes.

Now on Tiwarik I note the reddish tinge of the eclipsed moon and understand the biblical references to its turning to blood. At the same time, of course, I am captivated by the oddness of the phenomenon. It is so rare and completely unexpected I do not know quite what to do with it, so after walking about experimentally for some time I come back and sit on the top step and watch the first splinter of silver as the untrammelled disc begins at last to slide clear of the shadow. No doubt about it, this heavenly body has nothing whatever to do with the bleak satellite on which men landed nearly twenty years ago. That was merely the Earth's moon. But the brilliant mandala whose last segment of tarnish is wiped clear as I watch, this is The Moon. The Moon is an act of the imagination and will remain forever unmarked by the cleated boot-prints of interlopers. And from all around crickets burst back into song, the *tuko* calls, the sea breathes again. Now I can go to sleep.

2

When living in Kansulay I commute between the forest and the village by the shore, a distance of only a mile or so but quite enough to tinge things with the remoteness of the interior, the *bundok*.

The path from Kansulay takes me up a valley whose floor was long ago planted with coconuts. Eventually the path forks off, crosses a stream and climbs steeply up one side among wilder vegetation until it comes out on top of the bare ridge where my hut stands. From here I can look down into the valley without at any point being able to see its floor, only the dense crowns of the palms, infinite sprays of tail-feathers and the coconuts' amber gleam. Invisible beneath them are two huts several hundred yards apart. One is the house of my nearest neighbours, the Malabayabas family, whom I see almost daily. The other is a ruin and stands by the stream amid the pink–grey pillars of the coconuts. There with several pigs once lived Lolang Mating.

Lolang Mating was undoubtedly an exceptional person by rural Filipino standards in that although she was a grandmother (as the honorific implies) she chose to live alone, away from her family who were down in the village. She was visited daily by her son and her grandchildren who are now muscular teenagers with feet calloused from climbing trees. They came as much to feed the pigs as to see Granny but to all appearances relations between them were reasonably cordial. However, the old woman refused absolutely to go down and live with them. Probably nobody had actually pointed out that it was unseemly for a woman in her seventies to live on her own in the semi-wilderness: it would have been superfluous in a culture where the principle of family proximity is supreme and where the question *Who is your companion?* is habitually asked whenever any activity such as eating or sleeping or merely walking home is proposed. In a land where nobody does anything alone from choice, where a bamboo floor densely packed with sleeping bodies is considered far preferable to luxurious solitude, where superstition as much as a lack of torch batteries keeps people indoors after dark, Lolang Mating chose to live alone in her hut.

In time I became friendly with her as I went to and from the village for necessities such as rice and cooking oil. When I fetched water from the stream nearby in the mornings I would see her, patched skirts tucked up around bowed mahogany legs and with her grey hair done up in a bun skewered with a bamboo sliver, standing in the current washing her wrinkled chest. With instinctive decorum we would pretend not to have seen each other as I suddenly found something to interest me a little way off. Then she would call out a greeting and I knew I could come and lay my plastic jerrycan on its side in the stream and chat. By now she would have changed her blouse and be washing yesterday's with an end of bright blue detergent soap.

Those early morning conversations with Lolang Mating became a feature of daily life at Kansulay. We would sit on the low boulders with our feet in the current while the palm fronds combed the sunbeams as they fell on the water and butterflies floated on the air. She would talk and unaccountably fall silent, absently raising and lowering the blouse into the water, sometimes beating it with a paddle hacked from the spine of a frond as if to emphasise an inward voice. She would talk to me of the Japanese Occupation, of the anti-Japanese guerrillas, the Hukbalahap, whom she had once sheltered. She would talk of pigs and murders and Mayor Pascual who had been born without an arsehole – she knew because as the midwife she had delivered him – and the doctor had had to make one with a pair of scissors. She talked about the days when you could shop for a family with a single *piso* and when almost anyone who wore a proper hat spoke Spanish. She knew a lot about the magicians who lived in the hills of the interior and grew whole fields of *tintang luya*, black ginger, that rarest of freak plants whose properties were immensely powerful. Black ginger would help you cast spells or defend you against *mananang-gal*, vampiric horrors which squat in the rafters of huts where there are babies or the sick and let down their tongues to suck out the sleepers' livers.

'So aren't you frightened here at night?'

'Of course not,' she said.

'But believing in all those spirits and dwarves and ghosts and vampires?'

'I believe in them of course, I often see them. But I'm not scared of them. They'll never trouble me. They never have and I'm an old woman now. As long as I'm in my place they'll leave me alone because they know it's my place and not theirs.'

'Like dogs.'

'Like that.'

She told me she was born here. I looked instinctively towards her hut, its legs and walls bleached silver with age. It was not the house she had been born in, of course, but it was on the same site, as she explained on another occasion. To Europeans accustomed to nostalgia about old things Filipinos can sometimes seem strangely matter-of-fact about impermanence. In an architecture of light wood structures and grass or palm thatch, termites and typhoons between them make a fifty-year-old house an antique. Houses are quickly built and newness is valued as a sign that the family fortunes are on the up-and-up. A patched or sagging house speaks of poverty and low spirits.

Of the house in which Lolang Mating had been born not a trace remained but a blackened rectangular pit where she told me one of its four legs had stood. The original post-hole had been enlarged and was now used as a kiln for making charcoal from coconut shells.

'When I was born there were no coconuts here,' she said one day. 'This was all forest like up there where you live. We had a clearing where my father kept pigs. We found bananas and papayas in the forest and grew *kamoteng-kahoy* which we carried down and sold in the village. Then our landlord bought the land and decided to cut it all down and plant coconuts. I remember how ugly it looked, the

land burnt off and with tufts of coconut seedlings in rows.
Now of course it'll soon be time to cut them down and re-
plant them. They should have been re-planting all the time,
not waiting for them to become old at the same moment.'

This spot by the bend in the stream had always been her
place regardless of what vegetation came and went, and
about it she was not a bit matter-of-fact. She spoke of
Kansulay as if of some alien city, not as a small collection
of houses identical to her own a bare mile away by the sea
and lived in almost exclusively by her own relatives of
varying remoteness.

'Too much noise there,' she said. 'I couldn't live in that
house of Dando's' (Dando was her son). 'Children and cooking and drinking all the time, day and night. And I don't like
that electric light they want to put in. It hurts my eyes. Too
much light at night is harmful: you can tell because it
makes people look older, even the children. It does something to the skin. And when you go outside you can't see
anything for five minutes.'

A genuine solitary, then, recognisable at any time and in
any culture. The thought was not displeasing that I too
might end my days standing in a dappled stream at dawn
soaping my wrinkled chest and at night putting luminous
fungi in a glass jar to cast a soft radiance inside my hut. One
day Lolang Mating was found sprawled on the earth beside
her *kayuran*, the low wood tripod with a serrated flange
fixed to its beak used for grating coconuts. She was taken
down the track to the village and put to bed in Dando's
house. I went to see her a day or two later. She was ambling
about on her tough old legs but as if lacking a pig to feed or a
blouse to wash she could no longer remember where she
was going. There was talk in the family about 'high blood'; I
assumed a minor stroke. She seemed quite unimpaired but
there was a remoteness in her eyes that was new.

'They won't let me go,' she told me. 'They say I can't go on
living there, I might die there all alone.'

'I expect it's for the best,' I said ritually, but we both knew
it wasn't. She had been born there, why could she not die
there among the fireflies and the frogs and the crickets?
What was so special about having family faces stare down

at you and pester you with medicines?

'Lazy,' she said confidingly. 'They can't be bothered to come up the track and fetch me down to bury me.'

She made it sound a long way off to her land. It was obvious that had she lived in a world where one did not have to consider social rituals and pious custom she would have chosen to be buried there among the coconuts by the bend in the stream rather than in the cemetery at Bulangan where the salt sea breezes rotted the cement sepulchres and within ten years made them look sordid rather than venerable. She was cut off from the land of her death and quite possibly now at the mercy of an alien crew of territorial spirits. Each time I saw her she seemed more silent, more worn down with the sheer proximity of people.

'Take her home,' I urged Dando. 'Go on, even if it's only for a visit while you feed the pigs.'

And apparently he did, probably raising his eyebrows to passing villagers' unspoken enquiries with a mime of filial helplessness as his ancient mother walked back to her country. She was not allowed to do anything when she got there but sat once more in the doorway of her hut with her feet on the polished bamboo rung of the top step as she always had, looking out at the sift of sunlight into her glade and the lurch of butterflies in and out of the dapples. Dando and her grandsons bustled around grating coconut for the pigs, shinning up a tree to collect the bamboo flask of *tuba*. Now and again they glanced to where Lolang Mating slept the sleep of an old person after a long walk, leaning against the doorway with her head against the jamb. And when it was mid-morning and time to set off home for lunch they found she was not to be woken.

So they did cart her off down the track away from the fireflies and the frogs and in due time shovelled her into Bulangan. And there the salt sea-wind blows over her cement lid and the lizards run over the lettering carved with a trowel tip in wet mortar. And for many weeks afterwards I still approached the stream with caution out of sheer habit before going to lay the jerrycan on its side by the stones where we had sat. I would get back from the market in mid-morning and pass her hut and miss her intelligent gaze, for in the doorway now lolled the uncommunicative horny soles of a grandson as he snoozed.

Then I went away for some months and when I returned found Lolang Mating's hut canting and derelict. Her family had abandoned the site for it was more convenient to move the pigs and find another tree for palm wine closer to home. The roof had largely blown off in a storm and the slatted bamboo floor which had once been buffed by her bare feet was now black and spongy with wet, for the rains had come. In the mud nearby I found the ladle she had made for pigswill and took that up to my own hut where I still use it for boiling water. But it was not until I first passed her place in the dark that I found a strange thing. For there on a moonless night among the black pillars of this crypt Lolang Mating's hovel glowed softly. Presumably her habit of bringing luminous fungi into the house had seeded the whole structure with spores which, with the sudden coming of the wet season, had sprouted. Alive with yeasts her hut pulsed with cold energy while by day one remarked only a sad trapezoid of spars and slats.

It was not long before other people passing by at night noticed this and the predictable rumours circulated that the old woman had been a witch and that her familiar spirits or even her own spirit still haunted the spot where she had lived and died. The place was shunned, the hut fell down completely, and I was thought madder than ever to go on living at the end of a path which led through spookish wilds.

I went to Dando's on the anniversary of his mother's death even though I think he half believed I had helped cause it by overwhelming his better judgement. I went for the eating and conviviality rather than the prayers for her soul, which I had no doubt could take care of itself. Her grandsons had thickened with muscle and drinking; one of them had gone off to the town some miles away to work as a Petron boy, turning the handle of a petrol pump. Even the pigs had grown fat, roaming the foreshore at dawn to unearth the leavings of the villagers who decently waited until nightfall before defecating in shallow scoops in the sand, like turtles laying their eggs.

*

Only after she had died did I realise that throughout our acquaintance Lolang Mating had never once asked me what I was doing in Kansulay: a person of phenomenal discretion. Certainly when I first arrived I could not have told her had she asked. It dawned on me only gradually that she might have understood if I had said 'My father', since she was also living alone in the *bundok* because of her family and because of the person she was.

To explain it to myself, though, I would have to go back several decades and seven thousand miles to confront a few of those signal incidents which mark the trail leading here. I am old enough now to disdain the slow chronology of childhood and adolescence, most of it as boring to recount as it was to live through, and fix on a handful of events. I judge their importance to me in the way everyone does, by the manner in which they seem to echo down a life and go on appearing weirdly relevant and even influential in what one is and does. Drawing Tiwarik at the age of twelve was one obvious example of such an event. Another comes from a family summer holiday, that set-piece scene for so much collective friction in English family life.

This memory is of a particular skirmish in the protracted feud with my father which in retrospect seems to have begun the day he was demobbed and which lasted until his death in the week before my university Prelims. examination. We were somewhere in the West Country, having a picnic lunch on a beach. The day was warm, the Atlantic glacial. My younger sister Jane with her child's imperviousness to cold had earlier insisted on bathing, forcing at least one adult in with her to rescue her if need be from the green and pounding waves. I was sitting slightly behind my father, anxious not to be within his range of vision. He was slowly eating a tomato sandwich, gazing seawards as if at the fleets of ships he had always wanted to design in preference to a worthier career in medicine which presumably left the inner eye littered with nothing so much as corpses. Suddenly I saw the wasp which had settled on his sandwich and was busy in one of the doughy indentations of his last bite. I said nothing. I watched as without looking he took another mouthful and began his measured, irritatingly thorough chewing.

It was impressive. He spat out on the sand a bolus of goo flecked with red and yellow-and-black, itself shocking enough since my father was a stickler for table manners as well as having a horror of public scenes of any kind. My mother looked at him in amazement wondering what she had done wrong.

'Dammit I've been stung. Ow.'

'Let me have a look, darling.' My mother was an anaesthetist and had taught my father anaesthetics when he was a student at UCH just before the war.

'There won't be anything to see,' my father told the sand with his head between his knees. 'It's just damned painful.'

'Soft palate or throat?'

'God, woman, I don't . . . Sort of round about the uvula, it feels like. Oh,' he said, suddenly understanding. My mother had been thinking ahead. 'I don't think I'll obstruct. But it's swelling all right. I can feel a lump.'

We were a long way from the car which in turn was miles from the nearest cottage hospital. My mother persuaded him to submit to an examination.

'Ow,' she said in sympathy. 'Yes, I can see where it is.'

My father eyed her. Whatever the correct procedure should have been – such as running for the car – it was evidently too late now. He would simply have to weather it out. His voice was already hoarse and his breathing noisier.

'In the last resort you'll have to do a tracheo,' he told her. 'At least I suppose I couldn't be in better hands.'

'But . . .' my mother looked about her helplessly at the picnic things, at the jam-smeared spoons, the bakelite mugs, the thermos of orange juice. She picked up the bread-knife, a decent affair with a round wooden handle and a proper serrated edge.

'Come on you two,' she said to my sister and me. 'Daddy's going to be all right. You just go on down to the sea and play for a bit but you're not to go into the water yet, it's too soon after lunch.'

We left them willingly. Down by the foam which licked raggedly at the blotting sand Jane said:

'Is Daddy going to die?'

'Yes,' I told her with an elder brother's superior knowledge. She began to cry since she believed she was quite fond of him in the way children do. I was myself frightened by what I had done, quite rightly not bothering to distinguish between allowing something to have happened and actually causing it to have happened. We were both absolutely intrigued by the idea of the drama thirty yards away which we couldn't bring ourselves to turn round and watch: Mummy sawing away at Daddy's neck with a Harrods' bread-knife. After a tense five minutes, though, we could see her beckoning arm. The swelling was beginning to subside; beach surgery was not going to be necessary. I felt light with relief so perhaps I hadn't really wanted him to die either. (It was another ten years before he really did obstruct, this time lower down the alimentary tract, not from a wasp sting but from the pincers of the dreaded crab. Nor bread-knife nor all the glittering cutlery of St George's Hospital could save him. He was forty-seven, a scant two years older than I am now.)

Later that afternoon when the wasp business was all over my parents were lying like most other people on the beach in a kind of post-lunch torpor, soaking up the weak sun with that English fixity of purpose which recognises there won't be much more of it this year, next year, ever. I was sitting some way off making a corniche road with banked sand up the face of an outcrop of rock. Suddenly looking up at all those supine bodies it struck me they were already halfway sunk in sand. Supposing the sand were actually absorbing them as they lay dozing, that shortly there would come from all over the beach a series of soft noises, *flut! thoop! glup!* and I would look up to find it deserted of humans, of dogs, of parents, with only the faintest of outlines on the smooth surface to suggest what had lain there, like spoons allowed to settle beneath thick soup. I alone would survive ... I do not know much about Freud's theory of wishing one's father dead; I think my fantasy coming so soon after the wasp incident was very much to do with doctors. It is doctors who, above all, see themselves as survivors since it is their duty to minister to the ailing and moribund, and doctoring was in my blood.

Both my parents were consultants who were passionate founder-supporters of the National Health Service. Neither of them practised at home so there were no discreetly ringing doorbells and low voices or sudden gasps coming from behind the study door. Nevertheless the evidence for its being a medical household was plentiful. The magazines, advertising and – in those days – free samples of drugs which rained steadily on to the doormat six days a week were a part of it. Also a part were the anaesthetic machine and various accoutrements my mother kept in the cupboard under the stairs. The homes of schoolfriends I visited also had cupboards under the stairs but they were generally full of boring things like Hoovers and sewing machines and slide projectors. Nothing like as interesting as our cupboard with its gleaming equipment, all knobs and dials, the little cylinder of dreadedly-explosive cyclopropane, the bottles of waste ether and trilene which every anaesthetist of that era brought home for stain removals and putting down hamsters with tumours. There were blood-pressure machines and orange rubber bags and stethoscopes and catheters and old-fashioned glass syringes with rings to put the fingers through. By comparison my father's doctoring tools were feeble, consisting mainly of a rubber-rimmed knee hammer and about a hundredweight of file cards (he was doing research on Parkinson's Disease).

But it was not just the props: the medical ethic was plentifully there and, on my father's side of the family at least, fairly interwoven with the christian ethic of the Good Doctor as well. My father had been born of medical missionaries in China, like Mervyn Peake, and was sent back to England at a tender age to be educated at Eltham College where Peake also was, some four years ahead of him. My grandfather went on to be interned by the Japanese in China and tottered heroically through the war looking after his fellow-inmates of the camp. On his release he was a survivor, but only just. I remember him as an ill old man, very quiet and gentlemanly. His nervous system was being eroded by something irreversible; he died when I was about twelve. His nephew, my father's cousin, was a doctor; his son is a doctor. My father's younger brother my uncle is a doctor, so is *his* eldest son. My aunt was a pharmacist.

My mother was a black sheep, opting to be a doctor at a time when it was not ladylike for a girl who had been presented at Court to do anything as sordid as medicine. The medical ethic was strong in her too, the christian ethic vanishingly weak. She was something of a socialist in a devoutly Tory family (my grandfather was Conrad ImThurn, heavily involved in the Zinoviev letter affair of the 1920s). I grew up with her accounts of doing her midder in the Thirties in the St Pancras area, chiefly remembering her shock at discovering how the poor lived and her anger at herself and her class for electing not to have known. I especially recall her saying how common it then was to go into tenements north of the Euston Road and find the top floor inaccessible because the occupants had burnt the staircase for fuel. In such houses she would deliver the baby on sheets of newspaper (fresh newsprint being, apparently, remarkably germ-free) and tuck it up in one of the pulled-out drawers of a chest, there being nowhere else for it to go.

Actually my mother did have a great-aunt who was a pediatrician so she was not a complete loner in the profession on her side of the family. Nonetheless I honour the independence of her spirit. When I was growing up everybody except my parents took it for granted I would simply follow the family trade. But it was out of the question. I was already fighting my father: I could not have been a doctor had it been the last profession open to me. I made quite sure of this by failing abjectly in every science subject except Biology, which seemed interesting and neutral and which finally came to my rescue by allowing me to take up a place at university since I had ploughed 'O' level elementary mathematics seven times, then a school record for any member of the Upper Sixth and one which I would be proud to think remains unbroken to this day. It was not until my father's premature death partially released me from the obligation to be mindlessly contrary that I was able to exorcise the lingering medical ghost by working in St Stephen's Hospital, Fulham Road, where in all I must have spent nearly a year.

Kansulay has a water problem, relying for all fresh water on the stream which winds its way from the interior down past the place where Lolang Mating used to wash and where I still fetch my daily ration when I am living there. Further downstream it comes to where the coconut groves are more densely inhabited and finally flows through the village itself, under a shaky timber bridge and into the sea where it has created its own gap in the fringing reef off-shore. This stream is Kansulay's lifeline. Over the centuries it has eroded a bed for itself which is quite four yards wide and often more, but unless there is a sudden downpour in the distant mountains the water seldom fills it. Instead it meanders in a sub-riverbed within the larger bed, winding from rock to rock, pool to pool. Often there are wallows under the muddy banks in which buffaloes lie, their cool grey tonnage tucked into the curved recesses they have worn, muzzles resting on the surface, birds perched on their heads.

Upstream of Lolang Mating's old place few people actually live in the forest, as opposed to the groups who occasionally pass a night or two there while making copra from the furthermost coconuts. The water as I collect it is clean, kept so by leeches and by the little crabs, prawns and whelks which make nocturnal hunting trips (wading upstream with a pressure-lamp) a source of food. Sometimes one comes across a dead chicken or a loaf of buffalo turd but nothing to make one seriously doubt the water's fitness for drinking. Downstream from Lolang Mating's, however, it is another matter as more and more people use the stream for washing themselves, their clothes and their animals. By the time it has reached the village it must be carrying quite a lot of domestic waste; there is a steady incidence of gastroenteritis and worms, especially among the younger children whose habit of defecating in or near the water cannot much help.

The *baranggay* Captain there told me that all community development funds had been frozen by the new government: no projects were to be undertaken until either the national debt had been paid off or all local officers from the Marcos period had been investigated to find out what they had done with the money for similar projects in the past. Supplying Kansulay with drinkable water seemed rather more important than assisting international usury or national witch-hunting so I suggested to the Captain that if he could supply labour and technical knowledge I could probably squeeze the necessary finance out of friends and relatives in Europe.

Which was how I found myself one day walking in the woods not far from Lolang Mating's with a young Filipino graduate who had worked on the provincial government's water schemes in the days when there had been any. We were not expecting to stumble on an abundant source which could take the place of the stream, but it seemed to us that if we could find a steady spring we might pipe this down to the village to a series of stand-pipes where people could at least get their drinking water. They might still have to do their washing in the stream; and if they were unable to break their children's habit of crapping in it and drinking from it then natural selection would simply have to run its unemotional course and weed out the incurably brainless (there being nothing like low-budget good works for reducing one to a heartless pragmatism).

We encountered forest dryads, nymphs and sprites variously disguised as old men and women feeding pigs in a clearing, cutting a chicken's throat and digging up edible roots with a rusty crowbar. It was several hours before we came upon a hollow beneath a jungled hill which dripped and ran in a way which at once cheered my companion. After some loping about like a retriever quartering the ground for scent he announced we would have to dig a test hole to see if the flow of water justified building a proper concrete 'spring box'.

We returned to Kansulay to find men with spades willing to donate an hour or two's labour under their *bayanihan* system where everyone cheerfully chips in for a common project. There were plenty of volunteers, even a few cheerful ones, until we explained exactly where the spring was. All of a sudden people became unenthusiastic, looked at the ground or remembered other things they ought to have been doing. Tired and bitten I was swept by a churlish rage. I walked off to the river nearby where I pettishly threw stones at the piglets wallowing in the pools, indulging a savage inner monologue. *Typical. You take the initiative, get the Captain's okay, offer to scratch around for the money and spend hours tramping the jungle to find a bloody spring and you'd think after all that a couple of them might be willing to do an hour's work on it. I mean, who the hell's it for, anyway?* My *drinking water's fine; it's not* my *children dying of dysentery and worms. Right: they want to go on living like that, no problem. They don't want improvements, all they want is handouts. It's all the fault of the Americans fostering the aid mentality, that and those sodding charities. No-one can save the goddamned Philippines but the goddamned Filipinos and until they work that out they're going to have to go on living a hundred and fifty years in the past . . .*

And so on for quite some time. What was particularly disgraceful about this silent outburst was that it came as if from a reforming zeal I despise and which I dread may be in my genes. It seemed to put me firmly into that class of professional believers in Progress who must often have indulged similar passions of self-righteousness, whether they were Victorian social reformers tackling the rookeries of Tottenham Court Road, missionaries endeavouring to stop penis-eating among the Mbwele or Japanese soldiers trying to get a decent day's work out of British construction crews on the Burmese railway. Always there is that element of condescension, a disparity between doer and done-to whether cultural, educational, financial or racial.

Luckily there is no obligation on anybody to do anything for the right reasons, as the piglets discovered when I stopped throwing stones at them because there were no more left of the right size. In any case I was feeling better. The water expert was approaching.

'You were very wise to go. I think some of the people were ashamed in case you were laughing at them.'

'*Laughing* at them?' I say in real surprise.

'That's what I tell them. "James is very understanding," I said. "He never laughs at anybody." They know that but some are ashamed to you.'

'Ashamed.'

'Because of *nono*.'

And suddenly everything becomes clearer and it is my turn to feel shame. It was neither indolence nor feckless-ness which caused their change of heart, but superstition. The pantheon of demons, spirits and genii in which many of the villagers believe is vast: I do not think I have learned more than a fraction of it, and that fraction is merely a short list of names. Being able to identify spirits by name is but a beginning; what gives such beliefs their cogency and power is the mass of lore behind them, the myths and stories and inexplicable daily happenings which give them life. Each time I hear a new story I realise how ignorant I am of such matters.

Nono, then, are spirits whose characteristics seem to vary according to the places they inhabit although they may actually be of different varieties. They range from the reasonably neutral to the nasty: those associated with water as in streams, wells and damp places are reckoned the fiercest. This at once explained the men's reluctance to go to a part of the forest they anyway normally avoided and start attacking the *nonos*' residence with spades. That was simply asking for trouble, for displaced ghosts to light upon them. Certain other things began making sense. I had once been looking for wild guavas and chillies somewhat above Lolang Mating's place and, tired of crashing about, sat down by the stream to watch it for a while with my plastic bag of guavas at my feet. I am very easily entranced by water and must, watching its motion, have become motionless myself. In a short while Lolang Mating appeared wading slowly upstream, her torn dress bunched up in one hand as with the other she made sudden lunges into the water, coming up with small dark crabs she put in a plastic litre pot which had once held motor oil. She was talking out loud to herself, I presumed in the way most people do when engaged in something on their own.

'Damn you!' she said mildly as she bent down again. Clearly the crab had eluded her, only it hadn't for when her hand emerged it held a large specimen which she dropped into the pot where it scrabbled hollowly. But then she said 'Go away!'

She was not looking at me when she said this; furthermore she had used the plural 'you'. I had now left it too late to announce my presence. Embarrassed I sat without moving and hoped she hadn't seen me after all. Nor had she. After a moment she turned round, went back downstream and disappeared behind swags of dense greenery. Well, the old, I thought. Or we solitaries, perhaps; we're always addressing the people in our heads.

Weeks later I overheard a companion who was ahead of me jump over a rivulet and pause on the other side to light a cigarette. Before the scrape of match on box he said: '*Susmaryosep tabi nono.*' Seconds later when I caught up with him I did not ask him what he had meant but remembered the phrase since I had not heard the word '*nono*' before. '*Tabi*' meant variously 'edge' or 'to one side' and hence was used to tell someone to get out of the way. '*Susmaryosep*' was common enough, mostly as an interjection but usually with a hint of genuine invocation rather than as a mere expression of surprise (typically Filipino, of course, to call on the Holy Family instead of on something coldly cerebral like the Trinity). And now, of course, it made sense. Both he and Lolang Mating had been addressing the genii loci. Suddenly I began hearing everybody do it, which suggested that just as undersea creatures I don't recognise can remain invisible so speech I don't understand is often inaudible.

So there it was: Kansulay's water project seemed temporarily stalled for lack of diggers. At this point it became clear that not everyone was equally worried by the threat of *nono* and that a certain delicacy obtained in which nobody was mocked for believing. I was anxious lest the believers should feel that a foreigner with his natural immunity to such things would make fun of them and maybe even shame some of them into digging against their better judgement. In the event, however, nobody cried off for the simple reason that those who felt it essential took anti-*nono* precautions. Among effective charms were copper, salt, 'metal-shit' (i.e. swarf from a lathe), a kind of seaweed, incense, holy water and a cross made from a palm leaf. Several men, as they dug, told the *nono* to leave them alone but obviously felt secure enough with their charms to be amused when someone suggested that *nono* didn't understand Tagalog and that it would be better to address them in Latin like a priest. (*Nono* must have been apprehended and addressed differently before the Spanish came.)

In the event the test-digging was a great success. Not only did no-one fall ill but the expert said the water was welling up in sufficient quantities to merit building a proper cement 'spring box'. In short, the project was on. Would he, I asked, if he were in my position – in other words organising the funds – be as certain and as sanguine about it? Oh yes, he assured me. If lower down the pipeline we were to build a large collection tank which could fill up overnight, and if people could be persuaded to turn off the taps when they were not using them, there would be adequate drinking water for Kansulay. This was excellent news and we all returned mud-smeared and cheerful.

3

I wade on Tiwarik's upland through the wild grasses towards the patch of jungle where surely nobody has ever been nor goes today except to chop house-posts or pull firewood from its hostile and thorny fringes: my favourite place on the whole island because the hand of man has so evidently passed it by.

The type of rain-forest whose high unbroken canopy creates a gloom at ground level is often comparatively free of undergrowth. Not enough sunlight penetrates to encourage the growth of vines and bushes. But this patch of untouched jungle is not like that, mostly because it forms a cap on the island's abrupt summit which is exposed to storms and is irregular in its distribution of soil. Sunlight penetrates in shafts from all sides. The tangle of undergrowth is dense, reaching well over my head in places while in others needing only to be waded through but with due regard for hidden trunks rotted into fakes of sponge and mushroom which collapse and throw me into clumps of stingers. With a *bolo* I hack my way to the top for it is important to have visited every square inch of the island.

From the summit (whose exact location is not easy to decide: maybe I never did get there) there is no view at all. Splinters of blue light jab inwards from all over but it is impossible to say whether they come from sea or sky. There is a pungent smell of fresh paint from some plant I have cut. As I stand in silence the noises start up again, the crickets and tree-frogs and *tuko*s carry on their interrupted discourse. I wonder which of the massive trunks around me supports the sea-eagles' eyrie. I am immensely happy in my wild domain; it is like coming home.

Why? I ask myself as I slash my way out again. Why should it be like coming home? From where did I construct this landscape? Come to that, other than from English literature, where did I acquire any sense of landscape and place? In its near-unanswerableness this question merely throws up four separate memories which come to me as I regain the grassfield and the full glare of the sun.

The first, chronologically, is of Windlesham House, the private school in Sussex to which I was sent when I was nearly nine. Typically enough this was a substantial country house standing in its own grounds among the South Downs and cut off from the outside world by a long drive ending in a pair of iron gates. Equally typically I felt lost, homesick, bullied. Escape through the gates was impossible yet temporary escape via the farm at the back was not only possible but condoned. We were encouraged to go for long walks among those hills with their chalky scars, horse chestnut and beech woods, hummocks of grass littered with rabbit droppings, windy spaces and far-off glimpses of the sea. But what interested us was the spoor of war. The Army had used the area as a training ground in the Second World War which, when I first went to the school, had been over only four years. Behind them they had left countless unexploded smoke grenades now rusting through to expose a damp pinkish paste inside. We would collect the perforated metal tail fins of these canisters as well as live blank ·303 cartridges which could be found all over the place. We would bring them back to the school and, sitting on our beds in the freezing dormitories, lever open with penknife blades the crimped ends, pull out the wads and let the brittle cordite sticks cascade onto the blankets. In the two years I was at the school I collected many ounces of cordite in Stephens' ink bottles. We would explode the mercury fulminate caps with nails hammered into the base of the cartridges and set fire to cordite trails leading off across the floor among the beds. From the very first, I can say, my landscapes were associated with ordnance.

The second memory represents war of a different kind, the one with my father. Once again the occasion was a family holiday in the West Country, although it may well have been the same one since holidays tend to elide into undifferentiated scenes of squabbling and bad weather. We were possibly near Okehampton in our sagging grey Wolseley. I remember only the torrential rain, the irritable proximity of a family cooped up in a car with our breath misting the windows and the windscreen wipers' vain clack and slap. There was that clear sense of four individuals each asking themselves what they thought they were doing here: the dismay of two adults at being parents and that of two offspring at being, by the same token, children, all brewed up in evil weather and grim unspokenness. Finally the rain stopped enough for us to open the windows. Off the road to our right was a long valley whose windings were defined by a newly swollen river.

'Oh look,' said my father, probably quite privately to my mother. 'See how the river meanders down the valley.'

'Oh, *meanders*, does it?' broke in my hateful eleven-year-old's voice, heavily sarcastic from the back. 'How very *poetic.*'

My father was nettled, snappish.

'It's a geological word if you must know,' he said in a cold and tight voice. 'It's a technical word and I used it perfectly accurately. So it pays not to be ignorant if you're going to be so quick to sneer.'

He was very angry, perhaps because he *had* meant it in the poetic sense and suspected I knew. But for ever after – at least for the remainder of his lifetime – I experienced unease about acceptable ways of looking at landscape, refusing perversely to see anything pretty in Constable-esque pastures or, above all, in sunsets. I associated the whole conventional canon with a kind of grown-ups' unimaginativeness and even now I find it easy to avoid looking at meadows and sunsets, especially flamboyant tropical sunsets with the furnace colours and peripheral pastel tints. (A good many flowers, too, have abominable colours – all sorts of mauves and pinks – which perhaps look better to creatures seeing them at different wavelengths of light. It is hard to imagine a favourable position on the electromagnetic spectrum from which to view a monkey-puzzle tree.) Popular sights are, of course, matters of fashion, as are the various components of landscape such as clouds and soils which over the centuries go in and out of favour. My father was of his time.

The third memory comes from much the same year and is of my second boarding school, this time in Kent. It was here at Bickley Hall one June day in 1953 I was to draw Tiwarik in the back of a French exercise book. Once again an English country house, a not very distinguished eighteenth-century hall with one or two fine cedars outside its french windows. The grounds were large, much of the original park having been converted to playing fields, but a good deal of wooded bits remained, especially away from the main house towards the stables. These stables were built in a hollow square around a cobbled yard and entered through a gateway on the side opposite which a pretty wooden turret with a clock and weather-vane glittered on the roof. From this the stables were known collectively as 'Clock House'. Two sides of coach-houses had been converted into classrooms and the other two into a gym and a chapel. That the chapel had once been a stable was held by the headmaster to have some sentimental significance. Certainly its semi-circular windows had been left in their original shape and the iron tethering rings were still embedded in the walls. The windows had been set with modern stained glass commemorating the headmaster's name and his Cambridge degree but without, unfortunately, his likeness. Nearer the main house were a fine walled kitchen garden, partially made over into a grass tennis court, and the school shooting range which needed to have a policeman over on a bicycle to look at it since it was laid out across the drive in order to use the back of the kitchen garden wall as the butts.

What was odd about these grounds was that a screen of trees ran all the way around on the other side of which lay not the coloured counties but the leafy gentility and Stockbroker Tudor of Bromley, Bickley and Chislehurst. If one lay in the shade in an obligatory grey felt sunhat chewing squeaky grass stalks and talking dirty above the distant sound of cricket one could have been in the deepest of shires. And yet a few yards through that cordon sanitaire of elm thickets, hawthorn and elder the exploring boy came to a rusty iron railing and beyond that to well-mown lawns with circular beds of gladioli, bird tables and creosoted trellises. Since several of the boys at the school actually lived in the houses nearby there was of course no snobbery along gentility–gentry lines. All that happened was that certain expectations of exactly how houses should stand in relation to landscaped parks was set up so that for the rest of one's life one would instinctively know where to find the stables and the gardeners' quarters.

The headmaster, although not of the gentry himself, had about him an entirely natural sense of how life in an eighteenth-century park might go on. He used to stalk pigeons before breakfast with one of the school's ·22 rifles and when I became Captain of Shooting I sometimes joined him with the other. If nowadays it sounds odd that a headmaster and a boy wearing pyjamas should have been on the loose with Martini-action rifles shortly after dawn on the fringes of London suburbia I can only say it seemed entirely reasonable then and still does. I remember the headmaster stalking a pigeon and knocking it clean out of a yew while the bullet went screaming off over the roofs of commuterland. 'What an odd pigeon,' he said and then, 'Oh.' Later I heard him confess uproariously to the senior Latin master that he'd just shot the first cuckoo and ought he to write to *The Times*?

Some years afterwards I gathered the lease had run out, the bulldozers had come in and this little island of prime real estate had been obliterated, the rising tide of suburbia rushing forward and closing over it leaving, apparently, mock-Georgian houses with coach lamps on either side of their front doors. The Hall, Clock House, the Pavilion and all are no more. I hope the developers left some of the finer beeches but I don't suppose they did.

And the last memory I have of a formative landscape is of that outside Canterbury. Every so often the boys of the King's School (who were more or less forced to join the CCF) were marched in their borrowed khaki out of the Precincts through the Mint Yard gate and up to the Scotland Hills for training with the Buffs. To explain why at fourteen I was frightened of these outings it is necessary to

remember that in the mid-Fifties one's whole school career
was blighted by the thought of National Service. All over
the world there were real wars being fought in places where
the British still had interests and several boys I knew were
killed or badly injured in Malaya or Aden or Kenya, flying
Lancaster bombers against the Mau Mau and leading
jungle patrols against Communists. It was still only ten or a
dozen years after the Second World War and all the Army
instructors like the school's RSM had seen real action and
believed their task was to turn boys into men as quickly as
possible. Outside the Cathedral Close and the Precinct
walls lay a horrid, brutal, khaki world. The Buffs' barracks
lurked on its hill. At night the soldiers used to come down to
brawl and drink in town and one boy in my dormitory used
to climb out of the house and over the wall to join his
National Serviceman cousin in the pub over the road. Often
after his return the dormitory reeked of beer and Senior
Service smoke and vomit.

So it was quite possible to have spent the morning practising Weelkes, Mundy or Gibbons and that afternoon to
dress in thick khaki and march out of a safe and cloistered
world into the clutches of the professional Army. With the
school band blowing and banging away at our head we
would march in a long column up the road through decay-
ing Tudor streets (today no doubt restored and prettified
beyond bearing) while the thudding of the drums would
bounce back off the house-fronts, off little tobacconists'
with their bottles of Tizer and forbidden copies of *Reveille*
and *Health & Efficiency*, an echoing *thud*-thud for each
beat. Then the band up ahead would turn a corner and its
sound at once be cut off so that we were left with the sudden
naked percussion of our marching boots. And all the time
we were going slightly uphill, drawing ever further away
from that reassuring civilian heap of pseudo-Edwardian
clothing we had left piled on our desks. Then turning in at
the barracks the sentry-boxes, the whitewashed kerbs, the
brilliant red fire buckets, the stencilled letters everywhere,
another self-contained world with its own signposts and
bus service, policemen and cinemas.

'You're in the Army now!'

The mirthless grin on the cruelly-shaven face before it split into that terrifying parade-ground wail cut off by an explosive consonant.

'*Get* your fucking legs apart you 'orrible lot. You've got nothing to drop, you're not women. Though I've got my doubts about one or two of you. Oh, *comedian* am I?'

The collective glare personally interpreted by each boy in the squad, rigid with terror.

How silly it all now seems that we delicately nurtured little rulers of tomorrow should actually have felt aught might have befallen us. But we did and for as long as it lasted the square-bashing reduced all horizons to the wall of the nearest clapboard hut. It always ended in time for us to be marched off into the Scotland Hills to a landscape used exclusively for military manoeuvres and which in consequence looked as if it had been designed from the beginning with this in mind. When we had done our Bren-gunning, which I liked and was good at, we went up to the top for grenade-throwing and lectures.

It is the lectures which come back now most vividly. Not the content, of course, although I can still remember back-bearings and how to call in fire on a given target. It was the hours spent sitting on those bare hills in gathering winter dusk and the rooks flying down into the city below with its cathedral standing like a cool grey toy in the sunset. The particular quality of the chilly and deepening sky, the pinkish clouds, the slow and angular birds bending and unbending their way all stood as a pastoral bulwark against the uniform, the boots which rubbed, the idiotic talk about reinforcements and covering fire and the lecturing officers themselves who would take off their caps to scratch their heads and suddenly become ordinary bald and greying men looking forward to their tea. On one of these occasions I wrote my first sonnet on the inside cover of my Certificate 'A'pt. 1 instruction manual. I would like to pretend I can no longer remember its first line but I can:

'Twas there I sat, on heather-tufted mound,

it went. It would be nice for any writer to claim he had been

precocious. Alas for that. Or even truthful, since I seriously
doubt the heather. Alas for that too. I can no longer muster a
blush for my fourteen-year-old former self, at the revealing
conservatism of the heartfelt clichés. I do remember it was
a perfectly good sonnet in terms of mechanical technique
and that it was almost entirely about nature. So why in 1956
should the sub-Keatsian vein have suggested itself so
easily? Paul Fussell in his absorbing book *The Great War and
Modern Memory* has a chapter called 'Arcadian Recourses'
in which he assesses the relentless pastoral and floral
tradition in English literature and shows how in time of war
it became the most natural kind of language for Britons to
use to give irony to their descriptions of the indescribable.
The pastoral was set up as the antithesis of war. Quite
without perceiving it I had as a teenager lapsed straight
into this comforting mode showing that no matter how
dead the style might have been it was still alive and accessible at some subliminal level.

The only other thing I remember about my sonnet was
that it was interested in decay in a Tennysonian, *Tithonus*
vein, for even then I associated nature absolutely with
mutability and death. It was not until I read Paul Fussell's
book that I realised this, too, was peculiarly British:

In a brilliant essay Erwin Panofsky has discovered that
ever since the eighteenth century the English have had
an instinct not shared by Continentals for making a
special kind of sense out of the classical tag *Et in arcadia
ego*. Far from taking it as 'And I have dwelt in Arcadia
too,' they take it to mean (correctly) 'Even in Arcadia I,
Death, hold sway.'

This seems at first to exemplify a hard-edged adult
realism as opposed to sloppy Continental wishful thinking.
But it is surely the English attitude towards death and the
passage of time which is the more child-like in that it is the
response of a culture obsessed with loss. Nostalgia is very
much the home province of the English and when they tap
into its rich vein they become adult–children perpetually
grieving over some indefinable passing, a whole nation in

mourning for the pre-lapsarian. How easy it becomes to view a landscape in these terms and how full our school poetry-books were of its afforded vision.

'Right. First ten lines of *The Deserted Village* by tomorrow bedtime, word-perfect, or I'll send you to be caned.'

Thus a thirteen-year-old school prefect to a ten-year-old transgressor. Back it comes thirty-odd years later, word-perfect at bedtime in a bamboo hut in the South China Sea:

Sweet Auburn! loveliest village of the plain,
Where health and plenty cheer'd the labouring swain . . .

It was a homogeneous literature, a homogeneous landscape. Goldsmith's leas were such that Gray's lowing herd could have wound slowly over them without feeling remotely lost. What did it matter that Gray's darkness was occasioned by his sexual melancholy or Goldsmith's polemic by brutal landlordism? The lament for happiness lost descended once more on the English landscape – which could take it, being quite used to acting as a metaphor for this sort of thing. Less than two centuries later it afforded the poignant scenery for Housman's doomed bucolic lads in the depths of an industrial age, and half a century or so after that it supplied heather-tufted mounds and adolescent gloom to an unwilling recruit in the Scotland Hills.

Decades later I descend Tiwarik's uplands barefooted on the baked steep soil extruding thick waves of grass which flow snaggingly about the shins. I am wading through the island's hair, up here on its crown with blue calm ocean on three sides and the mainland passive in the torrential afternoon light. Do I feel nostalgic? Is there anywhere in me an ache for a glimpse of England? I can be quite specific now.

The nostalgia is undeniably there for a lost time, for imaginary lost content, for an actual long-ago happiness botched. It exists as a cultural trait defining my nationality, age and – let it be said – class. But whatever I may mourn it is revealingly not resident in any of the landscapes of my past. I do not miss the smallest heather-tufted mound of the English scene. I do not care if I never again see the South Downs, the tennis courts and patios of Beckenham, the hills and hopfields of Kent. Neither do I wish to re-visit the dank water-meadows of Oxfordshire, de-poplared Binsey, the ivy-clad alma mater. I wish very much to avoid Postcardland: Haywainland and Kendal-Mint-Cake-Wordsworthland and West-Country-Family-Holidayland.

I am aware of missing something, though; something which I was brought up to expect or to be, something nowadays so unfashionable and discreditable I almost find it hard to mention at all. For, unexpressed but implicit throughout my childhood and adolescence was the idea that sooner or later in this life one would have to *fight*. One day I should go to war. We warbabies born during the Blitz who grew up in a world of ration books, gasmasks and uniforms breathed a pungent atmosphere of evacuation and alarm. Our fathers were away being heroes, just as our grandfathers had been heroes in the previous war and *their* fathers had distinguished themselves in South Africa . . . India . . . the Crimea . . . and so on back for centuries. Not a generation but hadn't grown up knowing it would be called upon to fight.

As it turned out my own anxieties about National Service were unnecessary: it was abolished just as I was beginning to resign myself. Suddenly all that marching with the CCF, the Armourer's course at Catterick, the annual pilgrimage to Bisley stopped being training and overnight turned into grim recreation. We had been playing at soldiers after all. The promise of rigour and comradeship was back where it had always been, in the cockpit with Biggles or in the serials in *Tiger*.

Do not then (I tell myself) underestimate the hollowness of this cancelled expectation. You in your generation were brought up to anticipate war, no matter how much a pacifist you may be and no matter what vistas of actual napalm did to your fantasies of derring-do. You are thankful you never had to fight, you are fashionably mocking of the military mind, the macho politics of confrontation. Yet underneath it you are utterly cynical about peace, to which the human race is so genetically unsuited, since you have seen that the one thing at which man excels and into which he puts his whole heart is blood-letting.

Now the thought comes: in my private war with my own past the English landscape really serves as the battlefield. I love foreignness in landscapes to the exact degree with which they violently contrast with my inherited notions of how a landscape ought to look. Whatever my sense of loss it now needs other metaphors to express itself.

Which is why I am filled with pleasure by the millipede in my path, a very un-English affair (but with the contours of a London tube train), as thick as a small cigar, six inches long, glossy brown and with its yellowish legs seeming not to move individually but to produce waves travelling its length. I feel these waves ought not to be moving in the same direction as the millipede but backwards, rather as oar blades are left behind in propelling a boat forwards. The effect is disconcerting, like the wheels of cars in early movies. The millipede ambles off in his own familiar landscape of gigantic obstacles easily surmounted by his flowing legs and enemies to be dealt with by his nasty bite. He too is a gleaming fossil, very much alive in the sunshine.

No sooner have I explored Tiwarik than I must establish a daily routine to keep myself supplied with fish. An essential part of my scanty luggage brought down with me from Kansulay are my two home-made spear guns, the long one for daytime use, the short for nights. I am in love with my task, with the sea itself. I am also in love with the coral reef which surrounds the island, with the shocking beauty and variety of the living creatures it supports. This reef is the kind known as a fringing reef (as opposed to an atoll) which often follows the contours of an island or a coastline for miles at a stretch, broken only by such things as the mouths of rivers, for silt and fresh water are inimical to the polyps which form corals. There is also a fringing reef off Kansulay but there the reef slope on the seaward side is comparatively shallow and the bottom only about thirty feet

deep, a bed of sand which slowly shelves for a mile or more
offshore. Consequently there are fewer and smaller fish at
Kansulay for the coral forms are neither so elaborate nor
varied. Here at Tiwarik, though, the reef slopes steeply
beyond the shallows, a multicoloured cliff face dropping
abruptly into aquamarine and purple depths thickly grown
with algae and patrolled by deep-sea fish including several
species of shark.

Arman has arrived in the *Jhon-Jhon*: he and his crew of
four are going off round the far side of the island for a
morning's fishing. He has brought me two jerrycans of fresh
water and Intoy, who leaps off the prow into the surf holding
a spear gun of his own. Arman helps me carry the water up
to the hut where he examines my *panà*, trying the barbs
with his fingertips and stretching the elastic experimentally.

'You have a flashlight?'

I dig out the torch I have waterproofed by means of a
motorcycle inner tube and an additional lens cut from a
piece of glass. He examines it critically, testing the switch.

'We'll go fishing one night,' he says. 'Maybe tonight,
maybe tomorrow.'

'It'll have to be late,' I say, trying to remember when the
full moon had set. Darkness is essential for good night
fishing; moonlight makes the fish lively.

'About one o'clock. Did you see the moon go red? So
many people in Sabay were frightened. The young ones
thought the world was going to end and the old ones think
it's a bad omen because they say it went like that before the
Japanese came. We'll come and sleep over here so we can
all get up at one o'clock. Can you use a compressor?'

I have already spotted that the *Jhon-Jhon* is equipped
with a rusty air compressor which can be driven off the
twelve-horsepower Briggs & Stratton which powers the
boat by the simple method of slipping the drive-belt off the
propshaft and over the compressor's flywheel. On the narrow marine-ply decks fore and aft are piles of thin plastic
hose. It is the simplest (and most dangerous) system for
diving which exists. The diver takes the end of a hose in his
mouth and goes down, controlling the airflow with his

teeth. With a good pump and a lot of nerve it is possible to go down two hundred and fifty, even three hundred feet which is effectively the limit for scuba divers as well. To work in the dark for two or three hours with a torch and a spear gun at only half that depth is to become conscious of living on the edge. I tell Arman I have dived with a compressor. He has never before heard of a *'kano* doing so and wants to know where I learned. I name another province where I was three or four years ago. He is surprised.

'I didn't know they did it there as well. We often get Visayans here who have compressors, though. I think maybe it's everywhere in the Philippines, then. Typical Filipino cheap way.'

He sounds disappointed that the fishermen of Sabay and these parts are not exclusive after all, but proud to belong to that fraternity who get by without all the namby-pamby foreign clutter of scuba equipment. I am afraid we compressor-divers rather fancy ourselves. He recommends the submerged boulders beyond one end of the beach as a good place for daytime fishing and goes back down to his boat. On the way I tell him I prefer deeper water. He looks at me speculatively and pushes off. The engine starts and soon his hemplike hair disappears around the headland and the motor's noise is abruptly cut off. Intoy frolics in the shallows wearing goggles made from carved pieces of wood set with olives of glass. He grins as I pass on the way to fetch my spear gun. His mouth is full of white teeth, his eyes invisible behind flashing heliographs.

Intoy is good. He does not yet like to go much below twenty feet but he is stealthy and understands the habits of the various kinds of fish better than I do. I hang in the clear water and watch him a couple of fathoms below as he hides behind an outcrop of coral, lying in wait for a small school of parrotfish which as usual approach cautiously but full of curiosity. Just when I think he must be at the end of his breath he fires and hits a one-pound *manitis*, one of the goatfishes with the characteristic twin barbels beneath its chin. He comes surging up with it spitted on his spear, trailing spent air in glittering streams. He breaks the surface and pants, very matter-of-fact about his catch. Fish

are not at all easy to spear during the day, being altogether
too alert. The glassy water conducts every sound as if it
were a tympanum; it is like being immersed in synaptic
fluid designed to transmit the tiniest neural message, a
sentient bath so 'live' it is a wonder to get anywhere near a
sizeable fish. But with practice one can. After an hour or so
Intoy and I have enough between us for lunch and maybe
for supper as well.

We climb from the water, spitting, and sit on the rocks
with the sea lapping up over our feet. From slightly behind
him I watch the droplets run from the shining wicks of his
hair and trickle down his brown nape. Beneath the steady
pour of sun on our backs the surface of his skin doubles its
depth. A new layer stands off as though he were covered
with a dusting of light, a powdery membrane which
sheathes his whole body. The effect is similar to that when
eye and mind are allowed to drift out of focus and
undreamed-of textures float up towards them from ever
more deceptive distance. I think if I reach out my hand to
touch his slender neck it would pass through it and stretch
back thirty years. What resonance a life acquires as it goes;
resonance rising like a mist from what was not, the melancholy vapour of what was. And suddenly this endless
instant is compounded when he turns his head and smiles a
single, brief, unreadable smile. A sadness not at all at odds
with the sun is broken by his jumping to his feet.

'Come on. I'll show you where the big eels have their
nests.' And the great sea scours off all but the intent of this
new endeavour as we slip back between the layers of its
yielding glass.

In this manner the days pass.

At seventy feet and beneath the jutting coral ledge which
extends its sloping garden to the sunlit upper waters it is
dark and colder. I am at the extreme of my air, my lungfuls
of oxygen mostly burnt up in the effort of forcing my body
down to this depth. Time here is very limited: the urgency
to make each second's sense impression count, to observe

everything, is intense. It is partly scaring, partly exciting to know that shooting vertically to the surface is impossible because of the overhang. If mind turned responsibility over to body before winking out, then body would simply claw straight up and be caught among the juts and spurs on the underside of the ledge, swaying like weed in the currents there until eaten. Mind has to remain at its post long enough to get its blundering capsule to safety and the upper light.

Meanwhile the blundering capsule is suffering, but mind is busy admiring the gems of this hidden world. The sand is littered with empty shells, with nacreous spires and ginger fans, with spotted carapace and claw. Hands clutch and grab but then feet kick decisively off for the unending, swerving ascent which at last brings body bursting to the surface. There it lies, panting the sunlight in and out while the slower bubbles of its passage continue to prickle up from below and fizz around it. It is a minute or two before I can examine what my hands have found. Up here in the brilliance the objects are small and ordinary: common shells, parts of a dismantled crab. For a while a certain strangeness clings to them as to anything retrieved with effort which should never again have seen full light of day; then my hands open and the ex-treasures wobble their way down in the long fall back to their entombment.

The pleasure of this sort of retrieval is self-renewing. I do such dives many times, pure recreation amid the serious daily task of killing to eat, until they become a necessary habit. Now and again I come back up with something I keep. Mostly these gems are devalued as they cross over that barrier between the lower and the upper, like all souvenirs, like those hypnagogic fragments I so often awake with clutched in my mouth. I speak them on waking: significant phrases whose meaning quickly drains away until they are arbitrary jumbles of words and sounds. Occasionally they provide ideas, titles for stories, private jokes.

Face down in the water now I can no longer see the fragments I have released. Even the crab's shell with its gleaming white inner surface has been swallowed up. My mind starts working properly: that graveyard on the seabed might have accumulated because of the way the currents eddy at that point but more likely it represents the back-door débris of a creature's lair in the rock face beneath the overhang. Probably there is a good-sized octopus resident in one of the slots and fissures. I ought to go down again and discover where so I can come back and fight him.

Half an hour later I do so, this time armed with a long wire probe to take soundings. In a series of dives down beneath the ledge I quarter the rock face systematically. Several times my wire encounters something soft but the holes are too small. Eventually I do find the right hole. The probe quivers. A cloud of disturbed silt puffs out as the occupant shrinks back towards the island's roots. It will be a dangerous fight and impossible without a compressor. I doubt it is suitable for a solo effort. (Nor was it. This near-fatal encounter – albeit in a fictional setting – may be found in a short story, 'Compressor'.)*

Since a spear gun plays such an important part in my daily life on Tiwarik I shall have to describe it properly. It is a fishing tool which has been around for a long time: the oldest man in Sabay tells me he used one as a boy and that it was exactly the same as the modern ones except that in those days all the elastic was black. There may be regional variations in style but basically the classic Filipino spear gun is a wooden stock shaped like a child's toy rifle equipped with elastic thongs and a barbed metal spear. If the gun is for day fishing the combined length of spear and stock may be as much as five feet; if it is for a child or to be used for night fishing it is short: usually no more than a scant metre overall. The reasons for this difference are that at night most fish can be approached very close so less power is needed, also that the shorter the spear gun the easier it is to manoeuvre in darkness into holes and crevices in the rocks.

The top surface of the toy rifle is planed flat and a few inches of bamboo 'barrel' lashed to its front tip. To this in

*The View From Mount Dog, Macmillan, 1986.

turn powerful rubber strands are tightly bound with elastic. At their ends are loops made of nylon or stainless steel wire. These fit over a raised tooth near the rear end of the spear which is inserted backwards through the 'barrel' and held in place against the combined tension of the rubber by the sear of the trigger. The trigger itself will be one of two kinds. The simpler consists of a metal lip driven into the stock which engages with a slot cut in the underside of the spear. The butt end of the spear is held in a hole drilled in a piece of wood which pivots. The firer's thumb presses down on the end of the wood, the hole lifts the slot in the spear clear of the metal lip, the spear fires. The other kind is more of a conventional rifle trigger, the upper end of which emerges as a spike through the stock and goes into a hole drilled in the end of the spear. The firer's forefinger squeezes the trigger, the spike retracts, the spear fires. This is the pattern of all the spear guns at Sabay and is the type which I now use, having started some years ago in a different province with the 'rocking' kind of trigger.

I go into such detail because the fishermen take great care with the guns they make and the designs they use are now as perfected as is that of the bicycle. There may be improvements to be made possible by new materials but the basic idea is a beautiful balance of simplicity, ease of use, accuracy, cheapness and adaptation to the human body. The spear gun grows from the hand, the eye is at the tip of the spear (which is barbed, generally with a sharpened nail pivoting through a hole). The spears themselves are a matter for some competitiveness. The best are of steel rod, about a quarter of an inch thick, which flexes but will not easily become bent. The ideal rod is stolen from the core of local government power cable and bears the spiral shadow of the wires once wrapped around it. A good alternative is a light reinforcing rod. The cheapest and least successful spears are of mild steel or iron. They bend very easily so that at the end of a short struggle with a small octopus they are kinked throughout their length. On the other hand they are much simpler to work.

The strength of the propulsive rubber, the number and length of the thongs, is dictated by how strong the user is and how much power he needs. A heavy spear for daytime use needs an effective range of only about ten feet. This seems a tiny distance on dry land. Underwater it is hard for mere elastic to drive a steel rod much further than that with any accuracy: water slows projectiles abruptly as anyone versed in ballistics knows. Besides, the spear takes a measurable time to travel that distance and it is difficult to 'lead' a fish and outthink it when the mere sound of the trigger releasing is sufficient warning. The spear passes through the space where one hoped it might have been, except that it is now a good yard away and going in the opposite direction. It is because a spear gun like this is so 'low-tech' that the fisherman must compensate by acquiring knowledge of his prey: how each species moves, how each reacts, the subtle differences of behaviour. I cannot imagine what it would be like to hit every fish one aimed at as if shooting tin ducks. The fishermen of Sabay might yearn for such luck but after a while the fish would react by staying out of range. It must be at least partly because the present technique is so heavily in the fishes' favour that they continue to loiter and be shot at and this whole method of gathering food remains possible.

We have all spent hours speculating about ways of increasing our spear guns' power. Instead of elastic stretched straight back along the stock in the catapult principle, how would it be to build an underwater crossbow? But the objections are at once obvious: re-loading would be far too slow, the 'bowstring' would be impeded throughout its length by the water, the overall width would be cumbersome and out of the question at night. Springs, then? But these argue a much more complicated containing mechanism which in turn means concealed metal parts which will corrode. The power of a compressed spring is also released over a short length only; one of the advantages of elastic stretched so many times its own length is that the spear is driven and accelerated right up to the moment its tail disappears into the little bamboo guide.

A further issue is how to avoid losing the spear which is not, after all, an anonymous bullet but like a mediaeval arrow, a hand-made weapon representing hours of work.

One may most easily lose a spear by firing it out into a sudden deep or by hitting a fish big enough to swim off with it. Neither is likely to happen close inshore when the spear being used may not be much heavier in gauge than an average knitting needle. Either is very likely indeed when using a big spear gun for deeper work on the outer slope of the coral shelf, which is what I like doing.

Some years ago I finally made my own first spear of which I was greatly proud. Not that there was much craftsmanship involved, merely a sense of having triumphed over difficulties. I had had no tools other than a *bolo* and worked crouched over a fire: rocks were hammers, an old nail gradually banged into red-hot metal was a drill, a piece of broken cement paving was a file. Eventually, at the cost of an hour or two's clumsy labour, burns, cuts and a mortified fingernail, I was holding a serviceable spear. I took it out and in the first hour's fishing bagged a fat *tudluan*. The following day I hit a large cuttlefish which had just begun to pick up nervous speed the moment my spear pierced its bony plate. There was an ink explosion in the water ahead of me. I caught it up and groped inside the opaque cloud. Nothing. Then I spotted the cuttlefish moving steadily away towards deeper water, much hampered by the weight of the spear it trailed but making a good pace. Every so often it let out a pulse of ink which hung in the water as a twirling sepia nut. I set off in pursuit. At some point as it got deeper I stopped chasing a fine cuttlefish and started trying to save my spear. I had given up pursuing it underwater and was on the surface preparing for one last attempt when the dimming shape far below me stopped. I swam down. It made a despairing effort to escape but it was even more exhausted than I and I plucked both it and the spear from deep water.

This episode, ending as it did in a sense of triumph at having retrieved the spear just as it was about to become irretrievable, had a nonsensical effect for it made me more confident of being able to deal with such things in the future rather than serving as a warning. For another couple of days I fished on but without any spectacular catches. Then on the fifth day of my new spear I sank to about seven metres, to that gracious level where the human body achieves equilibrium in seawater, neither sinking nor rising and initially making one feel it would be possible to spend all day there without taking a breath of air. I lay behind a coral outcrop and waited for a knot of offshore fish to assemble in their curiosity. I waited so long I knew I could not last another ten seconds without air, let alone all day, and at that point a gigantic parrotfish swam slowly past, its eye swivelling to watch me from its blue socket. Startled, I fired even as I pushed off for my ascent and saw, incredulously, the spear miss. The parrotfish characteristically dumped a trail of excrement as it bolted while my spear fell in an ever-steepening arc out over the shelf and into the deep purple beyond.

The rest of that day I made numerous attempts to retrieve it. I had fixed its position in relation to a curious green toadstool of coral growing on the very edge of the undersea precipice. If I swam down to the toadstool itself, about thirty-five feet, I could just make out the spear lying at the foot of the cliff. I took great breaths and pushed myself down to fifty, sixty, seventy feet. But the spear must have been lying in a hundred and twenty feet of water and I never came closer to it than forty feet, from which distance I could see every inch of it in all its familiar detail: the scratch-marks from my improvised filings already beginning to go ochre with rust, the slight lop-sidedness of its barb. Had I been ten years younger, had I trained myself for depth diving, had I . . .

I exploded up to the surface, ears squeaking and ringing, head squeezed, rib-cage quaking. Had I nothing. Had I had the sense not to fire at all. Never would I have killed a *bonak* that size outright: it would in any case have swum away with my spear, probably shedding it within a hundred metres. But to have fired seawards at anything from the edge of a coral reef was fatuous and betrayed a complete lack of the right instincts. I had been so excited by the sight of a big fish close up that all I could think of was pulling the trigger. I meditated sadly on this unprofessionalism as I fashioned another spear, this time stabbing my palm with a hot nail. One learned with awesome slowness; but I did resolve to learn, for even then I knew there was a psychic investment involved.

Nowadays I, like all the other serious spear-fishermen of Sabay, have thin nylon cords on my spears, spliced through a hole in the end. These lines which are anything up to four metres long serve a dual function, enabling one to retrieve the spear and also providing a place for the catch. It took time to learn how to use a spear trailing a line. At first it seemed impossibly cumbersome. The tail snagged on corals, it fouled my plywood flipper, it drifted around my legs with the current. In fury I cut it off; penitently I later had to re-splice it onto yet another new spear.

The technique of using a catch-line is that until there are some fish on it one holds a gather between two knuckles of the trigger hand. One swims, gun loaded and arm outstretched, the cord loosely held in such a way that it can run between the fingers when the spear fires but be stopped instantly if a fish is hit or the spear is about to fall into deep water. I very soon learned not to tie it to my wrist or ankle. I once found myself tethered thirty feet down by unbreakable nylon cord to a steel rod whose barb was firmly embedded in coral. This is not an experience one forgets; in the last resort one always needs to be able to let a spear go and after some years of spear-fishing the circumstances in which this happens are not likely to make one lament the spear overmuch.

When the fisherman hits a fish he makes sure it is safely impaled through a substantial part of its body so that once on the catch-line it will not be torn off if snagged on a rock or kicked by a flipper. He passes it down the spear and onto the cord. Two-thirds along its length the line has a brass swivel spliced in to prevent the fish's body acting like a propeller in the water and winding the line up into kinks. The fish is now pushed over the swivel until it reaches the stop at the end of the cord. In practice the whole action of hitting a fish, sweeping it back along spear and line and re-loading the gun takes a matter of seconds during which time the hunter, who may still be deep under water, is looking about him for fresh prey even as he rises for air.

*

One night not long after my arrival on Tiwarik I wake just
after the moon has set. I get up and go out. There is nobody
else on the island; Arman has not come over to fish. I am
glad since I am not in the mood tonight. Leaving my spear
gun tucked into the roof I walk down to the beach through
swirls of fireflies. I do not know why fireflies are more
plentiful on some nights than on others, nor why phosphorescent plankton in the sea should be equally variable.
Maybe the weather, the temperature or barometric pressure have something to do with it; maybe it is merely a
matter of season. At any rate the night is now moonless,
overcast, utterly black except that in the blackness swim
these constant or winking insect lights.

I walk on into the still water which is the same
temperature as the air and can hardly be felt except as a
weight. I go on; the water comes up to my chest. Almost
without noticing it I have stopped breathing and find
myself heading downwards into equal black in which the
stellate points of tendril and plankton whirl and glow. The
island and the sea are not after all separate entities but one
continuous medium. In a while I no longer know for certain
if my head is breaking through into air or water.
Somewhere in this spangled firmament I take breaths. I
know only there is a great lid over this universe, or else an
unyielding bottom beneath it, and that if I keep heading up
or down for long enough my head will strike one or the other
but that if I steer a middle course I could keep on for ever,
dazzled by these infinite motes, by my passage through a
void in which mill the atoms of creation. In this pre-Genesis
my mind floats off and out. There is no longer any body left
to move in this nothing, only a cloud of electrons rap-
turously adrift in chaos.

Intoxicated, I am aware of motionless points of light. I
find I am on my back. The overcast is dissolving and stars
are coming through. Gradually their constant candle-
power outlines the dark heave of Tiwarik and everything re-
orients itself according to old conceptions of gravity. The
island has revealed another accuracy in its name but now
its bulk settles the right way up. Fathoms below my soles lie
the familiar marauding teeth and chitinous beaks among

the great sierras of coral. Far above me the forest and
grasses shed down their drifts of fireflies, a twinkling dan-
druff eddying lazily in and out of the thorny brushwood
above the shoreline boulders.

I love this place.

4

The more familiar it becomes the more the reef surrounding Tiwarik is unknowable, a disclosure of that *mare incognitum* without whose liquid setting the island would be a stone instead of a jewel. At Kansulay I was intrigued by the spectacle of Lolang Mating's ruined hut shimmering with cold fire, but they exist here beneath the sea, too, such luminous fungi. And just as in the woods one sees a glow and shines a torch to reveal some undistinguished mould, deep underwater a coral hill may bulk with a beacon on its peak which is much harder to find. In the dark I mark the place and switch the torch on but at the instant of light everything springs slightly to one side. Eventually I track it down: a tiny nodule of jelly lost among a tuft of weed. Still stranger are the lights on the sea bed which bring me down with my belly on the sand, flattened beneath black fathoms. That steady incandescence is surely a lure put forth by some poisonous predator bunched in waiting beneath the sand like a buried ray trailing its white quill. But no; it is so invisible by torchlight it needs a long minute finally to see it: something shaped like a sodden wisp of cellophane which, enveloped in dark once more, pumps out light as an insignificant flower its scent.

What is it for, this light? To entice, to warn, proclaim? We are in a foreign place and nothing may be taken even as language, still less as translatable. The light may simply be part of the creature's outline, much as a dog's four legs go towards defining its shape. On the other hand it may not be a creature at all but a fragment of one, a tatter mimicking autonomy like the severed tail of a lizard or the crawling blushes which run and pool on the skin of a dead squid. It brings me down with my nose to the sand time and time again. If scientists are right in claiming that algae were for

aeons the only living things on the newly cooling Earth,
maybe what we see now is the scattered remnants of a
former splendour, much as a skein of incandescent gas a
few light years across may mark all that remains of an
entire galaxy.

And now it is at night that the old Earth lives on,
threadily, at night and in the tropic seas. To take a torch
down among the reefs at night is to experience still other
things which suggest an ancient broodingness, a fragmented hegemony from whose visible signs you cannot
construct a whole. Even if that were not so you would be
chilled by the sound filling your ears. It is that of a million
creatures fiercely being alive. At times it seems like the
noise of limitless frying, the preparing of a million dinners.
At others there is an insistent, manic quality to its gravelly
roar like hearing a huge crowd in a far stadium, its voice
surging in waves so the imagination half supplies unseeable
events, half thinks to make out individual words. Just so on
a Roman evening must the villagers of that city's outskirts
have heard the barbarities of the Colosseum several miles
away borne to them on the soft summer wind.

The volume of this steady underwater black noise is
evidence of activity and violence far beyond what you can
see with a torch. Above it are individually-separable
squeaks, grunts and flutings. Something drums abruptly its
thoracic sac. Something else makes a nearly human yawn.
A shrill groan has you turning in shock, torch thrust out
defensively to see whatever carnage is about to embroil you
and there is nothing. Nothing but doused incandescent
points, the nocturnal species you already know, a crab
scurrying.

You soon recognise that, just as on land, at night other
creatures emerge and prowl the sea lanes. The hunter of fish
down among the reefs with a torch and spear gun gets to
know them, a different set of threats and prey. He is on the
whole not after them; he is more intent on looking into holes
and nooks to find the big fish he can seldom catch by day
when they are alert and on the move. There is experience
involved in knowing how to get them out since the holes
through which they can be glimpsed may be too small, the

real entrance hard to find. Useless to fire a spear into a fish that cannot be retrieved. There is experience, too, in knowing the sort of rock formations it is worth going down to inspect at close range.

But the real skill is learning to see things and knowing what it is you are looking at. When I was a novice with a spear gun I would go out on patrols with a skilled mentor. I would pass over bare rocks and featureless seabed and seconds later he would pass over the same patch which for him became a rich fishing-ground. His spear would streak before my eyes and quiver fifteen feet below into a patch of sand which would suddenly heave and flap and flash the undersides of white wing. In those days I would not have known how to deal with a ray even had I been able to spot it and would have risked the thrilling (and sometimes fatal) poisons of its lashing sting. But not being able to see it until it writhed around a steel rod was a clear sign of how far I was from being self-sufficient as a fisherman. And now, I think, if I went out with a neophyte he might in turn wonder that I saw things he knew were not there.

Of course I am still not seeing much of what there is; and allowing that far more experienced fishermen than I miss things I am made thoughtful by the rustlings in the marine undergrowth at night, at the constant roar of sound, at the evidence my eyes cannot see and my ears cannot hear of an unknown universe. I am always surprised at scientists' surprise when they discover that the sunless depths of the great undersea trenches are not after all barren wastelands. It is evidence on their part not only of a lack of imagination but of a profound sensory chauvinism, a certainty that what would be a blind and crushing void for humans must also be for other creatures. At different wavelengths of vision and sound, with other gamuts of olfactory response, an ancient world lives on in invisible splendour. We are too dogged by Genesis, by our own myth of the absolute polarity of dark and light, of the one meaning death and the other life, absence and Presence. Being prisoners of an extensive set of such dualisms has led us to deny what they cannot encompass. The cure for this is to slip into black tropical waters at night and head on down. Through eye and ear

pour exclamations; but as evidence of the world down
there they are only as the faint scratches in a radio astro-
nomer's headphones are to an invisible galaxy of suns. It is a
magnificently alien world which cannot be apprehended
by terrestrial instincts alone. It is difficult to recognise a
universe from inside another.

Even in broad light of day the island itself, despite its
smallness, offers unexpected asides. It hints at more than
surfaces. It took a while to discover that there is an enchanted place on Tiwarik, one which will remain for ever
unfound by any ordinary stroller or scrambler since it is
inaccessible except from the sea.

On the side of the island away from the mainland where
the ocean lies empty the cliffs fall sheer into a tumble of
boulders awash with suckings and surges. At one particular
point the angle increases beyond the vertical and there is
an overhang beneath which a spit of flat rock no more than
a yard or two across juts into the sea and so low it is covered
at high tide. Here, invisible from above, I can lie on my
stomach with my nose practically in the water and gaze
straight down eighty-one feet to where the island's roots
disappear into sand. With the sun at the correct angle and
with no wind to ruffle its surface the water becomes a block
of glass and through it I can follow a map of the land of
Drune.

Drune is essentially a desert country between two mountain ranges. It is a plateau from which the inhabitants raise
their eyes in every direction towards the great peaks which
glitter in the rarefied sun, surrounding and defining the
place of their birth. From these heights tumble boulder-
strewn gorges, screes of eroded rock. Harsh though its
outlines are in large-scale terms this is no sterile lunar
landscape. A closer view shows the mountains to be densely
wooded in places with thickets of emerald gymnosperms,
stands of amber fern-trees, forests of wand. At the mountains' foot along the edge of the desert are little white
jumbled villages whose people live industrious but not

grinding lives, tending their flocks and cultivating their terraces. They are respectful of but not terrorised by the vast birds which live in deep and mysterious caves in the mountains. These sleek-winged creatures traverse their skies at immense speed, occasionally pausing to nuzzle a village with their beaks, overturning houses by the hundred in clouds of dust, or browsing on the forests high in the hills. Drune.

Why Drune? I wonder as soon as the name suggests itself. And then I remember back and back to long, shapeless, mesmeric hours on a swing beneath whose oak seat was an area cobbled from pieces of broken flagstones. Above this I would slump, arms hooked around the ropes, head hanging nearly between my knees, swinging gently backwards and forwards until I became hypnotised by the coming and going of the ground beneath. I was a child of secret lands and arcane languages and from the cockpit of my aircraft I soon identified the patterned landscape of Drune. I knew each hedgerow of moss bulging up between the triangles and polygons of its fields; I knew each crack which was a highway leading between its towns and every hairline fracture which was a wandering path down which the villagers went their ways.

Sometimes I lay on my stomach across the seat and wound myself higher and higher off the ground until the ropes above me bunched and creaked. At maximum altitude I would begin my spiralling descent. High above Drune my little plane spun and spun while the countryfolk beneath stood in the fields with their heads thrown back and their mouths open. The spectacle! The control! Would he ever pull up in time! He always did, even though his head was plump with blood from the G-forces of his spin and he had broken through some barrier beyond instruments and clocks and had entered Drune itself, a different world where his whole body resonated with weird and piercing sense-impressions. It was Drune he loved to visit, and it was *Drune* because he loved playing with letters and in its own spelling Drune was Under.

That the demon pilot of Drune was also an inveterate sketcher of imaginary islands now seems perfectly consistent. Already he had begun his search for a land but it was not the traditional land of escape. It was not at all to be a place of comforting evasion but of harsh and abrupt edges, of ravishing and awful gulfs under skies of tropic blue but blown through always by that sad dark wind – in short, a land he might at last recognise as his own.

There was a curious legend at my first school, that country house among the South Downs. The house was one of those built without proper cellars but with a semi-basement lit by barred, ground-level windows with downwardly sloping embrasures inside. As far as I can remember this basement was largely given over to kitchens and laundry rooms and suchlike; if we went down there towards bedtime wearing a dressing-gown and a suitably pathetic expression there was usually a large woman with rolled sleeves to say 'Poor child' and give us a mug of unsweetened cocoa (sugar was still on ration) and a piece of bread and dripping. But anyone who then watched the poor child sipping his cocoa would have seen him wander about, his eyes on the floor, chewing abstractedly. He would roam through cavernous rooms forbidden him by daylight staring at the flagstones, peeping behind stacks of wicker laundry baskets held together by parchment thongs, straying if he were brave enough into the furthest unlit recesses brooded over by immense spiders and mouldering ping-pong tables stacked against the wall. He would be slightly emboldened by being a conspirator, for he was on a special mission which had been previously arranged in the dormitories up under the roof. The mission was to find the Lost Cellars.

The myth of the Lost Cellars was one of the first things a boy heard as a newcomer to the school. In effect it said that somewhere beneath the school was a whole level which at some time in the past had been deliberately walled up and forgotten about in an act of collective amnesia. What was down there was the subject of endless speculation in the dormitories after lights-out, ranging from boys murdered by a long-dead headmaster to an idiot daughter of the present Latin master who was chained there with an iron mug and a tame rat which had worn its teeth down to stubs trying to gnaw through her shackles. Unfortunately we never found any evidence for there being access to these nether regions: no new cement in the joints between stones, no iron rings, no fresh plaster. This did not stop the speculation, naturally, nor the handing-on of the myth. But we soon became busy with our cordite collections and with the Army surplus equipment which was then so cheap and plentiful: signal lamps and walkie-talkies were the most popular with their great batteries wrapped in brown paper beneath layers of varnish and what looked like laminations of fat.

The Latin master's idiot daughter is there to this day no doubt, fulfilling her unenviable destiny of representing unfinished psychic business. Her father must long since have died for even then he had been nearing retirement. But his daughter is not one day older. Very beautiful, very wild, she talks all day to her toothless rat, staring into the darkness with atrophied eyes and relaying to him with great clarity the events of the bright visions wherein she lives. For even as she hangs in her chains her freedom is complete, as witness the power she has to escape the Lost Cellars, cross nearly forty years and seven thousand miles to present herself on Tiwarik one night where she steps straight into my mind.

The odd thing was that when I moved to my second school, to the island amid suburbia, nearly the first myth I encountered was that of the Second Cellars. In this building the first cellars were proper underground ones without any windows and access to them was not limited since they held the changing-rooms and the hobbies room, the boot-room and the boiler-room in addition to a good many poky unlit annexes full of burst suitcases and mildewed copies of Ovid with 'P. Binsted, Summer 1938' on the flyleaf.

These cellars were reached conventionally from inside by a flight of stairs which was merely a continuation (on a far less grand scale) of the main staircase. Outside, a tradesmen's stone flight led up again into daylight. It was at the bottom of this flight that the evidence for the Second Cellars was strongest. There was a large flagstone which rocked hollowly under the combined weight of three boys (two, if one of them were 'Slug' Summerbee). Nobody had ever seen this flag lifted but it was known for a fact that an unnamed head boy had once been sent down to the cellars on some errand during morning classes and had seen a firm line of wet footprints leading from the stone's edge and along the passage to the boiler-room. This added greatly to the awe and horror in which we held old Bisley, whose duties in addition to acting as school groundsman were to tend the school boilers and clean the school's shoes. To help him with all this – for he was truly an old man all brown skin and sinews – was a mysterious younger man believed to be his illegitimate son. This was a sort of Heathcliff figure with long blueblack Brylcreemed hair and tattoos on his forearms. He looked like a gypsy and when he smiled he showed brilliant white teeth. He rode an AJS motorcycle with sinister skill and was rumoured to be able to make any girl pregnant simply by passing her in a corridor and smiling. Nobody knew where he and his unofficial father lived. Maybe they didn't live in the Second Cellars but they definitely knew something about them.

Wright was brave, no doubt about that. One day he simply went up to Bisley's son and asked him point-blank to show him the Second Cellars. A strange veiled look crossed the gypsy eyes.

'How old are you, son?'

'Twelve.'

'H'm. Wait till you're thirteen.'

'But I'm nearly thirteen now.'

'Wait till you're thirteen and just about to leave. *Then* I'll show you. And one or two of your friends, too, if they're lucky.'

But something must have happened in the intervening months because Wright never did see the Second Cellars; probably in the flurry of Common Entrance examinations and cricket Elevens he forgot all about them. Still, we would often be changing down there for some sport or other and look up with surprise to see Heathcliff lounging silently in the doorway, smiling secretly, surveying with his black eyes the little waxy English bodies.

However, certain boys were quite immune to any sense of threat this man implied. Ackroyd in particular was used to a very straightforward relationship with the sort of people who cleaned shoes and stoked boilers. We were down in the boot-room after lunch, a room lined with wooden pigeon-holes in which nested the school's shoes. The atmosphere was peaceful like a library, scented with leather and dubbin and Cherry Blossom polish. Old Bisley and Heathcliff were sitting in one corner, cleaning shoes. Bisley was putting on the polish while Heathcliff was buffing it off; the back of Bisley's left hand had a black tide-mark of polish across it. Ackroyd went to his pigeonhole, retrieved his shoes and examined them critically, moving beneath the ceiling bulb in its metal cage.

'I must say I don't think much of these,' he said.

The two men went on polishing.

'I say,' said Ackroyd. 'These really aren't up to much, you know.'

Heathcliff put down his wad of rags.

'I'm sorry young sir is not satisfied.' His voice was not very loud; I trembled and prayed for Ackroyd to shut up. 'You see, we've only got eighty-four pairs to clean.' But he should have known that this sort of mode is lost on the Ackroyds of the world.

'Exactly,' said the boy. 'Give me the cloth.' He took Heathcliff's rags and scrubbed at the toecaps of the shoes he was holding. 'There. Not very difficult, was it? It's called elbow-grease,' he explained.

The look Heathcliff gave him would have kept me – did keep me – sleepless for nights but Ackroyd was unconcerned. He simply put the shoes neatly back in his pigeonhole and walked out.

If old Bisley and the threatening Heathcliff added to the psychic resonance of the Second Cellars myth, then plausibility was given by the nearness of the famous Chisle-hurst Caves. Very occasionally when the school was deemed to have been especially good and deserving (plenty of scholarships and matches won) we were marched in crocodile along the scrunchy drive between the rhododendrons, past the gate-keeper's lodge and out into gracious suburbia. Downhill we went past fine examples of Gynaecologist Gothick set on an eminence amid their spacious gardens, down under the railway bridge by the little bosky station where poor drudges called commuters apparently had to go every day, down to where a densely wooded hill rose steeply on the other side. And there, under this hill, was the entrance to the Chislehurst Caves.

These were a natural cave system stretching – some said – for twenty-two miles. Or it may have been forty-two. An essential part of their reputation was that their full extent was not yet known, so terrifyingly labyrinthine was the network. Part of them had been used during the war (then only seven or so years before) as air-raid shelters and were equipped with barbers' shops, chapels, clinics and stores. At the entrance, a simple wooden gate which did not even reach to the top of the cave mouth, we were handed oil lamps and allotted cocky Dickensian guides, likely lads with the accents of Wapping and the Isle of Dogs who had learned their spiels by rote, including impromptu jokes and warnings.

'Several blokes 'ave come down 'ere nights and climbed over the gates 'oping to do it all fer free. Nuffing but a bicycle lamp wiv 'em. Poor sods.'

'What happened?' we ask, trotting down the passageway in a cloud of lamp soot, our figures thrown onto the walls by the flickering orangy flames we carry. The sense of drawing ever further away from warm sunlight is weighing on each of us.

'Ah, we always finds 'em *in the end*,' comes the voice from the darkness. 'Takes a bit of time, though. Last bloke it was what, Pete, five days?'

'Wha'?' shouts back Pete from somewhere ahead.

'That last geezer what climbed in, 'ow long was it before we finds 'im?'

'Six days, wannit?'

'Yus, that's right, six.'

'But wasn't he hungry?' asks 'Slug' Summerbee.

' 'Ungry? 'E was *dead*, wannee? They always is. Dead.'

'From hunger?'

'Nah, they go mad. Yer batt'ry lasts, what, three hours? Then yer thinks, better save 'er, use 'er as little as possible. But yer lost, aren't yer? All these passages looks the same. Yer panicks. Yer turns on yer torch 'cos anyfink's better'n that 'orrible blackness pressin' in and in.'

We can well imagine it now. The feet of the furthermost parts of our crocodile make a booming and sighing noise in the galleries which open off on either side. The air is cold, the chalk walls slick with damp.

'That last bloke, know where we found 'im? Only thirty yards from the entrance. *Thirty yards*. 'E was all – but I'd better not say.'

'No, go on. *Go on . . .*'

''Is fingers? They was all wore down to the second knuckle. 'E'd been trying to claw 'is way out, annee? But worse'n that, worse'n that. 'Is eyes? They was all stickin' out 'is 'ead like organ stops. Great big white starin' eyeballs and this terrible grin. Yer could go mad just thinkin' about 'im and I 'ad to look at 'im 'cos I'm the one what finds 'im, innoi?'

After a long time we come to a halt and various torch-beams pool on the uneven roof. What looks like a massive bone is sticking out of the rock.

'Dinosaur's leg,' our guide tells us. 'The rest of 'im's still there, buried in the livin' rock.'

'Can't they dig him out?' someone asks, clearly thinking of the huge and prized specimen which dominates the entrance hall of the Natural History Museum.

'Nah, 'e'd bring the roof down. Or it might make it unsafe so we'd all be buried 'ere for ever and ever.'

While everybody's attention is fixed on the ceiling I glance sideways in the reflected light and look at our guide covertly. He is not after all very much older than ourselves. I am fascinated by the smooth line of his throat as he gazes upwards, by the almost imperceptible bump of his Adam's apple.

'Funny thing,' he says in the silence, 'there's people what says . . .'

'Nah, Brian, don't tell 'em that one,' breaks in Pete. 'I'm

not sure I believes it meself and you'll only scare the little
'uns.'

'No, go on. *Go on* . . .'

'Well, there's people what says there's still dinosaurs
livin' somewhere in these caves, somewhere 'asn't been
discovered yet. They says they've 'eard 'em calling at times,
very faint and distant-like.'

'Dinosaurs . . . *alive?*'

'Sort of like the Loch Ness monster. Yer know, left over
from pre-'istoric times.'

A shudder runs through the entire school. The little ones
are indeed petrified. Unconsciously we huddle together,
the uneasy susurration of our feet whispers away along the
corridors and galleries, the caverns and passages, rebounds
from a hundred surfaces and sets inaudibly ringing the
stalactites and stalagmites which bristle in the dark like
limestone tuning-forks. And in a few seconds, as from an
unknown distance near the Earth's core, there comes a
faint echo which raises every hair on every head. For what
we hear is a deep, sad mooing. It is precisely the sound we
expect to hear from a prehistoric left-over, a saurian
Wandering Jew cut off from time and condemned eternally
to pace these nether regions, calling forlornly to its friends
of seventy million years ago.

'What . . . what was *that?*'

'Aw, that,' says Brian airily. 'Dunno. Yer hears it all the
time at this spot so yer kind of gets to pay no attention.'

'Is that the living dinosaur?'

'Dunno. Could be, I s'pose. We don't go any further along
'ere, see. None of us knows what 'appens if yer keep going
along this tunnel. Prob'ly nobody knows. Yer'd 'ave to be a
bit barmy to head orf into the unknown down there. They've
offered prizes, yer know. Farzend pahn ter the bloke what's
the first to make a proper map right to the end of the caves.
But nobody wants ter do it, do they? Anyone 'ere like to try?
Fink of it, a *farzend pahn.*'

A thousand pounds is a stupendous sum. A top managing
director like Cheveney's father gets three thousand a year,
and his Rolls-Royce cost five and a half, according to the
Observer's Book of Automobiles. But there are no takers

down here in the dark with the cold breath of dinosaurs filling our lungs. In addition to being terrified myself I am bewildered by the idea that even these caves, too, have their Second Cellars. Was there no end to this recession of underworlds? Was there no place which did not have its hidden levels? (Thirty-seven years later I ask this on Tiwarik and am rewarded by a submarine cleft leading straight towards the island's heart. It takes me three days to work up enough courage to hold my breath and go in.)

The reason why the underlying presence of the Chislehurst Caves made the school's Second Cellars myth plausible was because the cave system was so close to the school while known to run far down into Kent. Indeed Thompson's aunt who lived out towards Bexley had a cellar in the corner of which a never-to-be-lifted slab led directly into the Caves. Thompson was not a faint-hearted boy but whenever he and his friends were tempted to prise up the stone and look down into the welling black dinosaur-breath they remembered the fingers worn to the second knuckle, the mad eyes like organ stops, the melancholy and eerie mooing. Thompson once said he was scared that if he opened the hole he might be dragged into it.

'You know when you go up the Eiffel Tower you get that feeling you might *have* to jump?' he said. 'Well, like that. I think it's so dark down there it'd suck the light straight out of your torch so your battery would be flat almost at once. I bet those people's torches didn't last anything like three hours. That dark just sucks the light out of them.'

This observation of Thompson's remains as graphic a way of conveying an intensity of dark as I have ever heard.

A year or two later I was at school in Canterbury, living within the Cathedral precincts, surrounded by stories of underground passageways linking that with this. In particular it was rumoured there was a tunnel running right round the Cathedral past the Dark Entry (with its ghost of a walled-up woman), under the Green Court and away towards the school dining hall. We consulted Dr Urry the Cathedral archivist, a gentle and sympathetic man who gave lessons in paleography to boys who couldn't bear PT. Certainly, he said, we must be thinking of the Roman sewers; and he forthwith dug out a map which showed very clearly how they ran. We called them the Roman sewers but I think they were actually an aquifer the Romans built to bring water down from the Scotland Hills to their town. The question was, how could we get down them?

Dr Urry made it clear to us that because they had long since been abandoned they would be in an extreme state of disrepair and consequently *highly dangerous*. He then told us exactly where one of the entrances was: a manhole plain for all to see on the west side of the Green Court not far from Lattergate. We thanked him courteously, assuring him we would hold it to be an act of stupid irresponsibility for anyone even to think of exploring the passage, still more so to tamper with a manhole clearly in the jurisdiction of the Dean and Chapter.

So a week later half a dozen of us wearing games clothes and carrying torches heaved up this manhole in full view of anybody who happened to be passing and dropped into the hole. We found ourselves in a passageway we could enter only by stooping and which ran roughly along a north–south axis. We turned south towards the Cathedral and moved off, giggling. The floor was muddy but not deeply so; the roof was vaulted and mostly made of narrow Roman bricks. Every so often there was a stone archway complete with miniature capitals. The librarian had been right: the place showed all the signs of somewhere forgotten for centuries. The stonework was cracked and sprouted moss and ferns, the bricks were porous and flaking.

The roof became lower: we were forced onto hands and knees in the mud while the rotten brickwork rubbed off its snails and pink slime on our backs. The sense of claustrophobia grew more acute, the passage now being barely large enough to accommodate a crawling teenager. Word came from up front that there was a faintish patch of daylight ahead. It came from an overhead opening, a short shaft topped with a grating. We took turns to stand upright in this shaft. Beyond the grating was the underside of a car which some expert identified as a Morris. This made sense: from our direction and estimated distance travelled we must be beneath the Archdeacon's garage and this was

undoubtedly his ramshackle old tourer. The summer air
drifting through the grating smelt sweetly of oil and petrol
and roses. One by one we dropped reluctantly back and
inserted ourselves once more into the cold and ancient
tube. The closer to the Cathedral we came the more we
imagined the seep of charnel juices and the lower the
ceiling dipped. In many places the roof had fallen completely, leaving a mound of mud and bricks on the floor to
be slithered over and a dark wound of raw earth pre-
cariously above it.

Soon we had to lie on our stomachs and worm along. At
this point even the more intrepid started to lose their nerve.
No view ahead but the mud-caked bootsoles of the next in
line, the tender white gleam of the backs of his knees, his
smeared rump filling the hole. From up front came rum-
blings and mumblings which took on comprehensibility as
they were passed back: Can't go on. Effing floor's silted up
and's touching the roof. Go back and *get a move on* . . . There
was no mistaking the panic now that everybody had
decided to escape before the roof finally fell on our backs
and entombed us with two thousand years' of grave-worms,
toads, rotting monks, the gaseous effluvia of corpses. Probably at no point was the tunnel more than six or eight feet
down but we might have been in the deepest mine.
Somebody said we could fall through into the Kentish
coalfields. I was sure these came nowhere near Canterbury
but the thought once expressed persisted. The Second
Cellars again; the meta-tunnels which appeared to underlie
the solidest earth like wormy cheese.

The impossibility of turning round added to the panic.
Eventually we arrived back beneath the Archdeacon's
Morris, stood up gratefully one by one, drew summer air
into our lungs, turned round and continued at a crawl
which now felt expansive. Soon we were pushing up the
manhole cover and emerging into the dazzle of a June
afternoon. There, watching us curiously, stood Mr Sopwith, a vast old man who was the senior English master and
much revered because he had written some books. He did
not speak until we were all out, blinking and covered in
mud, and the manhole cover had been replaced. Then he

said mildly: 'But they will not dream of us poor lads Lost in the ground.' Since this was neither comprehensible nor answerable someone said: 'Er, school archaeological society, sir.' But Mr Sopwith merely repeated his line. 'Wilfred Owen,' he added, 'in case anybody's interested. I don't suppose anybody is.' And he walked off. By the time I reached the Upper Sixth Mr Sopwith had effectively retired but I sometimes visited him in his rooms in Lardergate, not far at all from where the Archdeacon's by now almost derelict Morris still squatted over its square of darkness.

It now seems hardly coincidental that the places which shaped my sense of landscape should also have confirmed my infantile sense that something always lay beneath. As quite a small child I knew the earth was not as solid as it looked, that trees for instance had been extruded from it leaving a hollow underground exactly corresponding to the bulk of wood above. Everywhere, I thought, was riddled and caved, the foundations of the hills bored through with secret fissures, unimaginable caverns. (I loved Verne's *Journey to the Centre of the Earth*.) Seven years ago I found myself on a lava-field below a semiactive volcano in the southern Philippines and, jumping, made the ground chime. Part of the enjoyment came from not knowing how thin this crust was, whether one might break through and plunge into sulphurous caves or lakes of molten slag. That sense of walking on a thin skin was what I had always known; it was inevitable that I would come to wonder what lay beneath the abrupt peak of Tiwarik.

The undersea fissure I eventually found was quite wide enough to swim into but entirely filled with water. The three days it took me to nerve myself to hold my breath and go in were coloured with imaginings of an unknown breed of sea urchins or some species of stiff weed whose inwardly-inclined spines allowed access but no backing out again. On the fourth day I took a torch and a deep breath and swam in ten feet. There at the end was a blank wall of rock. I turned and headed out again into the sunlight.

Now that I knew I could get in and out I swam in again more confidently. This time at the rock wall my torch was reflected from the underside of the water's surface. I came up cautiously, not knowing if the roof came to within inches of it. But there was nothing, only a cool marine smell. I shone the torch about, hoping for a massive cavern but finding there was no more than a fathom of air above my head. On all sides the rock fell into the water almost at arm's length. My secret cave system was no more than a sump ending in a pocket of ancient sea-breath. It was like coming up in the end of an inverted ice-cream cone. There were no peculiar sea urchins nor eyeless fish nor strange crystals glittering in the roof; nothing but a dunce's cap of air trapped in rock.

Later I perceived how childish my hope had been. More, it was stupid, and not simply because Tiwarik was igneous rock and not limestone. Had I not yet understood the significance of its being an upside-down island? If there were any secrets here outside the reef itself they surely lay not in chthonic gloom, in subterranean darknesses, but in the upper air, in sounds and light-beams running through the grasses. Here on Tiwarik I could actually breathe the hidden and be dazzled by the concealed, for there was nothing more mysterious than the drench of light onto the island, especially in the early mornings. I had never experienced light like it. It seemed out of proportion to the sun's low angle, out of keeping with what fell on the mainland when I crossed over first thing to fetch water.

Perhaps it is still the oddest thing about Tiwarik as I write this sentence in a dark room in some city or other, my head filled always with that astonishing light: that paradoxical quality it had of at once making surfaces more brilliant while producing transparence in everything. Uniquely on the island, as opposed to the reef around it, the world beneath the world is light and not dark. It is not a place of tunnels at all but of the invisible bright corridors rowed through by my pair of eagles as they return to their fastness high in the jungle, blood from the fish in their claws pattering in a line across my roof as it did one morning. I once took some half-hearted photographs of the island but in none of them does this transparent quality appear. Maybe the camera cannot tell a lie but it sometimes cannot tell the truth, for it sees neither with the eye of affection nor with that of knowledge.

5

Often when I pad past the Malabayabas' house in the groves at Kansulay Bini is singing somewhere inside. It is a cliché, a sentimentalism that people who have nothing should sing. Her voice rises above the hollow rasping of the *kayuran* on which she is squatting while chickens squabble over the tatters of white coconut meat spilling out of the bowl. Sometimes when I am up there in my hut on the ridge the wind freakishly lifts sounds from below through the fretted ceiling of fronds. Then I can hear the children playing outside Bini's house, can even distinguish the words of their songs. In the Philippine provinces children still play chanting games. Even girls of eighteen join in with the little ones, playing with equal absorption, concentric rings of children skipping in contrary directions, couples bowing to each other with odd decorum. The songs they sing are old Spanish nursery songs, Filipino folk-songs, snatches from pop songs and American musicals, all of them with the macaronic air of being in several languages at once, none of which is wholly understood. The games also give the impression of being at once firmly choreographed by tradition and utterly improvised.

One day I can hear them enacting a dashing Spanish courtship game where a row of eight-year-old girls ritually flinches and giggles at the statuesque advances of eight-year-old *caballeros*. Above their chanting can be heard an entirely Filipino descant of obscene advice offered by the girls to the boys, ribald suggestions by the boys to the girls, shouts of laughter from everyone. On another day a song in parallel text rises up through the leaves. It must have been written for use in schools but has now acquired something of the status of a genuine folk-song with its elemental storyline and innocent tune:

One day   *isang araw*
I saw   *nakakita*
ng bird   *isang ibon*
flying   *lumilipad*
I shot   *binaril ko*
I picked   *pinulot ko* (i.e. retrieved, not plucked)
I cooked   *niluto ko*
I ate   *kinain ko.*

Over the years I have become deeply attached to the
Malabayabas family. For a start I like their name, eminently
ethnic as opposed to Spanish. Just as *bato* means 'stone' and
mabato or *malabato* mean 'stony', so *bayabas* means 'guava'
and hence 'Malabayabas' is whatever adjective you could
derive from that fruit: 'guavery', perhaps. It is particularly
pleasing that their little house is surrounded by wild guava
bushes. Sising (from Cezar) is exactly the same age as I am,
born in late 1941 not long before the Japanese Occupation.
His wife Bini (from Divina, pronounced 'Dibina') is two
years younger, exactly the same age as my sister Jane. We
spend hours at each other's houses drinking *tuba* and eating
puppy, crocodile, fruit-bat or merely shellfish from the
stream, whatever is available. Some night I may be on my
hill-top when suddenly from over its curve a flacking
orange glow will appear as if a volcanic seizure were
sending sporadic flame shooting from fissures in the path
below. Then their voices, ascending beneath the blazing
torches of *lagi*, dried palm-fronds artfully bound into flam-
beaux with their own leaves. Sising, already a little drunk,
brings a long bamboo tube of palm wine, Bini a covered
plastic bowl full of boiled chicken bits. Nobody drinks
without *pulutan.*
'Good evening, James. Are we disturbing you?'
'Not at all. I was just beginning to feel lonely.'
'No wonder, living up here without a wife to keep you
warm.'
'It's quite warm enough without.' And we all laugh at our
by now ritual exchange; they are fanning themselves after
their climb, the sweat on their faces glinting in the dying
flames of the torches discarded on the ground.

Occasionally I have a bottle of *anisado* which I buy in town and which I now produce like a punctilious suburbanite his bottle of Cyprus sherry from a compartment in the radiogram. We drink and fan ourselves for the night is deep and sultry, a muddy lid of cloud closing off the stars and shutting the Earth in a cooking pot from beneath the edges of whose top flashes of lightning leak in from outside. This lightning below the horizon is constant, soundless and meaningless since it heralds no storm, no rain, no change, nothing but its own fitful discharge. We talk of the steady fall in copra prices, of their son's success with his catapult (four of the Philippines' national bird and a good solid hit on Kuyo's dog which was chasing their chickens), of the rumours that half the supplies of medicine for the little provincial hospital ten miles away have been sold on the black market by one of the doctors.

'*Ay!*' they laugh, shaking their heads as at the immutability of human behaviour. Sometimes I find their lack of outrage infuriating, at other times deeply admirable. It is a phlegm they need, for the Malabayabas family are tenants of the Sorianos.

I had heard about their landlords before I finally met them since shortly after Lolang Mating's death I decided to make life easier for myself by installing a hand-pump at the foot of the hill, hence not having to go so far to fetch my water. It seemed obvious the best site was behind Sising's house; in this way we could all benefit. I bought a Chinese pump, twenty feet of galvanised iron pipe, a couple of bags of cement, and after some strenuous digging which I avoided by being occupied elsewhere the pump was installed and within two weeks was drawing sweet clear water. So far so good; but I had forgotten about who owned the land on which it stood.

Shortly afterwards I was introduced to old Judge Soriano who lived away in town. He was a moulting old boy who spent much of his time sitting in a chair reading through his bound collection of Jehovah's Witness texts dating from the Thirties or looking at photograph albums with his cronies. He had married just after the war and his favourite pictures were those of his honeymoon spent in America. He handed me many albums of black and white photographs so that I should have plenty to occupy me while I sipped my *calamansi* juice and he described his grandiose plans for building a Kingdom Hall on what the province's government had officially named Capitol Hill, a jungly mass of bananas and rooting goats behind the market which had been earmarked for better things. There they were, Attorney and Mrs Soriano, beaming happily beside their rented Ford V-8 (it must have been just before the single-piece windscreen came in) at Ausable Chasm, Golden Gate Bridge, Niagara Falls, at all sorts of concrete diners in the middle of nowhere. In their two months' touring they seemed to have covered pretty much the entire continent but their smiles had never flagged, at least not when facing the camera.

I recognised Mrs Soriano at once when returning one day from town and dropping in on Sising and Bini with some cough medicine for their youngest. A stout woman in a blue dress wearing a good deal of jewellery and shoes with heels (in a coconut grove!) she was standing outside their house holding a stick. Nearby was a jeep whose driver was chatting to Sising and which must have been driven among the trees and across the stream.

'Good afternoon,' she called as I approached. 'You must be the famous Mr James.' We went through the rituals. 'Why are you living here?' she asked abruptly, smiling.

'Why not? It's nice and quiet up there on the hill. Seabreezes at night, no noise, no NPAs.'

'Where do you get your bread? Americans eat bread.'

'I'm not an American. Anyway, I like rice.'

She looked around in expressive silence at Bini's youngest children playing in the dirt beneath the house, at Bini's torn T-shirt, at Sising's threadbare shorts, at the worn-out rubber flip-flops mended with wire lying about, at the two old torch batteries placed on a tree stump to catch the sun and squeeze the last microvolt out of their exhausted chemicals.

'You mean you *want* to live here in the *bundok*?' she asked. She pointed with her stick at the hand-pump. 'You paid for that? For these people?' She was incredulous. 'Perhaps you are very kind.'

I said I had put it there for my own convenience.

'You should charge them for using it, you know. Are you with the Peace Corps?'

Questions, questions. I repeated that I was not American and explained how only Americans could belong to the Peace Corps. I knew it was a waste of time, that to her all white foreigners were *'kanos*, that she too thought England was one of the States. She was as bored as I; her attention was distracted by a couple of the Malabayabas' chickens. She pointed with her stick.

'Boks!' she called to her driver. 'I'll have those unless you can see anything fatter. Everything's so thin here.' Her stick-point wandered with her attention, pointing now at little Lito beneath the hut. I dared not look at Bini whom I knew to be eaten up with shame about her own thinness, about that of her youngest child and about what it said of her and Sising's failure to provide. Boks grabbed one chicken, Sising the other; they trussed their feet with stalks and tossed them into the jeep. Meanwhile Mrs Soriano's stick-point had lighted on a hand broom which Bini had just finished making out of frond ribs. It was beautifully bound at the handle with a triple plait of *nito*. 'That's not bad,' she said, her stick-point going from Boks to the broom. Bini surrendered the broom with a smile; it joined the chickens in the back of the jeep.

I could not believe what I was seeing and I could not watch any more. What I wanted to say would have rebounded on Sising and Bini. I turned and walked off up the hill.

'Goodbye,' Mrs Soriano called out behind me. I knew she was bothered and uncertain. People acutely conscious of their own status are necessarily obsessed with that of others and she could not yet place me. Nominally I ranked high as a *'kano* (rich, white, maybe useful for contacts and help with getting visas for the family) but I had spoiled everything by going native, by failing to recognise her as a fellow member of the middle class and by not having the sort of job to which she could assign a notional salary.

The real fact of the matter was that the Sorianos and I were separated less by a cultural or geographical gap than by a temporal one. They were still living in an era which was classically feudal and their relationships were those of feudalism. I thought back to school, to European history with its Jack Straws and Johnny Peasants confronting the tyranny of Lord and Lady Landowner, to sweet Auburn. I had never expected I might one day meet Lady Landowner and find her a fat Filipina with brown ringed fingers, a fake Dior handbag and a chauffeur-driven jeep with bald tyres. But then, neither had I expected I would be befriended by Johnny Peasant and brought palm wine and fried dog and the company of his family at night in case I was feeling lonely in my hut in the hills.

Mrs Soriano may for a while have been wary of me and puzzled but within six months the self-assurance of her class had settled the matter. I had to go to Europe for some time; on my return I found the old Judge was dead and the Malabayabases embarrassed and despondent. They pointed to a grassless depression in the ground behind the house.

'Where the hell's your pump?' I asked.

'Mrs Soriano took it. She came one day and said that now her husband had died she would have financial problems and needed the pump herself. Boks came and he and Sising dug it up. But they've left the pipe going underground; it wouldn't come up.'

I was still recently enough arrived to have newly laundered shirts and trousers in my luggage. I broke them out and walked furiously back down to Kansulay. It was the wrong time of day for jeepneys. Eventually I caught a *calesa* with high wooden wheels and a bony horse which trudged us into town in a matter of hours. I went straight to the Soriano house and the first thing I saw was the pump lying on its side in the front yard among the chickens and litter. Mrs Soriano was called by a houseboy and emerged smiling gravely, as befitted a widow. I was in no mood for condolences.

'That pump, Mrs Soriano. I want it back.'

'Oh. I see. I understood you to say you had given it to the Malabayabas family?'

'No. I said I had installed it for my own convenience. It just happens to be convenient for all of us, so I want it back.'

'Let us go in, Mr James. I would like you to meet my eldest son.'

Not having met Attorney 'Cads' (for Ricardo?) Soriano before, I felt able to commiserate perfunctorily with him on the recent death of his father. His mother was not in the mood for small talk.

'Mr James has a legal difficulty regarding our pump,' she prompted him. Cads looked unhappy; I suspected that like the old Judge he was more at ease drinking with his *barkadas* and indulging in congenial small-town malice. Indeed the law scene in Manila might well have been a bit too fast for him and it crossed my mind that his father's death may not have been wholly unwelcome since it would entitle him to retire to this quiet provincial backwater while appearing selfless and dutiful. Certainly as he sucked his gold-and-ruby fraternity ring it was barely possible to imagine him plotting shrewd deals, still less successfully confronting their victims.

'Not exactly *your* pump,' I said in case leaving his mother's adjective uncorrected constituted a legal admission of ownership.

'I think my mother wishes to say, er, please sit down. Will you have coffee, a soft drink, *calamansi* juice? I am so sorry, you must be hot after your journey. Kansulay is very far. I used to go there a lot as a boy. We went to pick the *duhats* when the season came.'

'Cads,' said Mrs Soriano.

'Don't rush me, Mom. Mr James is our visitor and we haven't met before although I have heard so much about him . . . Er, I think my mother wishes to say that the pump, having been installed on our family's land, was with effect from that moment *our* pump. This is Filipino law. It is unfortunate that at the moment my mother had urgent need of it you were out of the country.'

'Urgent need? It's outside the window there, rusting on the ground. What was it urgently needed for, a chicken perch?'

'Ha, a chicken perch,' laughed Cads. 'That's a good joke.'

'Plans change,' said Mrs Soriano.

Perhaps emboldened by so recently having been in

Europe that I still felt a sophisticated globe-trotter's immunity, perhaps thinking of Sising being made to remove with his own hands the pump he had helped install, but most likely not wanting to go all the way to the river once again to fetch my own water, I abandoned caution and took the line I thought most likely to succeed.

'Mrs Soriano, I don't know whether you are aware of it but for many years I was a journalist and I still have a great many friends in the European and American Press.' This was completely untrue. 'If that pump is not back, installed and working at Kansulay by tomorrow evening I shall make it my business to ensure this story gets printed in the newspapers and that the name of Mrs Soriano is given global publicity as that of a wealthy Filipina who finds it necessary to steal a hand-pump from the penniless peasants who work her own estates. Believe me,' I lied, 'Associated Press and Reuters will leap at a story like this, especially now that the Marcos regime is starting to get a bad press.'

Mrs Soriano blinked. Cads was sucking his ring hard. 'That's the world-wide angle,' I went on. 'Now as regards the local scene: I happen to be quite good friends with an ex-Minister' and I named an old member of Macapagal's government which the Marcos dynasty replaced. He was truly a has-been but still respected in many quarters as a serious man of culture and integrity who had survived the Martial Law persecutions with his honour intact. I noticed from her expression that Mrs Soriano knew exactly whom I meant. 'Also, I believed the Governor of this province when he told me personally over dinner about his concern for land reform.' This was outrageous. The man in question had indeed expressed concern, but I suspected it was *lest* land reform should ever be implemented. Nor did I point out something which Mrs Soriano would later work out for herself: that owing to my recent absence I had to be referring to the previous Governor, not the one who had just been installed in an attempt to redress some of my host's flagrant misdeeds and repair the ruling KBL party's public image.

But it appeared my shameless and mendacious name-dropping had had its effect. Mrs Soriano was now all smiles.

'But don't you see, Mr James, it has all been nothing but a misunderstanding. I think I didn't explain myself well. Thank goodness you came here so we could clear the matter up.'

'I came here to get the pump back.'

'Of course. But what I have been trying to explain, only I am so bad at it, is that it's fine now. *Ayos na.* It's okay. Good as new.'

'What do you mean?'

'I think,' said Cads, 'my mother is saying she had the pump dismantled to carry out maintenance. It was broken.'

'That's right,' said Mrs Soriano. 'Broken. No water would come. I said at the time they dug it wrong, they did not put a filter so sand gets in and wears out the *balat* . . . Cads, what is *balat*?'

'Washer,' I said wearily. 'I understand perfectly, Mrs Soriano. That was very thoughtful.'

'No, no. Those poor people.' She was relaxed now, her rings flashing in the light from the louvred windows. Both sides had been allowed to lie their way onto neutral ground; faces were saved but I had won. That would not be forgotten at some future date. What I really wanted to say to her was *Ano ka na, suwerte?*, now a slightly dated piece of *kanto*-boy slang but which could still mock and deflate. It might be translated unidiomatically as something like 'What are you, lucky or something?' meaning, 'Did heaven shit gold on you?' But stressed with just the right inflection it really asked the same thing as that English phrase, inflected with equal subtlety: *Who the hell do you think you are?*

But that had been two years ago. Now Kansulay's water project was about to move on a stage, entering the sphere of local politics. The morning after we braved the *nono* in their lair my engineering friend and I go off to our test dig and find the hole full of dusky water, overflowing away towards the eroded gully of the stream. Actually I am impressed by the quantity of the water and the speed with which the pit has filled. Not wanting to make my enthusiasm the pretext for his assent, however, I opt for a restrained, judicious note.

'Well,' I want to know, 'tell me again: is it worth spending real money on a proper spring box here? Plus of course, what? a good kilometre of two-inch PVC pipe? If we decide to go ahead we'll be getting into real money even allowing for all the work being done *bayanihan*.'

He looks up at the forested hill above the spring and thoughtfully produces a calculator from his hip pocket. I am easily impressed when people produce the tools of their trade on-site; it denotes seriousness of intent. My father, who after all was not a surgeon, used a scalpel to sharpen his pencils. (Even I, carrying my home-made spear gun down to the beach at evening, walk in a little glow of professionalism.) I now notice my friend's calculator is a scientific one, covered with buttons labelled for arcane functions. I want to feel confident in him.

'I think,' he says at length, 'I think there will be enough water. But only for drinking. People must still do their washing in the stream.'

'It's as marginal as that?'

'Yes. Also another very important thing. You know who owns this land? The Sorianos. If they want to make a *kaingin* here, *ay*, no more water.'

The air suddenly seems loud with the clapping wings of metaphorical pigeons coming home to roost. In those intervening two years I had only seen Mrs Soriano once or twice in the market, long enough for each to bare teeth judiciously at the other, to enquire after the other's health in that way which makes solicitude seem like bad taste. Who the hell does she think she is? I had wanted to know; and now here am I hoping to see the village's new water system installed on her land. I know who the hell she is, and she me. My friend has correctly spotted the weak link which could break the entire project. For if indeed the Sorianos did decide to make a *kaingin* and grow cassava where before there was merely a tangle of vegetation dotted with wild bananas and papayas, then that was undoubtedly what would happen.

Kaingin is the most basic form of cultivation: slash-and-burn. It offers short-term rewards and long-term disaster; naturally people opt for the rewards. It is an easy way to clear a patch of land and the natural fertility of fallow ground is supplemented for a while by the potash and nitrates left by the burning. But on the steep hillsides of this province the rain soon washes away the topsoil once its cover is gone, silting up the streams and even altering the offshore fishing. From the air much of the Philippines is visibly scarred by this primitive form of agriculture. Some provinces are nearly ruined by it, whole populations having been forced to move from the wastelands they have made. Here at Kansulay's potential source of drinking water it is easy to imagine what would happen should at some future date one of the Sorianos look at this unproductive hill and spitefully decide to get a couple of years' worth of cassava out of it before turning their attentions elsewhere. Shorn of its lush green vegetation the bare soil would parch in the sun and the water which at present percolated the earth would be drawn upwards to boil invisibly off into the tropic air. Similarly when it rained the water would run straight off since there would be nothing to retain it.

'What I'll do,' I say, trying to sound measured and responsible although I am already, unworthily, becoming a bit bored by the whole business since it has so quickly led into potential feud-and-trouble territory, 'I'll tell the *baranggay* Captain what you say about the water only being enough for drinking and also that I will agree to start spending money only when he has extracted a written undertaking from the Sorianos that they will not turn this hill over to the *kaingineros*.' How decisive that sounds. How dubious I really am about 'written undertakings'. An 'accidental' fire ('I have of course punished the offender') and Kansulay will go back to drinking contaminated stream water.

When I think of Sising and Bini or of my friends at Sabay, I come up against ordinary affection, the urge to do them justice. I finally think the way to do it is not to describe their lives as they see them, in terms of a daily struggle against poverty, though I am no stranger to the details. How well I know Sising's income from his eleven rented *karitan* or *tuba*-yielding palms, his entire pay for three days' copra-making of 84p, the average monthly sum from all sources coming into his household of about £12.[2] I know exactly what his cigarettes cost, the soap, the matches, the little bags of brown sugar, the essential rice. I know the price of kerosene which fuels the decrepit Coleman lantern he uses for finding crabs in the stream at night, which is why when I visit him after dark I often find their house lit with the smoky orange flames of *tangan-tangan* beans from the castor oil bush, 'Nature's candles' as Bini blithely describes them. I also know why even the most selfless mother thinks twice before spending fifty centavos on a small Band-Aid dressing to put on her child's wounded foot: even less than 2p is a recognisable portion of the family's daily budget of 35p.

This is how they themselves describe their lives to an outsider. With the utmost trepidation I will not do the same. There is always a gap between how people portray their lives to differing audiences and how they actually live them. Poverty is all; and yet it isn't. It grinds away daily but doesn't explain the hours spent gossiping, laughing, yearning, being utterly diverted by a hunt for a wood-wasp's nest. It is just as sentimental to misrepresent the poor as obsessed all their conscious hours by poverty as it is to depict them as always singing. Nevertheless it is an inescapable convention of the times that rich and poor should confront one another on territory bare of nearly everything but bleak economic factors. It can take a long while before that terrain fades and is replaced by something else, by affection and shared experience. That I have to deal with my own useless guilt as well as love where my friends here are concerned is my private misfortune and not their responsibility. It is something anybody from a developed country living in an undeveloped must face. The important thing for me is that Sising and Bini no longer talk about themselves as they once did, as representative poor confronting representative rich. We now allow ourselves the latitude of humour, of gentle mockery even.

'H'm,' says Bini one afternoon, peering closely at the side of my head where the sunlight strikes it, 'grey hairs. Time marches on and still no wife.'

We are knocking back ESQ at the table outside her house.

'Steady on,' says Sising, but his wife is not to be steadied.

'No, but really. Half the girls in the village would give their teeth to make him a wife.'

I observe that half the girls in the village seem already to have done so: their extreme beauty is often marred by endemic tooth decay. This makes Sising laugh and he says something encouraging about being unlucky in love.

'Unlucky can sometimes hide Unwilling,' says Bini. This old saw gives a glimpse of how she will be at sixty if she lives that long: too knowing to be really sententious but probably rather implacable all the same.

'God save me from peasant wisdom,' I say defensively.

'He has,' says Bini in triumph.

This exchange breaks us all up and our laughter scares the piglets and brings the children running to hear the joke. When they see the rum they go back to what they were doing. The afternoon wears into evening; night falls and our improvised party stretches on into supper. Sising gets out his home-made ukelele and our songs rise in the clearing, lurching and ungainly like the hens trying to get into the trees. Events become a bit blurred. I vaguely recall a dearth of matches and one of the children whispering to me the suggestion that he raid the door-post. (This was a reference to the bamboo hinge-post of the house door. It is a custom, now dying out, of the older people in this province to put small coins through the slots for the door's cross-members to bring luck to the house. Bini's old father always did this when he visited. To the children, though, this secret hoard building up in one of the internodes represented a piggy-bank rather than a fund of good fortune. They were always trying to winkle the coins out with knife-blades when Sising and Bini weren't looking. It was a conspiracy I shared with them not to tell their parents.)

Next morning I wake headachy but early – so early that

the valley below remains full of inky pools where the chickens are no doubt still coming down out of the trees. There is unexpected whistling from the path; visitors or passers-by at any hour are rare. I wait in the dew, barefoot, holding a half-eaten banana. It is Sising.

'I think last night you didn't believe me.'

My brains are drowsy. They can remember nothing of last night. Sising opens the old plastic bag he is carrying and shows me two lengths of bamboo, the halves of a single tube about two inches in diameter split lengthwise. One has a long slice taken out of its rounded upper surface so that the internal wall is very thin. There are many scorched holes in this wall. At once I remember: I had expressed scepticism when he told me he was not worried to be caught without matches because he could always make fire. I thought of fire-making as an aboriginal accomplishment, maybe still practised in remote areas of the world almost out of perversity rather than from necessity. I associated fire-sticks with ethnology museums and rubbing pieces of wood together with jokes about Scouts.

Sising produces a handful of dry tinder which looks like (and probably is) kapok and within two minutes has a small flame dancing on the earth floor of my cooking area. He smiles up at me. His look is neither triumphant nor smug but merely suggests, 'There, that's how it's done.' Politely refusing a cup of coffee he gathers his tinder and sticks into the plastic bag, accepts a banana and goes. I hear his whistling descend the hill, become swallowed up in the rising chorus of birds in the waking groves, dissolve into the distant bleating of his own nanny-goat and his own children's cries.

I discover later that retaining this skill is not by any means purely a generational thing: plenty of youngsters in the woods of this province can still make fire. Once more I am reminded of the irrelevance of the distant capital, of the complete independence of people who can survive typhoons, the rise and fall of governments, all sorts of disruptions and calamities and go on living in circumstances which for many would not be noticeably worse than usual. In Western countries with their dangerously centralised economies where the standards of living even in rural areas are little different from those of the cities, each citizen is indissolubly a part of the body politic. If the system ever collapsed beyond a quick retrieval people would begin dying. At the very least it would once again become a commonplace – as it must have been in England until the nineteenth century and as it is here in Kansulay any day of the year – to see people go to each other's houses to borrow fire, to meet a woman hurrying past with a single stick whose end is a glowing ember, trailing a wavering line of smoke.

My admiration for these survival skills, this independence, is considerable. But I know also that it is sentimental yet again to represent it as being born of anything other than necessity. It is a virtue for that reason alone and for none other. Likewise it is not thrift which sends Sising's child to the village shop at evening to buy a quarter-*lapad* of cooking oil or a few spoonfuls of soy sauce in a knotted plastic bag; half a kilo of rice in an old biscuit tin; a single small onion or one cigarette.

If the gap between the lives of Sising and Bini and their landlords the Sorianos is vast, that between theirs and my own is unimaginable. Time and again, despite friendship, despite the intimacies of five years, I am brought face to face with it. That I have chosen to live so much in their world ought to make them deeply suspicious or at least to resent bitterly the ease with which I can buy their children Band-Aids.

As I contemplate this unpalatable fact I remember occasions when circumstances – an injury, a week's torrential rain, sickness – have magnified the ordinary hardships of living to the point where they seemed overwhelming for a day or two. The last time it happened I had sprained my ankle so badly I could not go up and down the hill. Sising lugged my water for me, the children brought me vegetables and guavas, Bini came with plates of dabs and leaf compresses. Once I imagined I caught the vestige of a look on her face which brought to mind a passage in Michael Herr's *Dispatches* where he deals with the incomprehension of the GIs in Vietnam when they learn that he and other correspondents are over there to cover the war voluntarily, that they are running the same dangers and living in the same conditions but that they could be on a plane home that very afternoon if they chose. Sometimes Herr intercepted a look from a wounded soldier or from a man who had just lost a friend, 'the look that made you look away, and in its hateful way it was the purest single thing I'd ever known . . .'

At first, I got it all mixed up, I didn't understand and I felt sorry for myself, misjudged. 'Well fuck you too,' I'd think. 'It could have been me just as easily, I take chances too, can't you see that?' And then I realised that that was exactly what it was all about, it explained itself as easily as that, another of the war's dark revelations. They weren't judging me, they weren't reproaching me, they didn't even mind me, not in any personal way. They only hated me, hated me the way you'd hate any hopeless fool who would put himself through this thing when he had choices, any fool who had no more need of his life than to play with it in this way.

It was probably the first time that precise phenomenon had been so accurately recorded. Correspondents in previous wars no doubt felt occasional guilt at making a living from others' deaths, as any journalist might at the scene of a disaster. But that was before electronic newsgathering and satellite links, before the whole world became a voyeur, before any image viewed on a television screen had attained the same inconsequential level of fiction. Just as air travel changed for ever the world which was flown to, so electronic newsgathering has changed for ever the world which is reported. Coming from the world of the voyeur it is no longer possible to take a step backwards and become a mere observer again. The rôle of the describing writer is different now despite all he might like to believe. It was still possible for Christopher Isherwood to play at being a camera amid Weimar decadence just as it was for Graham Greene to lie in hospital with a novelist's chip of ice in his heart recording the behaviour of parents around the bed of their dying child. But now we are video-cameras: our subjects know what it is like to be part of the audience, the actors are themselves viewers. They understand what happens to the pictures swallowed up by the lens, they perceive a world in its armchairs whose insatiable need for images has put forth tentacles in the form of cameras and cameramen, journalists with their tape recorders, writers with their deadlines. Above all they know that briefly to be the centre of someone else's attention, even the world's, does not necessarily presuppose either interest or concern but finally has more to do with good programming, selling products, entertaining.

So it is fine to note how people sing, their cheerful resourcefulness. It is all very well to remark on their dignity in the face of suffering. It is inspiring to watch them (on television) sitting down like Manileños in 1986 in the path of tanks and APCs, just as it is to observe (in actuality) their delicious improvisings in the face of disaster. But a disaster it remains, the life of the people of Kansulay and Sabay and all those like them the world over. That it is a slow, unclimactic disaster goes on being true independently of the lives which may be lived happily, contentedly, sadly or miserably in its shadow. I chat to Bini while she is washing the clothes; I follow her eyes as they rest in resignation on the too-thin body of Lito. When her singing drifts up to me I no longer think about the indomitable human spirit, I think of a national health service and that there are certain basic things the human spirit should no longer have to contend with at the fag-end of the twentieth century.

Many times Filipinos have asked me: 'Are you writing a book about the Philippines?' In the past I have truthfully replied, 'No, I don't know enough,' and glimpsed a passing look of relief before the conventional expression of disappointment, that surely the place is significant enough to interest someone *out there*? That look of relief is the first acknowledgement that the new era which Michael Herr so eloquently heralded has dawned here too, a growing suspicion that a writer might do something as cynical and prudent as to invest a good deal of discomfort in a book which may later make him money.

This is the crux: the eavesdropped world now wants to know who is listening and why. Anyone could have come to Kansulay with a journalist's writ ('Get the background, the *real* grass-roots feel') or as a doctor, a worker with an international charity, an adviser on some construction project. But to have come as none of these, neither intentionally to write about the scene nor yet completely as a voyeur but simply to *live*: this reduces everybody, myself included, to incomprehension.

Yet I now know that I did imagine that look I thought to see cross Bini's face as she brought me food up my hill. What Michael Herr saw I have still to see in the faces of my friends here in Kansulay and Sabay although it would be incredible had the idea of resentment not crossed their minds in private. If so, and they still allow no evidence of it to show, then all I can say is that it betokens an astounding generosity of spirit which characterises my entire experience of their country. This generosity of spirit is indeed the most angelic of the Filipinos' qualities. In terms of their own ruthlessly exploited history it is probably their greatest flaw.

But there again maybe that, too, is a sentimental construct. The more one tries to make sense of one culture in the terms of another the more the whole issue disintegrates into polemic. The fundamental oddness and unknowableness of human beings, their sheer otherness, is what remains. I think of the (to me) mysterious private world of Sising and Bini and their children living amid the coconuts, nowhere, anywhere, dancing their dances and singing their songs. That part of them which I can put a price on – their few commodities, their labour, their aspirations to have at least one of their children working in Manila or married abroad – that I know. But there is another side, far more alien, which has only a little to do with *nono* and the whole range of peasant beliefs. It has rather more to do with confronting death and typhoons and landlords, with living uninsured in a world of disasters for which there is no redress. It has to do with ancient cultural norms which once, not so long ago, existed in Europe but which now are forgotten or out of fashion.

One day another song makes its way up through the trees, sung by the children to a tune which for me has become wistful. Among the young voices I can identify that of Marisil, Bini's fifteen-year-old daughter. She produces angular sounds which are entirely Eastern; in their scraped quality the words carry intact through the leaves:

> *Ali, ali, namamangka,*
> *pasakayin yaring bata;*
> *pagdating sa Maynila*
> *ipagpalit ng manika.*
>
> *Ali, ali, namamayong,*
> *pasukubin yaring sanggol;*
> *pagdating sa Malabon*
> *ipagpalit ng bagoong.*

Suddenly the words are no longer those I know by rote. They become immensely sinister. Just as underneath certain of Grimm's fairy-tales lurks the true savagery of the human psyche so this artless song strikes me for the first time with its terrifying threat of the stranger to whom bad children might be handed over, the unknown to which anyone might be consigned for summary metamorphosis:

> Old woman, old woman, paddling
> your boat,
> Give this child a ride;
> When you reach Manila
> Change it into a doll.
>
> Old woman, old woman, beneath your
> umbrella,
> Shelter this child;
> When you reach Malabon
> Change it into fish sauce.

The obliqueness haunts me, the children singing of 'this

child' but not meaning themselves, singing as if they were already parents conjuring a bogeyman with which to threaten their own offspring. I look towards the invisible singing, across the valley with its canopy of fronds beating back the sun in green and gold spears and concealing all sorts of primal rawness. Having glimpsed an elemental and unchanging world and in the temporary grip of afternoon melancholy I ask myself what on earth I think I am doing messing about with water projects, what kind of parental ghost I am myself appeasing by this idiotic way of life.

6

Back on Tiwarik I have been spending a domestic morning making a fish-drier: four lengths of wood from the forest supporting a chest-high top of woven rattans. It is a few metres from my hut, angled to catch the sun and near enough to deter the sea-eagles as well as the crows which now and then flap across from the mainland on the scrounge.

Keeping food edible in the tropics without refrigeration is an art. After a bout of night fishing it is possible to hang the catch up in a tree for the rest of that night without gutting, scaling or salting it and still find it fresh in the morning. But the moment the sun rises it must be cleaned or cooked. If after a greedy breakfast there is still fish left over the best thing is to dry it.

I have become very fond of sun-dried fish although much can depend on how it is marinaded beforehand. First, though, the individual fish must be properly cut. Small or flattish fish are opened down the spine so that they hinge apart at the belly. This ensures the thickest meat along the back is fully exposed to the sun. Thicker fish such as eels are cut twice so the fish may be opened out into three flaps with two thin hinges of flesh. The fishermen of Sabay can do this with great dispatch and dexterity while scarcely watching what their hands are doing.

Next the sliced fish are carefully washed to rinse off any blood and pieces of internal organ and put into pans to soak for several hours. If only salt is used as a preservative the solution must be strong enough to prevent the growth of bacteria but not so strong as to render the fish inedible. The correct degree of salinity may be judged when the fish float in the solution rather than lie under it. Personally, I prefer a more elaborate marinade of chopped onions, garlic, crushed peppercorns, soy sauce and *tuba* vinegar, the salinity brought up to strength. A few chillies add interest. Then the fish are laid out flat in the sun on a *tuyuan* such as I have been making. When thoroughly dried they can be kept a long time although care needs to be taken in damp weather lest they 'sweat': being hygroscopic the salt absorbs water from the atmosphere. Kept dry, the fish are crisp and papery. They rustle when sorted and are delicious fried. It is provident to keep some by one for lean and future days, besides which they are always readily saleable as *daing*.

While at work on this drier I have all the while been conscious of occasional explosions somewhere in the background. Every so often a thud shakes the air about Tiwarik and the echo of a dull clap falls to the beach as if, having bounced tiredly off the peak, it lacked the energy to go any further. At the same time I have had a tune running obsessively through my head in the way that happens sometimes when one's hands are occupied. It is a tune I have not consciously heard in decades, something released from childhood like a trapped pocket of prehistoric air returning to circulation from the heart of a smashed flint. A particularly loud bang from close around the nearest headland has jarred the association loose in my brain. An especial quality in the explosion, something reminiscent about its *timbre*, enables me to identify the piece of music as part of a Mozart sonata for four hands. And suddenly with a rush an entire memory comes back of Mozart and detonations and bright sunlight. Once again, it seems my present life on this curious island has evoked a private past.

There was a summer long ago just before I went to Canterbury when my friend Howard and I shared certain interests, two of which were music and explosions. In the long holiday we spent much time at each other's house where we did more or less exactly the same things. Often we sat at the piano earnestly inventing ever more elaborate descants for well-known hymns or playing Mozart duets. Then a different urge would take us out to the garage to make bombs.

I still had some of my original cordite collection left,

Howard (whose elder brother was a National Serviceman) a lot of empty ·303 cartridge cases. We would drill a small hole near the base of these and feed in a length of Jetex fuse which was available in those days for setting off model rocket motors. Then we filled the cartridges with a mixture of sodium chlorate weedkiller and sugar and crimp the open end in a vice. These little bombs made an immense noise, tearing apart into ragged brass petals. Sometimes when set on their bases on a wooden surface they blew out the ignition caps and took off like missiles, leaving a gleaming copper disc embedded in the wood. No boffin at Peenemünde working on his Führer's programme of rocket-propelled retribution can have experimented more carefully than we did, varying the proportions of mixture and writing it all down in an exercise book. We cross-referenced the different explosives with the way they were packed, too, for we not only used rifle cartridges: we tried lengths of gas-pipe, jam-jars of plaster of Paris, balls of clay, a roll of lavatory paper with both ends bunged and the whole encased in yards of the elasticated webbing Howard's father treasured for the roof-rack of his Humber Super Snipe.

That summer rang with tunes and bangs. I can remember adults only peripherally. Howard's elder sister Judith seems a presence, less because she was a very pretty sixteen-year-old with blonde hair she could practically sit on than because our noises frightened her pony. She didn't like Mozart and she thought boys with bombs were silly. We didn't like ponies and it was universally acknowledged that girls constituted a category of silliness such as to re-define the word. Our mines threw up clods of earth at the feet of her horse, sending it cantering with flared nostrils to the protective shade of an elm in the corner of the paddock in whose branches there nestled a 'blinder': one of our better devices full of magnesium powder which burst with immense lightning and crack. Shattered twigs and elm foliage rained down behind it as the horse took off once more, eyes rolling, for the far corner of the field where it tore through the hedge and vanished.

We set bombs off at night to watch the flash; we sent them

up on the backs of gliders and kites to see what an explosion in the sky looked like. We even sacrificed Howard's oldest control-line plane, substituting a bomb in the cockpit for the plastic pilot whose moulded head and shoulders had been glued beneath the canopy. The realism of this explosion exceeded all expectations: it ignited the fuel in the tank and the entire plane blew apart in mid-air while travelling at speed. To children brought up on movies of the recent war it looked entirely authentic: the severed wings fluttering to earth, the E.D. 'Bee' engine shooting forward from its mounts and plunging through the greenhouse roof, the trail of smoke across the summer sky.

And still we were not satisfied. I filched ether from my mother's bottle of waste anaesthetic, Howard stole petrol from his father's Atco motor mower. How we never blew ourselves up was a miracle but we never between us lost more than an eyebrow or two. No neighbour complained, no parent intervened. Presumably they were all too busy elsewhere being doctors and lawyers to notice what their sons were up to. 'That sounds nice,' said Howard's father vaguely one evening after we had played some duets. 'Better than those fireworks you keep letting off. I didn't know you could buy them in August. Never could when I was a boy.' My own father, too, was oddly tolerant. The only time he objected was when I embarrassed him. This came about one evening as he, my mother, my sister and I returned home from seeing a film and dining in town. It was late, a dark summer's night. For some reason I was carrying one of the cartridge bombs in my pocket. While my father was putting the car away and the others were sleepily opening the front door I let it off in the front garden to see how much of a flash it made. The noise was very satisfactory and I went through the hedge into the orchard with a torch to find the torn metal casing which I had heard rattling through the apple branches. Within minutes there were sounds of conversation from the front. I overheard my father saying 'No, I'm afraid it was my son letting off a firework. I'll certainly speak to him. I'm sorry you were bothered, officer. Goodnight.' I made myself scarce for as long as I could without risking being locked out and went in to find my father white with rage not because I had been exploding bombs but because he had had to explain to the local bobby who arrived on his bicycle in a lather of sweat and trembling with dread of being the first on a murder scene. Giving an innocent policeman a nasty turn, making my father apologise on my behalf – far from becoming a family joke such was not a laughing matter. On the other hand I now suspect that my mother, true to her more subversive nature, was secretly amused.

In the meantime Howard's and my days were endless, our friendship without bounds. Yet my memory of that summer is not that it was conventionally carefree. Henry Ward Beecher's observation that despite their intent energy 'boys have hours of great sinking and sadness' applied to us well enough but especially to Howard who was older than I in an unchronological sense. Already he had glimpsed the future and one night he was not to be consoled. In the dark of his bedroom he worked himself into a peculiar mood of despairing seriousness which I associated with adulthood and which ended with him in tears. He said that soon we would never see each other again; he was going off to one school, I to another. He said he knew we wouldn't still be friends in five years' time. He was 'frit' (our slang) about having to do his National Service. Suddenly five years seemed nothing. It was as if men in khaki would be coming round any day now to tear us from our homes and march us away as even now his brother William was exiled and being shot at in Malaya.

Until then I had not glimpsed this future for myself but Howard's words now filled me with his contagious panic. I was upset by his upset, frightened by his fright. For a long time we both lay in tears, each staring at his private vista of never-ending uprootings and separations which we knew to be our common lot. The seemingly endless world of childhood was finishing, as it does not when children do precocious things with grown-up earnestness but when tomorrow first begins to weigh upon today. Temporarily adrift somewhere between mourning and panic we indulged ourselves splendidly with a kind of solemn hysteria. What were we really doing? What but making a hostile sea of the future the better to make an eternal island of the present. What but whipping up a storm to earn ourselves the luxury of consolation as young lovers might do while the summer moonlight fell across their bed like a cold scythe. The next day we were up early and making bombs with strange intensity. That morning we must have got through pounds of Howard's mother's granulated sugar and bags of his father's weedkiller; when that ran out we moved on to their fertiliser. I remember crouching beside Howard as he tamped a bomb into a hole in the earth. I remember watching not his hands but the edge of his ear with its bright curve of fine hairs, the light down on his forearms, the caramel smell of burnt sugar which hung about his hair, the vulnerable neck in its Aertex collar. In the afternoon we hit belatedly on the idea of underwater explosions, lowering bombs into the water-butt, a vast oak barrel once used for molasses. By tea-time we had devised a way of keeping the fuses dry and had sent up stained gouts of water into the sunlit air, falling as rain across a bed of nasturtiums. We had inadvertently killed a goldfish he had won at a fair and forgotten was in the tub as well as a couple of newts which had also been there. We didn't discover about the goldfish for a day or two when bacteria brought it to the surface with a bloom of white saprophytes around its gills.

That night I felt it my turn to work up a storm, but it was not the same. It was too self-conscious, too much an attempt to repeat something which had happened spontaneously, inevitably, in its own time. We went through the motions and again the summer moonlight fell across our bed but this time it suggested instead that we got up and went out into the warm air smelling of night-scented stock to look for Yellow Underwing moths with the ultra-violet lamp from under the stairs.

We never did see each other again; Howard had been right. We were neither of us the type who keeps in touch with gangs of friends or goes to reunions or Old Boys' dinners. We might have made a pact but didn't. Probably each of us was daunted by visions of an awful meeting between two gangling sub-adults making that preening

gesture with one hand at the neck as if to check the latest shave and affecting the formal insouciance of our class: 'Christ, it's Andrews.'
'By God, it's H-P. Well I'm buggered. What are *you* doing here? Oh, I'm awfully sorry, this is Felicity.'
(In fact, though, whenever I had fantasies about seeing old schoolfriends the meetings usually took place abroad as if foreign travel would set the seal on one's adulthood. I envisaged running into people on the Champs Elysées, in Shepheard's Hotel in Cairo, on the campus of Berlin University. Or we might find ourselves with our respective girl-friends on the same Rhine steamer or in the same cable car high above Kitzbühl. 'Good Lord, it's . . .' 'What on *earth* . . .' 'Well, let's all have dinner . . . Sorry, this is Lisl.')

I can still remember the music we played, though. On distant, piano-less Tiwarik it suddenly all comes back, summoned from the attics of memory by explosions. These are soon explained as Arman's *bangka* grounds on the shingle. He and Totoy Matias spring out looking pleased with themselves, as well they might since the bilges are full of a slithery mass of silver and pink fish – mainly *dalagang bukid*, a small herringlike variety of *Caesio* whose charming local name means 'country maiden'. A successful morning's dynamiting has earned them a good lunch. Democratically (for he is the *Jhon-Jhon's* owner and skipper) Arman sets about cleaning fish. He has been acting as bomber, Totoy Matias as aimer. The other two crew members who are rather slower out of the boat have had the more strenuous task of swimming down to retrieve the catch. Silo in particular looks done in and even rather cold. Non-smoker Arman tells him he ought to smoke more, since there is a widespread belief that smoking gives a man energy and keeps him warm.
Since I have firewood and utensils we cook and eat in the shade at the hut. The fish is as good as it only ever is when taken straight from the sea. Not the most instant of quick-freezing processes preserves that unmistakable flavour. It is

not a matter of bacteria or decay; it is almost as if the life still present in the fish's cells at the moment of cooking had a taste of its own, a brisk marine ghost which otherwise fleets away. We also eat *kinilaw*, marinaded raw fish, which confirms my fanciful thesis for it is even more vibrant with cellular activity. At once I understand primitive ideas of incorporation (anthropophagy, Holy Communion). Maybe I shall now swim better. Soon we drowse over the remnants of an illegally-fished lunch.

The people of Sabay are practised bomb-makers, as I discover one morning when I paddle over to buy rice and matches and find Arman cooking up what he calls 'dynamite' in a large wok over the fire in his kitchen area, surrounded by empty gin bottles, helpful colleagues and children. Strictly speaking the explosive is no longer dynamite but *ammonium*, the cheaper and more legally available ammonium nitrate fertiliser they use for mango trees. It is white and granular, not unlike that powdery snow which falls as tiny balls rather than flakes. To increase its explosive force it is roasted with ordinary kerosene much as rice is fried. The junior pyrotechnician in me is reactivated after lying dormant for decades.

I tell him about the bombs I used to make when I was thirteen, also using various kinds of fertiliser and weed-killer, but mixing them with sugar rather than frying them in paraffin.

'We used to use sugar too,' Arman says. 'Then some fishermen from the Visayas came here and stayed for a week on Tiwarik and told us you could get more power by using kerosene. So now we do it this way. They're very inventive down there. Most of the bright ideas for fishing seem to come from the Visayas. It was they who taught us we could make our own igniters so we didn't have to rely on the Army keeping us supplied with blasting caps.'

I didn't say so but their igniters were hardly new, having been described in OSS field manuals dating from the Second World War. Arman shows me how they take a torch bulb and rub it against sandpaper until a hole is worn in the glass, enabling the bulb to be filled with powdered match heads before being buried hole-downwards in a gin bottle packed with the still-hot fertiliser.

There is a story that it was the Army, in the form of a squad of rogue soldiers, which forced Sabay's villagers into illegal fishing. This account has the air of a half-truth. I have no doubt the incident occurred, as similar incidents have occurred all over the Philippines. But for years before that dynamite fishing had been a way of life at Sabay and had evolved into a sophisticated art. As long as I have been living on Tiwarik I have remained in two distinct minds about it. One of these minds runs thus:

If I describe myself as a spear-fisherman, hunting for my own food, then I believe in terms of time and energy expended, in terms of sheer physical attrition I earn every ounce of my food. I eat my successes – generally in a matter of minutes – gratefully. My failures account for unrecorded hours which at present amount to my days. To take on wily and evasive sea creatures with an elastic-powered spear is a game loaded heavily against the hunter, whose life is under constant threat from an alien medium as well as from certain of its denizens. Kills which he makes on such unequal terms have often a sublime quality to them. To have out-thought and out-manoeuvred an animal in its own element means for a brief moment having stopped thinking like a middle-class Englishman, a university graduate, a writer, a human being even, and to have partaken actively of that anarchic amoral will which lies beneath all there is and all one pretends to be. The painstaking stalking of a parrotfish, the keeping its interest aroused by scooping up handfuls of sand from the bottom and stirring little clouds of silt; the allaying its fears by turning one's back on it for half a minute and motionlessly lying in the water twenty feet down gripping a knob of coral; intriguing its colleagues and bringing them circling cautiously in at exactly the moment when one must go up for air or die, scattering them with that rise to the surface: that endlessly-repeated cycle is so much an analogue for stalking sexual prey it is impossible not to feel a strange bond with the fish which usually escapes in the end but which very occasionally is caught.

The complete antithesis of this private combat is the use of explosives. After that underwater gasp followed by a slamming concussion the immediate area is an anonymous battlefield. The seabed is littered with corpses since not all dynamited fish float conveniently to the surface belly up. Some lie on their sides on the bottom presumably because the same shock-wave which ruptures their vascular system also deflates their buoyancy sacs. Whether a fish sinks or floats seems to depend on several things, among them the temperature and salinity of the water and the species of fish. *Tulingan*, for example, a year-round staple food fish in these parts, is a little member of the tuna family without an air sac which invariably sinks in the deeper waters it frequents and is consequently one of the many species unsuitable for dynamite fishing. Meanwhile at the scene of the explosion there are always some fish cavorting horribly across the scene, their brains broken. To break a fish's brains by firing a steel rod through them is, to be sure, no better for the fish. All the hunter can say is that the victor of hand-to-hand combat is not left as tainted as he who soars scathelessly overhead and drops his undiscriminating bombs. And when one of the bombers miscalculates and his bomb goes off too soon taking with it an arm, a hand, the head of a companion with screaming shards of gin bottle, the hunter on hearing this tale of tragedy from up the coast piously says how awful it is – as it is. But inwardly he sides with his beloved prey instead of with his own species and cannot suppress a deep and secret thought: 'Serve them right.'

That is one of my two minds. The other readily recognises the imperative of feeding not just a lone hunter but an entire family, of earning enough money to buy essentials. It readily recognises how disgusting moral stances are when taken by outsiders like myself who, no matter that they choose to submit to the rigours of that life, still do not have to. It also recognises the skill of Sabay's dynamiters, for theirs is no indiscriminate bombing. They discovered years ago that if their charges were too large or set to go off too deep they damaged the corals and that stocks of inshore fish depended entirely on healthy reefs. Furthermore they generally aim for one particular species at a time, most often *dalagang bukid*, and select their target with care. It is astonishing after that horrendous concussion to see the bottom strewn with dead *dalagang bukid* but with the other species swimming around above them apparently unharmed. This is not because *dalagang bukid* are particularly susceptible but because they have been so skilfully hunted.

The modus operandi is that a boat drifts, one man wearing goggles lying across it with his face in the water looking for a shoal large enough to merit one of the precious bombs. He signals directions by waving a free hand behind him in dumb semaphore while a companion with a paddle steers accordingly. In the prow stands the bomber poised for the throw, armed with a light (if they are using a conventional fuse) or wires and battery if not. This drifting and signalling under the blazing sun can go on for hours, the patient watching informed by a good deal of knowledge about fish behaviour, for all these men are spear-fishermen too and theirs is the craftiness of long experience. Often they will go home without dropping a single bomb, occasionally they will strike lucky within minutes.

When a suitable shoal is found the tension goes up for this is the moment of greatest danger. This is because *dalagang bukid* often move quite close to the surface. The bomber must control the depth at which his charge explodes mainly by judging how long to delay his throw after lighting the fuse, sending the gin bottle glinting over and over in a high arc into the sky or holding it while it sputters in his hand.

The moment is dangerous not just for the waiters and watchers in the little boats gathered around, all of whom hope for a share in the catch. It is so for any nearby swimmers or divers who may have gone unobserved or who may themselves have been too preoccupied to notice the sudden activity on board the quietly drifting craft. I was once down at fifteen or twenty feet behind a coral outcrop when a revolting noise went off in my head followed at once by a shock-wave I felt over the entire surface of my body. I came to the surface in a daze, my head ringing, not knowing where to look, for the noise and the impact had been completely directionless, afflicting my body simultaneously inside and out. When I crawled shakily onto the rocks expecting to find blood pouring from my ears and nose I saw a knot of boats at least a hundred metres away. To this day I cannot imagine how it is that fish survive a matter of yards away from the point of the explosion but I know that they do. The noise is excruciating. Sound travels oddly in water: I have often been deep beneath the surface when bombs have exploded a long way away, half a mile, a mile, even. The first thing one hears is a sharp hiss like a sudden release of soda water and only then the great bang of sound. If one comes up quickly enough one may often hear the same bang again, conducted more slowly through air.

So just before the bomb is thrown cries of '*matera!*' or '*hagis!*' ('throwing') go up, warning even those merely staring over the sides of their own boats to take their faces out of the water. There follow the glittering arc, the splash, the breathless wait. Then from the sea twenty metres away a short white spurt of fume and spray leaps up and the wood of the boat slams into footsoles and the backs of thighs. Scarcely has the foam fallen back than the boatman of the bombing crew starts his engine, now driving the compressor. The retrievers bite their air-hoses, snatch up hand nets and jump overboard.

But already the hangers-on are in the water, swimming down to see how many bodies they can gather before the boys with the air-tubes and nets arrive to make their methodical sweeps of the sea floor. Everything depends on the depth of the water. Very few of Sabay's fishermen will swim down to more than thirty feet to retrieve a few *dalagang bukid* since the energy they expend is hardly worth a handful of small fish especially if there is a current running. Once down, the freebooter finds the fish hard to hold: they slip easily out of his fists, wriggling feebly as some still are. And always at his back is a swift-moving boy with twin plywood flippers, bulging net trailing behind him like a park-keeper's litter sack, the gallons of exhaled air gushing in fine prodigality from between his grinning teeth. Generally the bombing crew will allow hangers-on to keep what they can scavenge provided it is no more than half a dozen reasonably sized fish and provided that their own haul is good. In the old days I used to get away with a couple of dozen fish until they discovered I was a non-smoker and my lungs would happily take me down to forty feet in a succession of dives. Now I am a notorious vulture and they laughingly but rigorously search my boat. Mostly, though, I watch impotently as the compressor takes them down to sixty, eighty feet for as long as they want. Instead I scour the coral ledges for minor fry while below me, his hair streaming in the currents and lifted by gouts of air like any Pre-Raphaelite Lady of Shalott's, a boy with his net turns and sweeps and gathers from the steep hillsides and rocky gorges.

Sometimes a single bomb will net no more than fifty fish. If the bomber has no motor in his boat and hence no compressor and has miscalculated so that his victims lie in deep water, retrieval is such an effort he can virtually make the same claim as the hand-to-hand hunter: that each fish was earned the hard way. If anyone doubts this they should try swimming down to fifty feet in order (if they are lucky) to come back up holding two small herrings, and then repeating it nine times. By the end they may also be in the second of my two minds over the issue of dynamiting fish as it is practised here at Sabay. In any case it has long since become a vital part of the place's economy. If it were suddenly stopped an already poor community would be practically ruined, for while conventional fishing methods could probably keep them alive they would offer no hope of advance, allow of no improvement, pay for nobody's medicine, no child's education, buy no petrol for a single fishing boat.

This being said there is, of course, a conservationist case. To say the catches of the bombers of Sabay are paltry compared with those of the Japanese ships crammed with high-tech. fishing devices which infest the archipelago is both true and irrelevant: this I know. I know that neither technique is desirable, that both will have future consequences. It is safe to predict that the consequences will unfairly be worse for the villagers than for the Japanese, who can always trawl elsewhere. Meanwhile, listening to the right-minded gentlefolk of Europe I do occasionally find myself wondering if because their supermarket fish fingers and cod pieces come deep-frozen in neat geometrical shapes boxed with pictures of peaceful marine scenery they think the fish have been gently farmed and humanely killed. Presumably they must think vast factory ships don't trawl swathes across the ocean, sweeping paths clean of practically all living creatures and leaving long empty corridors. Likewise they must assume those creatures are not suffocated or frozen to death and then pulped, mangled and processed into acceptable products ranging from fishmeal to fillets.

Meanwhile I keep the company of dynamiters while wandering my island like a Balkan king made uneasy by the sound of Anarchists growing ever closer. Intoy, in his way the purest little anarch of them all, is a devoted jester. He springs out from behind a rock, his head breaks what I took for empty water, his laughter floats from trees.

By now the reader will have the impression that life here is indeed rather chappish, unrelievedly masculine. But there is little alternative for the unattached male who does not wish to do anything as blunt as importing a girl from another region as if she were one more of the essential stores for island-dwelling. In this respect the Philippine provinces are not at all what a foreigner familiar only with Manila might imagine, being in general passionate but proper. All sorts of wild flirtations abound but they are taken account of down to the last detail. Pious Catholic parents and in-laws still value virginity on the wedding-day but they value honour and financial understandings more. I have twice attended weddings nominated as *ninong* to the child the bride was visibly carrying. There was never the least hint that things were less than ideal: everyone was far too pleased the right thing had been done, that a romance had been blessed in the sight of heaven and the offspring would be legitimate. Many foreigners who stray into the provinces with ideas of dalliance discover quite soon that all but the most innocent of flirtations are taken quite seriously, not least because on various counts foreigners tend to be valued (not to say costed) as potential husbands. Girls after the age of puberty are usually chaperoned by their friends on any occasion which involves calling on a single male. Even Marisil Malabayabas, whom I have known since she was ten or so, has only very rarely brought me something at my hut in Kansulay unaccompanied by a little sister or two, although this may quite possibly be due to no more than the Filipino dislike of doing anything on one's own.

In consequence, needing to stay unencumbered by such things I elect when I am here to live a life which is the butt of fairly gentle jokes and gossip: I am *monastic*, I am *virtuous*, I am a *gentleman*, I am *self-controlled*, I am *cold and sexless*, I am *baklâ*: one takes one's pick. Of course the more knowing that people are the less they like enigmas. Where sexuality is concerned the Filipinos are very knowing indeed and from the earliest age. Thus my friends are irritated and intrigued that in my case they seem unable to settle the matter and I have heard that many a discussion on this inconsequential topic has raged around the drinks-table. Apparently *kapitan* Sanso's old father once snorted and said 'Why does he have to *be* anything? Why mightn't he just be *sensible*?' For that I salute him, or rather his memory since he died not long ago.

Meanwhile on Tiwarik I go on living a life whose company – when there is any – is necessarily male, except when wives and sisters come over for visits or I go to their houses on the mainland. Many days go by when I see no-one of either sex. I might be dreaming on the uplands or fishing when somebody lands on the beach for an hour or two. I arrive back to find only a keel-mark and footprints, a cigarette end by my hut or the gift of a plastic pitcher of *tuba* left inside. However insecure my position in the marriage-market of Sabay I cannot doubt that I do occupy a place of my own in the economy of its affection. Reciprocated fondness does not, after all, seem such bad terms on which to live a life even if everybody is left faintly puzzled.

On other days Intoy might well come across in the early morning with my water. Since I have now acquired four jerrycans this no longer need be a daily routine. He really has rather taken me up and if I did not discourage him gently from time to time I think he would come and live on Tiwarik. This despite my having made it clear that I am not about to pay him extra for further duties simply because there is nothing more I need beyond his bringing water and running the odd errand to the village shop. But I do not think it is purely a matter of money for him. Maybe it is status or just pleasure at the oddness of observing a foreigner at close range. Whatever the reason his permanent presence would not suit me. Apart from anything else he ought to be at school most days, for his schooling has been of the skimpiest. Now and again when his parents could spare him and could afford to buy the odd pencil and exercise book he has attended the village school in Sabay. Over the years he has picked up smatterings of this and that but where schoolwork is concerned he has never learned how to learn.

Surprisingly, nearly two hundred children of primary school age to twelve or thirteen attend this school, many walking several kilometres each day in all weathers along the paths leading from outlying hamlets hidden among the groves and forests on the lower slopes of the cordillera. It is at this level of village life that one encounters a deep yearning for administrative stability, for official encouragement, for progress. There is a profound respect for the idea of education; there seems not to be the least degree of cynicism about it to the extent that questioning the existence of God would hardly be thought more subversive than questioning the value of education.

The school at Sabay is a long bungalow with a verandah running its length whose roof is patched with *cogon* where the corrugated iron has rusted or blown away. Around it runs a border where flowers have been planted by the pupils: some are in bloom, others have been rooted up by the pigs and chickens and goats which scavenge the village between school and seashore. There is a flagpole in front of the bungalow with a few whitewashed stones around its base. Inside the school it is cool and dusty with bright shafts piercing from structural chinks. The classrooms are bare: there are not enough desks or chairs or tables, there is never enough chalk, the text books are few, tattered, out of date or just plain bad, as in the case of several books about Philippine history and culture which are thinly disguised hagiographies of the Marcoses. For some reason these rooms remind me of Clock House in my second school: perhaps they are the same size as the converted coach-houses. Certainly the contrast could hardly be greater. The classrooms in Clock House were efficiently-appointed little educational factories for producing the quality product parents were buying: entrance to public school, to university, to the gravy train of life. Here in Sabay, though, nobody would ever mistake these classrooms for factories. Rather, they are outposts of literate civilisation with their children's paintings around the walls done with the beautiful pale colours leached from the hearts of expired felt-tip pens on the insides of multi-pack cigarette cartons. There are also exemplars of handwriting and sums as well as some charts left over from the last BHWs' (*baranggay* health workers') meeting listing the incidence of TB, worms and gastroenteritis in nearby barrios.

It is here, as in thousands of provincial schools like it throughout the Philippines, that monstrously underpaid men and women teach. Many of them are, as they themselves sadly recognise, barely educated. Trying to extract supplies, pay rises, even recognition from the bureaucracy in distant Manila is like beseeching the moon. Often they are forced to buy the chalk they need out of their own pockets. But they carry on, year in and year out, and a steady stream of children leaves their hands able at least to read and do sums. That is a triumph; the very existence of such people in the villages is a solid thing to set against the barbarianism which so often seems likely to engulf the country. It is at this level, of *baranggay* officials, priests, teachers and BHWs, one can most often see the legacy of the more radical and enlightened of the Spaniards and Americans who colonised this land.

From time to time Intoy has attended this school in Sabay but at thirteen or fourteen (nobody seems sure which) he cannot read or write at all well. Too often his father has needed him to help with fishing or planting rice, just as seventy years ago in England children were kept away from Dame school to help on the land or merely throw stones at crows. I want so much to help him, but offering to pay for him to go to the High School in Malubog would be pointless since he couldn't keep up even if they could be persuaded to admit him. In any case he has nearly reached that stage of being a professional drop-out. Being educated is a habit and it is one Intoy has never acquired. Instead he is *bulakbol*. He lounges, he looks at comics, he climbs sixty-foot palm trees with laughter in high winds, he has all sorts of rural competences; he fishes with divine address. He will probably soon become a precocious drinker and smoker and maybe by the time he is eighteen he will have to marry. He often has fantasies of going to Manila, one more of the country migrants hoping for – what? Money, jobs, pleasures; whatever.

Sometimes, thinking about it all and about Intoy in particular, I become depressed. It is so predictable, so intransigent. But there again I wonder if this is not yet another form of sentimentality, worrying overmuch about how other people live their lives. Meanwhile Intoy glitters in the sun like Ariel. He gives no hint that he may, like Howard all those years ago, have had a sudden black insight, a vision of his own future. He runs and laughs and dives. He lies on his back in the hut and makes dozens of *nito* rings of varying sizes, plaited with amazing dexterity. He tells awful jokes. One day he turns up with a bomb-making kit for land rather than sea. His idea is to go after the large crabs which tuck themselves into the crevices of rocks just above the water line and he has brought several small bottles and some fertiliser. Do I have any sugar? String?

In my bomb-making days I never tried using brown sugar but Intoy assures me it works. Simple fuses made of string soaked in kerosene complete a couple of these devices and we go off to dispose them experimentally in holes. The first makes a soft bang and a cloud of white smoke but evidently lacks blasting power: the rocks remain intact. The second does little better, leaving merely an enlarged crack smelling of burnt jam. We return to the hut to blend the sugar and fertiliser in different proportions. After an hour or so we have achieved a mix which produces a most satisfying blast but I am far from convinced Intoy is going to get many crabs with it. This particular morning I have been marinading last night's catch; I now begin to lay the fish out on the drier while Intoy runs off with his bombs to try his luck.

After a couple of bangs when he has not re-appeared I go to see what has happened, dreading to find his mutilated remains. Eventually – heart-stopping moment – I see him sprawled face downwards on the rocks above the water line, one brown foot washed by the wavelets. But he is only trying to spot crabs in their holes. A match flares, a thin smoke curls, fragments of rock leap in the air and spatter the sea. Intoy jumps out of cover and goes to peer into the crater. He reaches in and comes up with a huge fighting claw; the rest of the crab has been atomised or else has dropped beyond reach. But he is well pleased with his morning and, having roasted the claw, presents it to me with a proud and graceful gesture.

One afternoon Totoy Matias paddles over in a small *bangka* to fish. Arman has gone to Malubog to buy supplies, Danding is taking the *Jhon-Jhon*'s carburettor down, so today it is up to Totoy Matias to get his family's meals solo. He always strikes me as a gloomy young man: he has a heavy presence as if life had done him a personal injury and he were still awaiting compensation. But as well as his nets he brings a copy of *Magix Komix* which he and Intoy read together on the floor of the hut with exclamations of surprise and pleasure, fingers poking at details in the pictures. Getting food can wait.

Totoy Matias's life and reputation were transformed the day the morning jeep bumped into Sabay with a packet for him containing the new issue of *Magix Komix*, but they had to wait for their transformation until he had read through the story which took up the first half of the comic. This concerned a girl who had thirteen fingers, each with its own identity. At moments of crisis (i.e. every issue) her fingertips blossomed with monstrous heads, some multi-eyed, some snouted, some blank but for a single tuft of hair and a mouth. In this particular issue the girl was raped by an ill-advised fellow who discovered too late that what he thought were her defenceless hands clutching at his back were really transfigured digits grinning at each other in glee before their fangs ripped and tore the living meat from his rib-cage. On page four he expired messily and Totoy turned to the heading 'I Love You Corner'. The first letter he read ran thus:

To: Sandy Mariano
027 Batisan St
Batangas City

'From nothing we were born, and soon again we shall be nothing as at first . . .' Happy, happy birthday on March 6.

Gary Piswig
581 Merchan St
Lucena City

The second was electrifying:

To my one and only,
Totoy Matias
Sabay

Hi! Hello! my love! I hope you're in a good condition. Dito ko lang masasabi sa iyo na you're my inspiration. Take care 'coz I care!

Still Loving You
Vangie
Mary Immaculate Academy
San José

The first time one sees one's name in print it produces a glow unlike any other. The indifferent and illimitable world has suddenly given back one's image. Totoy was over-whelmed with pride and pleasure and carried the issue of *Magix Komix* around with him for days, showing it to everyone he met which in turn created pleasure for since the previous issue people were longing to know what new adventures would befall the girl with the thirteen fingers. It was impossible not to feel pleased for him, even for Vangie, since seeing her printed name had reified her existence for

Totoy in a way which no mere posted letter from her could have done. I was disinclined to question him but not two days beforehand I had overheard him being chaffed by his friends about a girl in Malubog, the next sizeable town up the coast. It was a smart move of Vangie's to have immortalised herself and Totoy; it left the competition in Malubog with a lot of catching up to do.

At length the excitement wore off. A new issue of *Magix Komix* arrived without a single mention of his name. The girl with the thirteen fingers savaged an old woman who was really a witch trying to put a spell on her. The finger with the pig's snout burrowed its way into her ancient ear and ate into her brain. I wondered what happened if the girl absent-mindedly picked her own nose, or worse.

Totoy became his old disconsolate self again. 'No money no honey,' he would say, his one English phrase, when I asked him how he was.

'Never mind. Let's go fishing tonight. Maybe you will catch a big shark and sell it in Malubog market for lots of money.'

'*Ay* . . . Maybe the shark will catch me.'

'There's always that.'

Now many issues of *Magix Komix* have gone by but still Totoy Matias reads it much as a retired general pores over the latest number of the gazette which long ago listed his promotions and awards for gallantry. After a short sleep, quite worn out with reading, Intoy and Totoy Matias go fishing together. Their voices drift over the water in the evening quiet. Intoy is still slightly too young to do anything but inhabit the present which he does with sparkle and largeness. Totoy, though, is as if waiting for something which may never happen. Wherever he goes he induces an atmosphere of instability, of impermanence which people find infectious because all of a sudden they begin to talk of their own plans to go to Manila, get jobs as merchant seamen or radio operators, break up, go away, fly apart. Wives and families sometimes join in these discussions, the ones who will be left behind with children and infrequent remittances and with not much to say in the face of such unquestionable priorities: work, money, a future. Thus throughout the Philippines a million families connive sadly, excitedly, at a collective dream of their own fragmentation.

The voices of Intoy and Totoy Matias die away as their boat rounds a headland. They do not return. Night falls and I make my evening meal alone, expecting to hear their chatter from the beach at any moment. It is one of the pleasures of Tiwarik, how sounds arrive from outside. Explosions and piano tunes from the past may reach the listener's ears at any point on the island but there are otherwise two aspects to the place in that on the seaward side one may imagine oneself alone in the universe – or at least cut off from the main body of mankind – while on the side facing Sabay when the air is still and the sea calm the sounds drift across with a strange poignancy, remote yet clear, coming from another world. The crowing of cocks on the mainland has woken me at dawn in my hut a mile away. In late afternoon I have heard the sounds of basketball being played on the improvised court near the school where the headboard and ring are nailed to a palm tree. At night I have lain awake in the dark and listened to the skirmishing of Sabay's dogs. I have speculated that in the nearly five seconds their yaps and howls take to reach me the outcome of the particular fight I am hearing is already known and that over in the village an uneasy temporary silence has fallen even as on Tiwarik the audible savagery reaches its peak.

This night I remember belatedly that I have not yet brought in my *bislad* and the dew must already be falling on the drier. I go out and collect up the fish by starlight: they are practically dry anyway. As I do this there come faint sounds from the strait: voices, paddles. Out of the darkness three small *bangkas* arrive bearing Intoy and friends. It turns out they have already eaten with their families in Sabay. Of Totoy Matias there is no sign; he has long since gone back with his catch. Instead a party of six teenagers (two of them not even that, probably) wants shelter for the night so they can start fishing at dawn. They have brought *tuba* (a present from Arman's wife), several packets of fried salted corn called 'Chikinini' (from Captain Sanso) and a pack of pornographic playing-cards. These, so worn the pictures on their faces are barely discernible, were brought back a year ago by Danding's nephew who went to Olongapo where he won them from a US sailor.

We unroll the mats and play cards on the floor by lamp-light, somewhat jammed together with a glass of drink doing the rounds. One or two of the younger ones become mildly tipsy and frown as they concentrate on a game which seems not much more than a sort of Tagalog 'snap'. The winners punish the losers, totting up their forfeits and administering *pitik*, flicks of the nail on the backs of the finger-joints of proffered hands. Intoy rolls on the floor in mock agony while the others gleefully accuse him of being *baklâ*. From time to time I wish they would all go away so I can stretch out and go to sleep. Then I feel churlish and think that without their visits I should become dreary and crazed with introspection.

Eventually the lamp goes out and in the darkness we lie almost indiscriminately on the floor, fitting together into the available space with a good deal of jocularity and simulated complaint. A silence falls in which a dog over in Sabay can faintly but clearly be heard. '*Si Biloy*,' someone says. 'Bokbok's cat always sets him off.' There is a short discussion about the village cats and dogs. A ghost story is begun but it is too unfrightening and has obviously been lifted half-digested from a comic. They subside in giggles. Softly from the walls comes a lizard's *chuk-chuk-chuk*.

In the black hours there are abrupt turnings and murmurs, re-arrangings of limbs as from the depths of sleep, stealthy shiftings of unknown direction. In the greyish light of cockcrow we get up between quite different neighbours and go about lighting fires and boiling rice with a certain gleeful elasticity of movement. The sun is up, declaring everything erased. We are starting afresh in fresh day.

Shortly after this Totoy Matias comes and announces he is going to Manila to look for work. He says vaguely that a cousin there will help him but he has no companion for the journey and is too unconfident to travel alone. He supposes I am not planning on going to Manila soon? I hadn't been, but on investigation discover I should. My visa will shortly need renewing so I tell him we can travel together. He is very cheered by this. Two days later I hear he has told everyone I have offered to pay his fare. I can't quite bring myself to feel aggrieved but it is a near thing since he is not someone to whom I feel especially close.

In due course I walk up to the grassfield and tell the island I shall not be away longer than a week, less if humanly possible. Out in the strait I can see the *Jhon-Jhon* drifting and can barely make out the bronze mop of Arman's hair as he hangs it in the water, his legs sticking out on the opposite side, motionless in his search for a shoal. It is a familiar scene. I paddle over to Sabay and wait with Totoy Matias for the jeep which arrives late in a rush of sand and coral gravel. Fishwives hurry forward with baskets of the night's catch as well as the *daing* they have been drying on their roofs. They clamber aboard with much shoving, carrying rusty pairs of scales behind which they will preside for the morning in the market at Malubog.

As I myself climb aboard I catch sight of Intoy hanging back in the shadow of a house. He looks anxious, I think, but maybe it is merely envy. From across the strait comes a flat report. Everybody reflexively looks towards the sea with a buzz of interest and speculation. *How far away is the* Jhon-Jhon? *Is it worth trying to get there to scavenge the odd fish?* The jeep pulls out of Sabay to waving hands on the first part of a long and uncomfortable journey involving many more jeeps, boats and buses which slowly bring us ever closer to the capital, a city I have never much liked.

PART TWO

Manila

7

The Manila which ex-President Ferdinand Marcos left in late February 1986 was, like the man himself, a notorious mixture of wealth and decay. His regime and family had become like the prestige projects they had from time to time dotted around the city to impress visiting popes, potentates, world bankers and suchlike. Their very prominence drew attention to flaking exteriors and gave off great wafts of savage dismay like the dank toadstool smell of air conditioners. On the reclaimed foreshore was Imelda Marcos's pride and joy, her Cultural Centre of the Philippines to which the great and good of the world's artists, opera singers and ballet companies came. Behind it on the inland side of Roxas Boulevard was the high-rise row of international hotels, gap-toothed here and there where a night-club or massage parlour had been burned to the ground. Several safe miles inland lay the upper- and middle-class enclaves, the opulent residential suburbs of Forbes Park, of Dasmariñas Village and Wack-Wack with its golf course, as well as the pocket Manhattan of the Makati Commercial Centre. In between, among the tumbled concrete breakwaters of the foreshore, in burnt-out ruins, even in trees and clumps of bushes, the squatters shrugged themselves into cardboard and plastic sheeting, their infants laid out asleep and black with flies on pavements amid passing feet. It was a city in which even the world's bankers had lost faith.

I arrive in this place with my head still full of silence and glittering air, of unconfined spaces, which are at once smothered and forcibly replaced by crowds and carbon monoxide. Manila has to be faced. It is impossible to write anything about the Philippines without at some stage dealing with this extraordinary city. This is not from any conventional courtesy whereby a visitor pays tribute to his host nation's capital – far from it – but for two other reasons. One of these is that most of the knowledge the world has of the Philippines comes via Manila; to a large extent the city mediates the national image and the consequences bear looking at. The second reason is the almost mythic position Manila occupies in the minds of Filipinos themselves. Maybe this is a common phenomenon in any country where rural poverty drives people centripetally towards its chief city. Certainly wherever one goes in the provinces one begins to get the feeling that scarcely anybody wants to remain where he is but is merely counting the days until the right quirk of fate will pay his passage to Manila, give him board and lodging there, help him out with a bit of *pakiusap*, offer him a job.

Sometimes from the way this desire is phrased it is possible to extrapolate a Manila which is no more than a necessary first step to emigration. If America remains the Promised Land for so many Filipinos the rest of the developed world still offers a worthwhile exile. The newspapers are full of advertisements for agencies and fixers who will wangle visas, see to the paperwork, back-handers and red tape involved with getting a passport, interview applicants for jobs abroad. Among the saddest of all recurrent tales in a nation of hard-luck stories is that of the young man in the provinces who applies for a labouring job with a construction company in Saudi Arabia. The agency in Manila handling the job calls him for interview with a letter full of hopeful signs. All the applicant has to do is present himself at an address on a date with some photographs of himself and an application fee of several hundred pesos to show he is in earnest and to pay for the processing of his papers. The young man is crestfallen: he can never lay hands on a sum like that. But he has a whip-round of his family, his friends, his parish priest, anybody. He beggars himself. He scrapes together his fare. Somehow he at last manages to turn up at an ad hoc office in Manila, is welcomed together with thirty or forty others like him. They all fill out forms, hand over their photographs, hand over their fees, are asked to call back at 3 p.m.

It is not unusual to read laconic newspaper accounts of men like him found dead, leaving suicide notes (in one case of an illiterate, written by an amanuensis) saying there was no way they could return home to those families, those friends, that parish priest. No way, either, to describe the impotent rage and shame when at 3 p.m. they went back to find a locked door and nobody who had ever heard of 'Gulfcon Recruitment Enterprises Co.' Yet other than the relatives of those who die, how phlegmatic most Filipinos are when they hear of such things. '*Ay* . . .' They cluck once or twice, the same noise the English make to gee up horses but which here signals distress, then laugh slightly. That's what happens; that's how the world is, full of swindlers and cheats; better watch out; trust neither policeman nor President unless they're members of your own family, in which case be doubly careful.

Such tales apart it is a melancholy enough business for any fond visitor to contemplate a country of great beauty and natural wealth most of whose inhabitants seem desperate only to leave and turn themselves into the world's servants, its nursemaids, its amahs, cooks, chauffeurs, houseboys, labourers, bar-tenders, bell-hops and waitresses. It must signify something, this near-romantic dream which almost at times transcends matters of mere money. The southward urge to the land where the lemon-trees flower which the German romantics characterised as *der Drang nach Süden* has its counterpart in the modern Philippines as *der Drang nach Ausland.* 'Abroad' is good on any terms since it is better paid. But a mere skivvy's wages in a London Wimpy Bar, magnificent though they are compared with what Sising earns in Kansulay, still hardly seem quite enough completely to explain how the mere act of being abroad is equated with success and status back home. There must be something else involved, some jackpot dream of treasures without limit for the myth to go on surviving the reality of merciless exploitation, the coldness both metaphorical and literal which pushes ordinary culture shock over the edge of the bearable and sends so many Filipinos in the UK into mental institutions.

Meanwhile Manila itself remains a goal for the unqualified, a halfway house for the more plausible, a positive clearing-house for those with degrees and qualifications. Of the emigrants few have no dreams of returning one day, typically and wistfully to the small pond of their rural origin in which their new wealth will make them very big frogs indeed (The envy! The adulation! The delicious settling of old scores!). Of the transients who harbour similar fantasies most seem to stay and after some time find they have crossed into the category of residents. This must be true since the city goes on growing.

It is conventional to make the point that Manila strikes most Europeans as disturbingly without a centre. The Second World War and the elements have destroyed much and the old vernacular architecture of wood and *nipa* thatch was by its nature impermanent. It appears to them a shapeless, confused and unrelievedly twentieth-century mess strung out along a reeking bay. Some visitors are better informed, in which case it becomes conventional to discern amid the sprawl distinct villages still organised into *baranggays* exactly as they would be in the provinces from which many of the inhabitants have so recently arrived. These visitors might also have read a book or two by Nick Joaquin, one of the best known of contemporary Filipino writers. Amongst his collected journalism, much of it written under his anagrammatic *nom-de-plume* of 'Quijano de Manila', are scattered pieces in which, full of affection and nostalgia, he wanders around his city disinterring points of interest.

It is Quijano rather than any guide book who can set a traveller down on a nondescript corner of this howling city and help him put out a few tentative roots. It is precisely not the guide book places which touch one: not the old Spanish inner-city fortress of Intramuros, nor the hotel where General MacArthur occupied a suite, nor even the national shrine on the spot where Dr José Rizal was executed by the Spanish in 1896. Above all the sunsets in Manila Bay are clearly fakes achieved by some vulgarian with the aid of Technicolor. Since there is little left in Manila which a European would consider at all old he turns to Quijano to glimpse the palimpsest beneath. In default of buildings and monuments he must rely for re-making the city on such things as the courses of certain streets. By some fluke the principal commercial and fashionable street of the late Spanish period – Escolta – still exists, and under its own name. It is now on the edge of Chinatown and is a desultory place of watch-shops and restaurants. But for nearly everywhere else Quijano is needed to make sense of streets whose names have changed and whose present undifferentiated squalor conceals a historic individuality. Calle Azcárraga, for example, which only some twenty-five years ago was re-named Claro M. Recto after the late nationalist intellectual. Writing of this street's Tondo end Quijano observes:

Today, the Divisoria, Tutuban station and the various bus depots have turned this part of Azcárraga into Babel town and its uproar, stinks and turmoil are, for provincial newcomers, their first taste of Manila life.

Around Tutuban used to be a *nipa* village. Here, Bonifacio was born; here, the Katipuneros [nationalist revolutionaries] held their first meetings. Just past Tutuban, near the corner of Reina Regente, was a *bibingka* stall that was the most famous in the city during the 1920s. Renaults and Studebakers succeeded each other at night in front of that humble shop, where a couple of old women took what seemed hours to cook one perfect *bibingka*.

A pleasurable sense of history is hard won in Manila and one doubts that even for a committed Manileño like Quijano the *bibingkas* were quite what *madeleines* were for Proust. Perhaps the pleasurable is out of place, even irrelevant. Certainly one pauses on a bridge near the Post Office above the deep khaki Pasig River, feeling the concrete vibrate uneasily to the immense stream of traffic for which it was doubtless never designed. The substance below is scarcely water at all even though it bears on its swarming and iridescent surface bunches of foliage as a reminder of its far-off inland provenance. To be plunged into it would surely be to die instantly. Certainly one pauses there, if only to reflect that this poisoned sump is the very river from which some etymologists derive *Tagalog*, the name, the tribe, its language (*taga* + *ilog*: inhabitants of the river). At this point it has just flowed past the gardens of Malacañang Palace.[3]

I explained at the beginning of this book that I originally came to the Philippines because it was one of the places in South-East Asia I had not visited at the time of the Vietnam War and which was to some degree involved in that war. Consequently Manila has for me a powerful ability to invoke a time nearly twenty years ago, not least because it is in some ways so old-fashioned. The awful concrete architecture, the scabby trusses of overhead wiring, the jeepneys which look like (but which mostly no longer are) re-bodied Second World War jeeps, the beer-houses and nite-spots and go-go bars and the rest are all reminiscent of an Asian re-creation of an American garrison town. It is largely post-*South Pacific*, although some of it by not much. It may be a modern international city as the guide books and handouts say; it may exhibit all the newest wrinkles of contemporary urban drift and crisis as the sociological studies assert; but for me Manila exudes the smell and the feel of another era. When I am in Manila I am also, however slightly, in the past in Saigon or Bangkok, an illusion strengthened by the US-style uniforms worn by the military. The shoeshine boys, the squalor, the violence, the shootings, the beggars, child prostitutes, 'hostesses', pick-pockets are the same; the occasional crew-cut Asian heads are suggestive; the burnt-out bars and hotels and massage parlours only too similar.

Do I unconsciously look for it and therefore see what I look for? Worse, am I myself in the grip of some squalid nostalgia? I do not think so. Certainly I am astonished at how it all goes on, noisily, vividly. I am less astonished by what overseas visitors do not want to know. Reading what lies beneath the surface argues not knowledge so much as that glum lack of personal investment which permits knowledge. It is both pleasanter and easier to spend money than ask questions. It is still too soon after the self-styled 'People's Revolution' of February 1986 to know whether Manila itself will change out of its hackneyed role as whorehouse of the East as if it were still ministering to troops on R&R who magically remain invisible. Very probably an era has indeed passed. But it is harder to see how the economic imperatives will themselves change at all quickly. The thought occurs to someone like myself for whom this city remains so strangely dated that it is not after all caught in some cultural time-warp but quite simply stagnating from lack of the right kind of spending. It is as unmysterious as that.

In the late Seventies and early Eighties – that is to say in the declining years of the Marcos dynasty – the country appeared superficially to be in a state of stable anarchy brought about jointly by the rigours of Martial Law and the untrammelled freedom of public officials to do pretty much what they liked. In this strange political half-life Manila had some of the high, wild, *fin-de-saison* qualities ascribed to other famous cities under regimes in their lapsarian heydays: Batista's Havana, Faroukh's Cairo, even Mussolini's Salò. 'Ah, I remember Manila then,' old hands will reminisce in thirty years' time, the semi-scandalised tone of their original narratives long having given over to a sundappled worldliness. 'My God the place was wide open. Anything went and I do mean *any*thing. Provided you had the money, of course. But you hardly needed very much of that. Oh well, it couldn't last, and quite right too' (the token responsible citizen); 'the poverty and abuses were sickening' (the obligatory humanitarian). 'But . . .' (The wistfulness, the wistfulness).

What a city, what a whole country turns into at such moments is Fantasyland, a far-off place on which the rest of the world can superimpose its unbridled dreams. There in the distance beckon baroque structures of vice, Disneyesque set-pieces of outlandish appetites gloriously catered for, a shimmering vista of carnality. It would have been a venereal Las Vegas except that even Las Vegas has laws; this country, this city had none for the paying foreigner. If his activities were shameless it was precisely in the way

that fantasies are without shame since without consequences. Neither the country nor its capital were real for
those who flew in, got drunk, were massaged back to
consciousness, unloaded their seminal vesicles into an
'escort' and flew out again. Later they shook their heads in
rueful male complicity in the less hectic bars of Hong
Kong, saying only 'Whew!' as they belatedly discovered the
loss of a gold tiepin or the acquisition of NSU.

Neither were Manila or Manileños real to the huge pale
pederasts – the German, the English, the American, the
Swedish, Dutch, Australian, French pederasts – who sat
about the air-conditioned shopping malls while small girls
and boys in very new jeans and training shoes gathered at
their tables packing in as much food as they could before
the bill was called for and their beaming host lumbered off,
towing one or two or three according to fancy to the
seclusion of his room in the Hilton, the Hyatt, or a rented
apartment in Dakota Mansions. The most notorious of these
shopping malls was Harrison Plaza which later 'burned
down' (Manileños supply their own inverted commas for
this phrase whenever referring to a place razed to the
ground for the insurance money or as part of a vendetta). A
new Harrison Plaza has since arisen from the ashes on the
same site and with many of the same stores but it is a very
sanitised and gelded phoenix. For all that the Marcoses
were to linger on for two or three years interested parties
will maintain that to all intents and purposes the old Manila
(their old Manila) died with the first Harrison Plaza. Apart
from anything else an innocence has gone. A new breed of
kid has arisen, they say, tough, streetwise, dangerous,
maybe even with AIDS. *Sayang.* It could not last.

A correct perception, this. Part of the pleasure of a
fantasy lies in knowing it is time off, untime in an unworld
bought against ever-encroaching reality. There was a
certain haste about those visitors like that of the metaphorical child on the loose in a sweet-shop. If there was a
certain innocence, too, about their public behaviour it was
because there was quite evidently no sense of guilt. Of
course they were not monsters: they were helping the
child economically . . . In any case the child had no real

existence of its own since it was part of a fantasy already older than itself. So while straight tourists strolled with their handbags and cameras through Harrison Plaza evincing outrage or a painstaking sophistication at the sight of men who were probably their own countrymen fondling and lolling and flirting with children who often looked (and often were) no older than ten, the fantasists seemed not even to have to affect unselfconsciousness. That had all been left behind as they passed beyond the last of the police at Schiphol, Heathrow and Frankfurt. The KLM, BA and Lufthansa storks had borne them safely beyond all legal clutches and delivered them babe-new into the sunny land of their wilder dreams. To all else they were oblivious. It was only the earnest, het couples from Iowa and Darwin who were so conspicuously un-born again, eyeing them aghast and sniffy with their sun-tan oil, righteousness and Hong Kong Nikons.

In order not to waste a moment of their fortnight or three weeks these men used to bring with them copies of typescript pamphlets with titles like *The Boy-Lover's Guide to Asia*, typically published in Amsterdam. These booklets were part of the fantasy too, the injunctions and advice in them entirely un-ironised. Much could be read between their faintly printed lines. In their way they did their level best to fix a single-minded gulf between the cultures, to preserve the fantasy intact, to make sure an object never became a subject:

> The Filipino boy is full of smiles and affection. Simple, warm-hearted and eager to please you, you will find he is intensely loyal. But do not fear you will break his heart if next time you will prefer his friend. He will be happy too.

Nothing about the common Asian convention by which smiling and laughing may hide embarrassment or anxiety, simply the engaging amorality of the sweet-shop. Not much, either, to suggest that intense loyalty might not be unconnected with economic necessity, with a dependent family. Mark Cousins once posited an imaginary, wittier and more ironic Bosie by proposing 'the love that dare not name its price.' *The Boy-Lover's Guide* was less reticent:

> The going rate for a boy since before time in memorial is twenty-five pesos [then roughly US$3] and only we would beg you not to exceed this. To the boy it is a great money even if not so much to you. Also, by increasing money the price will rise and you will spoil the market for those who come after you. If you become especial fondness for a boy it is better to buy him a new jeans or a shoes. A T-shirt will be a big thing for him.

Is there something special about the position occupied by shoes in the imagery of racial contempt? One was suddenly reminded of the immortal remark by US Secretary of Agriculture, Earl Butz, forced to resign in 1976 for observing 'the only thing the coloureds are looking for in life are tight pussy, loose shoes and a warm place to shit'. In any case the gentle reader sipping his *calamansi* juice in VIP's and eyeing the passing trade was not told about the men, often armed, who took their cut from the boys' ₱25. Nor did he learn about the street gangs which effectively controlled (and still control) Manila, even Harrison Plaza, and whose tattooes on the boy's shoulder or buttock he might later stroke with a jocular remark, provoking the child to pretend it was done as a joke by his brother. The Boy-Lover would still be unable to read the blue letters SSC or the cougar's head as signifying the Sigue-Sigue Commando; nor the UFO sign as that of the Sputnik gang; nor the tartar's head with horns and beard as belonging to the Bahala Na gang, famed as the 'suicide' gang whose street fights could leave half a dozen dead. Nor could he read OXO as a gang sign, nor BCJ as identifying the Batang City Jail where any child on the streets who was not obviously middle-class was (and still is) in danger of being hauled at any time of day or night by a policeman needing cash. Once in jail the child is free – indeed urged – to send a note to any next-of-kin, friend or remote acquaintance to beg them to stump up ₱50 or ₱100 to buy his release. Those unable to write find a jailer or gang member to act as amanuensis (for a cut, naturally). Many boys and girls are able to buy themselves out in a day or two. Others are not so fortunate and have to contend for rather longer with the cockroaches, slops, violence, to say nothing of the theft of their new T-shirt, jeans or shoes.

The deadly loyalties of members to their gangs, the deadly rivalries between the gangs themselves as between them and the police, the slum as village and battleground governed by obscure oaths, codes of honour and debts of obligation – such things are, of course, a part of the city which underlies the Manila the tourists see. In just such a way are the old streets Nick Joaquin celebrates disguised beneath new names and contemporary concrete, now so lost as practically to constitute a world of the imagination like Drune. The Manila which represents Fantasyland for rural Filipinos seeking their fortunes is a different city from the one which is Fantasyland for tourists, but occasionally the two overlap and are glimpsed by both sides as a battle-field. Fantasylands and battlefields have a good deal in common apart from the commingling of blood and passion, Eros and Thanatos, the Enemy and the Beloved and all those other celebrated couplings. Above all, they must de-personalise or the whole thing becomes impossible. Thus, Gook gets killed and Boy gets paid while somewhere in the middle, on that shady grey ground which both separates and mediates such economies, obscure *mafiosi* wheel and deal. To certain classes of outsiders it is vital for a country and its people to remain figments, real only in the rôles cast for them: *hostess, call-boy, bar-tender, bell-hop, waitress, peasant*. It is, after all, the essence of tourism.

Today in Manila there is indeed a strange crew, mostly foreign and left over from that old Manila, who are des-cribed in newspapers as the 'Malate Mafia', Malate being the particular area of the Ermita tourist belt which con-tains among other things Harrison Plaza. The Malate Mafia are characterised as people who have taken up residence and now largely control various rackets such as child prostitution and drugs and have become prime targets of post-Marcos reformist zeal. Catholic leaders and self-styled concerned citizens inveigh against them publicly, their power (Economic? Crony?) frequently alluded to as the reason why their disbanding seems so difficult to achieve. Whether or not they are protected, and by whom, is uncertain. More certain is that they could hardly be as immoral as the poverty which ensures their survival.

Manila remains the nipple from which the world takes most of its information about the Philippines. Maybe this is inevitable. It has certain results in terms of the accuracy with which the country is perceived. This was especially noticeable during the famous Snap Election of February 1986 which brought to an end the twenty years of Marcos dynasty.

I was not in Manila at the time. I was not even in the Philippines but up a mountain in Tuscany, by turns apprehensive and relieved as news came in over the BBC's World Service of crowds facing tanks and the tanks not firing. For a week or more every news bulletin was headed by the latest from Manila, the correspondents there filing dutifully and copiously, and by the end of that week I had the strange impression I was listening to descriptions of a country I had never visited, let alone lived in. The terms were familiar enough, of course: the Government, the People, the Opposition, the Armed Forces, the Police, the Church, the Authorities (how the British, in particular, love this phrase!). But the State they were describing was somehow unrecognisable, and the more one listened to journalists reifying their own descriptions the more one knew it would remain so.

It was perhaps not the journalists' fault. Being shunted about the world from one newsworthy crisis to the next is scarcely conducive to knowledge. It is not easy to be over-respectful of the opinion of a 'South-East Asia correspondent', on the same grounds that we would mistrust a South Korean newspaperman whose beat was 'Europe'. Britain would be merely one of the many countries which fell within his bailiwick. No matter how many sedulous months he had spent in a library in Seoul we might well doubt he knew much about Britain if he had only ever lived

a month or two there, including the obligatory couple of
days in Northern Ireland with the Provisionals. We might
be even more sceptical if he relied entirely on interpreters
and guides. Had he lived with Yorkshire hill-farmers? Was
he familiar with the preoccupations of commuters in pubs
on Saturday evenings in Westerham or on the Hog's Back?
Did he really appreciate the subtleties of the various trade-
offs made by a million families deep in the grip of deficit
financing? Above all, did he actually understand the
politics?

Yet the Philippines was perhaps the one place in the Far
East where many Western journalists evidently felt the
pressure to do additional homework was not so acute.
Enough to give it the old experienced eye for a week or two
from – for the best of professional reasons – a large hotel; be
urbane and amusing and readable while doing the couple of
days' up-country NPA bit and flashing the old humanist
credentials over the slums in Tondo. They all did it. How
else, to be fair? That is journalism. Was the place not a
quasi-American satellite? Plenty of old hands to give them
the run-down. Apart from anything else a familiar friend
had already been identified, a polarity they recognised: the
Corrupt Dictator vs the Downtrodden People. In fact their
typewriters and modems were still warm from the same
story only a matter of days before in Haiti.

Among the reasons why journalists must have felt comparatively easy about this new assignment were religion
and language. The Philippines declares itself officially to be
90 per cent Christian and 100 per cent English-speaking. As
an ex-Spanish, ex-American colony, runs the assumption,
the culture must be reasonably accessible. Like Hong
Kong it is an honorary part of the West but unlike Hong
Kong it does not have that aspect of a Chinese majority
behind whose significant dragons and complex ideograms
so much remains hidden to all but the most expert. The
Philippines, by contrast, must be *comprehensible*.

This very accessibility constitutes a strange barrier. The
West's insistence on holding up a linguistic mirror to the
world and seeing its own flawed reduplication makes this a
difficult barrier to perceive, let alone to cross, especially

when talking about these two subjects, religion and language. The Philippines's version of Christianity is often a religiose form of Catholicism full of elaborate superstitions and, at Easter, crucifixions. It is thus of a dated kind which many secular Europeans find considerably more foreign than Buddhism. To them it smacks of the mediaeval when they hear of the devout poor further pauperising themselves to buy a handful of fake pearls to sew on the stiff little cope of some crude effigy of the Santo Niño or Our Lady of *Biglang-Awa* (Sudden Mercy). So it does when they see the pictures in Good Friday's evening papers of a pious carpenter from Tondo hanging for three hours nailed to a cross he himself lovingly made, of a provincial mayor penitently thanking his God for the failure of an assassination attempt (the bullet struck his rosary) by crawling three kilometres with spiked blocks strapped to his naked back. It all sounds too much like the Holy Week flagellants in Spain: unsophisticated, dark, hysterical. It is certainly very untwentieth century.

If these same secular Europeans happened to pass through Kansulay on Good Friday they might see Tatang Naldo testing his own powers which according to tradition ought then to be at their height. On this day he eats glass and devours bars of Superwheel as well as (I am unreliably assured) frying eggs on the front of his T-shirt. '*Demonyo*', say the people of Kansulay respectfully. Precisely related to this phenomenon – repeated in a thousand barrios up and down the Philippines – was an incident related in the papers of Holy Week 1986. An off-duty policeman in Manila offered to test lucky charms by firing at them with an M-16 rifle on a waste lot. The climax of the story was not really the child who was killed by a ricochet but the failure of the majority of *anting-anting*s to resist a ·223 bullet travelling at 3250 ft/sec. They were obviously fake charms and their wearers unfortunate dupes. Two charms were apparently undamaged, presumably living up to their owners' claims that they could deflect any weapon. As to what an off-duty policeman was doing with an automatic rifle and a stock of ammunition at large on a slum lot was not clear. It was Good Friday, not a day for questions of that sort.[4]

Where language is concerned, too, the Philippines' claim to be the world's third-largest English-speaking nation is extraordinarily deceptive but is one which the visitor to Manila might not find time or even reason to doubt. American English is very much the language of the middle-class educated, of the élites of government, commerce and administration. Most of the capital's serious newspapers are in English as are the main American-style radio stations. Since it is recognised as an élite language English is aspired to and pretended to so that a Filipino may give an impression of understanding far more than he actually does.

The official language of the Philippines is Pilipino, which is essentially Tagalog with loan-words from other dialects. Tagalog was the original language of the people who had settled the area of Luzon in which Manila lies. In 1936 it was adopted nationally as the basis of Pilipino against strenuous rival claims from other large linguistic groups, especially those in the Visayas. Today's Pilipino is sometimes disparagingly described as a fossil language whose purity – like that of French – needs to be preserved by an academy. Critics like Nick Joaquin make a distinction between it and *Filipino*, which they say is the language colloquially spoken by half the population as their mother tongue and by the other half as a lingua franca: a mobile, energetic Pilipino full of *argot* and borrowings and inventive formulations.

That, then, is the nationalist point of view. As regards the American English often learned at mother's knee by phrase rather than with any real linguistic fluency, an expedient daily compromise is reached with 'Taglish', a bastard hybrid used by broadcasters, government officials, anyone fancying themselves as at all sophisticated. The Tagalog carries the colloquial and comprehension element, the English the kudos. At its worst Taglish is mere pidgin-Filipino and pidgin-American, as witness this extract from a film review in the magazine *Babae* (Woman):

Expected na something colorful ang presentations of awardees nang gabing iyon dahil sa emcee pa lang na sina Nova Villa at Rowell Santiago, expected na some-

thing to watch ang Annual Sining-Himig Award na ito.
Call it 'palpak' or problem ng mga people behind the
scenes, unang naging problema ang script ng show na
hindi mabasa-basa nina Nova at Rowell dahil kahit
malinis ang pagkakamakinilya nito, na-mangle ang
script sa sari-saring insertions at pagtu-twists ng number
ng mga presentors at awardees. Kagagawan naman ito ni
Greg Ritual na Chairman on awards ng BAMCI.

The main purpose of this mindless stuff is not to convey
information so much as make the reader feel she is 'where
it's at' (another favourite Taglish phrase). On the other hand
at its best Taglish can show an easy familiarity with both
languages which often hinges around word-play, undoubtedly one of the hallmarks of relaxed and civilised man. A
banner in a demonstration in the run-up to the February
election read: *Kailangan Bigas Hindi Teargas* (We Need
Rice Not Teargas), a phrase whose pungency would have
been lost had it been purely in either language. As for
'na-mangle' and 'pagtu-twists' in the extract above, con-
noisseurs of etymology will take pleasure from such cross-
lingual declensions, as from the notice *Bawal Umistamby*
which means 'Loitering Prohibited' (by extension from the
phrase 'to be on stand-by'). Thirty years ago as we plodded
achingly off the rugger pitch we would say 'Je suis utterly
knackeré' or 'Shaggé, c'est moi.'
One cheering thing I learned on my return to Manila a
month after the election was that during that tense week
many of the radio stations of the capital reverted to
Filipino. It was as if at a moment of real crisis all preten-
sions were dropped in the urgent necessity of being fully
understood. It was also Manila's way of acknowledging that
the rest of the nation which might be eavesdropping could
well have a genuine problem understanding English.
But at the time, when the world's journalists were filing
their reports, 'Manila' must have served them all too readily
as shorthand for 'the Philippines' just as they made their
own familiar nouns describe entities quite unlike those at
home. It became apparent that the Philippines is most
dissimilar to a Western country at the exact moment when

it is being described by Western journalists – which accounted for my sense of puzzlement in distant Italy. For when a Briton hears phrases like 'the Government', 'the Army' and – and how! – 'the Authorities' he knows in his heart it means the legitimately constituted, orderly, impartial Authorities of Great Britain. Transposing to a foreign country, he assumes that there, too, the Government's writ runs the length and breadth of the land; that the Armed Forces are answerable for their behaviour and unswervingly loyal to the Crown; that in turn they are supported and obeyed. Similarly, the Briton assumes that basic services and impositions are para-governmental and that their implementation will be uniform. Barring calamities water is always on tap, the electricity always works, postal workers do not on the whole rob the mails or take unfranked stamps off envelopes and re-sell them for their own gain, nor do tax collectors go from door to door collecting income tax in cash and paying off their own gambling debts with it. Come to that, the tax collectors are seldom *fake* tax collectors, any more than the policemen are fake policemen.

I am not being deliberately obtuse. Of course journalists qualify things by referring to 'Army factions' (a very un-British concept) and 'the Marcos Government', and of course the intelligent Briton knows perfectly well that things are done differently abroad, especially in the more anarchic areas of the world. Unfortunately the vocabulary remains the same and cannot help having inappropriate echoes. The mere use of words like 'Government' and 'Authorities' sets up an expectation of something familiar, no matter how distorted it may temporarily have become. This can produce an inner hiatus, a brief moment of blankness, as when the listener to the BBC in London learns that 'a spokesman for the Philippine Armed Forces is pleased to report the number of private armies in the Philippines is probably no more than 133.' Suddenly he is on unfamiliar ground; there's a contradiction somewhere, something he hasn't been told about. Who, then, might 'the Authorities' refer to?

At last in increasing bewilderment and scepticism he is

beginning to approach the wavelength of a Filipino who asks himself that very question year in and year out, according to local and national circumstances. Shootouts are common between rival police forces in the nation's capital, between real policemen and fake policemen, between good policemen and bad policemen, between ones on the take and others who want a slice. Units of the Armed Forces engage each other in firefights over claims of legitimacy, secret plots, over fiefdoms they have annexed as their own. Provincial governors and mayors run rackets, private death squads and goons; they keep slaves, siphon off development funds. In short there is no single writ of Authority which infallibly runs the length and breadth of the Philippines (in size the archipelago is, conveniently, comparable to the British Isles).

It is hard for people from the democracies of the industrialised West to remember how their own countries once exhibited such phenomena, and not so long ago. Surprisingly it remains hard even when there are large-scale scandals at home to remind them that the anarchy they so readily identify abroad is never far below the surface anywhere. Even in a European country like Britain, which in certain respects has arguably become *over*-governed, there have been scandals: corruption by provincial bigwigs (Poulson), by Cabinet ministers (Stonehouse, Maudling), by London's incorruptible Metropolitan Police (the great vice-ring shakeout of the early Seventies).

But perhaps the hardest thing to imagine is a country where there can be so little connection between the governors in the capital and the people in the provinces. As suggested earlier, a distinct rusticity can exist even in Metro Manila itself behind the whitewashed hollow-block walls erected to screen the slums from the gaze of tourists, while immemorial village life begins practically at the city limits, at least in attitude if not in aspect. From the provinces the capital is infinitely remote. What happens in Manila has almost no bearing on the way real life is conducted. Marcoses may come and go and the Manileño middle class can describe their uprising as a 'People's Revolution' but in the real world the people are busy planting rice and catching fish; the mango season arrives and improvised parties are held among the coconut palms. News of external events scarcely percolates.

Out in the country old skills remain unforgotten. What kind of disaster can befall a people who can get by even without matches? Who rely on their own abilities and on each other and never on a distant government which has seldom visited them with anything good and often with corrupt mayors, with thieving and murderous troops? If there is a national insouciance about tomorrow . . . *bahala na* . . . it must be at least partly because even quite urbanised Filipinos are often still close enough to their rural origins to feel that in the last resort they can always go back to the provinces and feed themselves. The streets of Manila are full of young people – Totoy Matias now among them – who are only months removed from a life of climbing palms and ploughing paddies. In a devastating economic crisis they might well desert the capital and its governors just as at a moment of constitutional crisis they deserted an alien language.

Knowing all this, how is one to treat those phrases like 'The Will of the People' or 'National Sentiment' or even 'Popular Feeling' when used, as they all were, by Western journalists about a country such as this? In Britain, a state linked to itself by television which almost everyone watches, by newspapers millions read, glutted with opinion polls and phone-in programmes and protest marches and all the democratic ways of ensuring that there actually is such a thing as a majority national opinion about almost anything, such phrases mean something. But how is consensus to be reached in a nation divided by eighty major dialects and eleven main language groups, linked by no reliable telephone network, where travel is laborious and often dangerous? A nation which in percentage terms reads little but comics if it reads at all, and from sheer force of habit mistrusts its own Press? Loyalties are to family, to *barkada*, to gang, to community, to ethnic group. They cannot reliably be used for extrapolating anything as coherent as 'The Will of the People'. In this context the phrase means nothing so the country to which it was meant to apply was, when I heard of it from Italy, not one I recognised.

What was it, then, this country which coincidentally bore the same name? It was largely an invention of those Western journalists who, by turns cocky and earnest, produced yet another of their homogenised Third World nations for breakfast-table reading. In almost complete historical, political and cultural ignorance of the country they were describing they relied extensively and unconsciously on the American version. No-one is surprised at this; everyone ought to be deeply shocked. It is astonishing that a modern independent nation is seen almost entirely from the view of its old Colonial rulers. It is – for example – as if present-day Indian politics could only be explained to the world by Englishmen whose ears were still attuned to the trumpetings of the Great Durbar and Lord Curzon, for thus the long-ago fictions of General MacArthur's version of Bataan and Leyte do indeed still echo down the corridors of the State Department and hence, ghostily, over the wires of Reuters and AP.

It is America, of course, which underlies the Philippines' history throughout this century. Or rather, it would be more accurate to say that America *overlies* the Philippines, as its strategic and economic taxonomy of the globe overlies so much of the objective reality of states and nations. In this way the entire Philippines is in one sense a palimpsest whose faint outlines stubbornly appear and re-appear beneath the guises American foreign policymakers have chosen for it: anti-Communist bulwark of South-East Asia, unsinkable American aircraft carrier, the land of Del Monte's pineapple estates. So if one describes the Western Press's view of the Philippines as largely its own invention, the amount of inventiveness is actually very slight. It is more a matter of *con*vention. But this convention still images an unrecognisable country just as tourist brochures do to the lands they are trying to sell.[5]

If this is true of Manila it is doubly so of the rest of the country. For if the Philippines ever explains itself to those who have the time and inclination to listen, it does so in the provinces and not in the capital where all sorts of subtly

distorting lenses – domestic and foreign – project lurid
images to suit all fantasies: city of gold, historic city, city
of sin, developing city; cultural centre, seat of government,
groves of academe, banking and commercial nexus, heart
and soul of the nation. All are true and untrue. All, claiming
everything, mean almost nothing.

What has Manila to do with Tiwarik?

I have tried to suggest how utterly remote is an islet off an
island which is itself off an island province. Yet even that
islet exists as a political entity, is involved in the politics of
everyday living. Some years ago – long after the declaration
of Martial Law in 1972 – troops stationed up the coast near
the provincial capital turned up one morning in Sabay. It
was merely a day's stopover on a leisurely tour they were
making of the province, which must have been a dull place
for them since there was no political opposition there, no
NPA guerrillas, no angry students or farmers. To fill the
time they made an effort to improve their own living
conditions and came to Sabay on the scrounge. They
requisitioned Arman's father's boat for an afternoon's
drunken fishing and, having caught nothing, shot it full of
holes and let it settle on the rocks off the beach. For a time it
looked as though they might shoot its owner too.

Since then they demand that *baranggay* Captain Sanso
give them fresh fish regularly on the plausible grounds that
Army food is atrocious and one of their officers is anyway
selling canned stores destined for his own troops in the
market at Bulangan. The quid pro quo is that the soldiers
keep the village supplied with blasting caps and demolition
fuses so the fishermen can use dynamite. This ensures their
catches are sometimes large enough for another officer to
sell off any surplus in the market at Malubog.

If dynamite fishing had already been part of the way of life
of Sabay (as throughout much of the archipelago), this
episode made it an impossible habit for the villagers to
break even if some of the more observant fishermen were
beginning to worry about dying corals. The unofficial

threat of a handful of official troops became one more of the interlocking imperatives which entangle the lives of a socially complex, isolated community.

And thus a familiar view from Tiwarik. A small boat drifts on the glassy calm, its occupants muffled against the sun, hanging over the sides, gazing down for hours. The sea is molten, nothing moves. Then beneath it a great door slams, loud enough to bring me out of my hut to look in all directions. But there is nothing much to see: a wisp of steam and spray dissipating above a patch of foam on which other boats converge, their occupants already slipping purposefully overboard with sleeve nets.

Far away in Manila there is a law ratified by all sorts of governmental and international bodies which says this sort of thing is completely illegal. But here at Sabay it is at the express command of 'the Authorities'. It is as if they had known all along I would one day come to live on Tiwarik and were adding that touch of ordnance and war without which my arcadian landscapes are never complete.

PART THREE

Tiwarik and Kansulay

8

The journey back alone from Manila is somehow less arduous. My heart lightens with each turn of the wheels leaving the city behind. The first glimpse of the sea – even if it is framed by the scummy reaches of an estuary where we embark – is a benediction. By the time I reach Bulangan in mid-afternoon the following day I am transformed, lighter by the weight of generalised anxiety which has slipped from me along the way. In Malubog I greet a shopkeeper with perhaps too much effusiveness; pleased as I am to see him it is only eight days since I last did so. I cover up this lapse by buying from him several tins of Alaska condensed milk for families in Sabay: it is not done to return from any trip without a *pasalubong*.

In so doing I nearly miss the last jeep of the day to Sabay. This is just leaving, already laden past the point where it is worthwhile to wonder how it functions at all. Glad I do not have to wedge myself inside and look sheepish for being so huge I stand instead on an empty fish-box roped to the tail grid and cling to the edge of the roof-rack which is itself piled high with luggage and children. The bright air whizzes past, we duck beneath sprays of leaves. From my eminence I look down at the boy beside me who has just clambered on and found a toehold. I recognise one of Intoy's younger brothers. His small hands are clenched around the edge of the polished aluminium roof, tendons standing out. The brown and serious face stares into the wind. From this angle the fine silk on the side of his cheek and the corner of his upper lip is a pale powdery nap. More extraordinary is his hair whose straight Asian jet shimmers in the airflow. Its movement is continuous like a stream of water, like the slide of water seen from over a boat's edge, a hypnotic lively rush. It is as if hair in an unending bow-wave were bursting from his temples and scurrying back off his head with its passing glints and lights and flecks of foam. I almost expect to look behind and see a growing wake of tresses in our following dust.

That night I walk the shore of Tiwarik alone, seeing my footsteps agitate invisible grains into momentary phosphorescence, living granules stranded by the outgoing tide. The shingle is alive with hermit crabs, a constant seethe of tiny castles lurching and jerking across a battered terrain which remarkably affords them rich pickings. I salute them for their life on the edge, being neither wholly of the sea nor of the land, living in cast-off forts, scavenging their sustenance from anything left by sea or man. Here and there two engage in battle, overbalance, roll down into the water. Others bump into each other, pass, following their own wandering courses with implacable purpose. How could each have a separate, valid path to pursue over those hillocks of dead limestone, among those valleys and crags and boulders? Is their progress merely random? Do they become confused and distracted by all the olfactory intertwinings? To understand what each crab is doing, exactly why it goes where it does, would be to understand something significant. Here in the moonlight by the still sea it is possible to glimpse an end to the world, aeons after the last human corpse has yielded up the ghosts of its last aminoacids, the hermit crabs still busy with the sea's mullings, shuffling and clicking their tangled paths which with the terrain they cross are daily washed into new configurations.

The sun next morning is not the same star which baked the photochemical smog above Manila into a pale brown dome. It is utterly direct and clear. It bleeds away the terpenes from the forest above, it strips off any human folly which I might have draped about the place. In that brilliantly-lit discourse between land and water something other is going on which I long very much to follow. For above all else the light reminds how unsatisfactory it is to look at the sun and say 'sun', at the sea and say 'sea'. It is no use pretending they don't have metaphoric status, that the rocking dazzle of noon about Tiwarik does not also contain all manner of *departures* from light. Thus one glimpses behind any landscape a fleetingness as if something not visible to the eye were racing through, something which nearly *was* the eye, amorous and transient, intelligent and thirsty.

This is the eye to cultivate, the way of looking which leaves behind the ego. The proper eye does not care to be liked nor does it feel it has to amuse. Tern-like it drifts on the thin gale amid arctic glaciers or stares into holes beneath ultramarine fathoms. When it looks at skin it marvels at the easy rubbing away of desire but knows of longing forever unassuaged. Uneasy winds blow through all it sees and can leave very clear and unexpected outlines. Tiwarik at noon has the contours of a mind, massively quiet and sentient with its humming surf. Like some mysterious vehicle at rest it waits, ticking over. The passenger goes up to his hut, sits on the floor in the shade. A different kind of journey has begun.

On this journey, which takes place at any time, he learns he has no right to expect a free passage. The landscape carries him along but it is not going his way. His desire that it be ravishing or mystical is only his desire he tries to foist onto it; the landscape couldn't care less what he wants. Underneath it is proceeding in its own way with extreme energy and economy, entirely self-aware and entirely uncompassionate. In the forest, on the beach and among the reefs it goes, in a manner which looks to a human observer like war. But the complexity of what is happening, the sheer beauty of the huge structure has nothing to do with human interpretations but merely encompasses the raw terms of life. The bristle worms fluff out their brilliant feathery crowns; the coral algae are busy with their photosynthesis, the polyps with their daily routines of chemistry and light. Outside the reef a hammerhead glides like a priest. He is quite clear from the bluff above the head, unhurried, not hungry, for he passes over the deep blue trench within a few metres of half a dozen bluefin. Both shark and fish must be perfectly aware of each other but whatever the means of communication it bears a message which allows them to continue their separate routes which

so briefly crossed. The bluefin do not alter course. Like
the hermit crabs they are purposeful, on the way somewhere or merely on the way through miles of sunlit water.
Slowly, too, the hammerhead fades. I watch him in his
magnificence growing dim, becoming a faint shape
scribbled across by surface ripples, his image erased by
wind.

From my vantage point I can look down and speculate
about the million messages carried on the currents below,
intercepted and acted on, heard, smelt, tasted, seen,
palpated, received. Some of the messages are highly
dangerous in themselves, cytotoxic and neurotoxic
venoms leaked from a variety of sting-cells, spines, fangs,
glands. Such messages are often received by human swimmers and the fishermen of Sabay answer back in kind, for
in addition to being accomplished bombers they are
poisoners as well. It is only at these moments the reef
becomes a battlefield, when man deploys weapons
designed for effects on a different scale and on different
terrain.

How resourceful they are, these people who have learned
hard how to stay alive by such a variety of means. Not only
can a Sabay fisherman turn his hand to agriculture on the
steep slopes behind the village, planting rice and cassava
when the rains come, fishing with net, spear and explosive
when the sea is right, but he has yet another source of
income. This is from two distinct activities known collectively as *similya* or 'seedlings'. One involves children trudg-
ing up and down in the breakers at certain seasons towing
behind them billowing nets of the finest mesh to catch the
tiny fry of *bangus*. The *bangus* or milk fish (*Chanos chanos*) is
greatly prized in the Philippines and has been elevated to
the status of National Fish. It is expensive and hence much
farmed. The fry are bagged in plastic and shipped off to
agents for rearing in fish pans.

The other kind of *similya* is the gathering of live speci-
mens of coral fish for export to dealers abroad who special-
ise in tropical fish for the world's aquaria. Once again the
methods of the Sabay fisherfolk are illegal and ingenious.

The technique this time depends on *sodiúm* or *kuskus*: sodium cyanide which is smuggled in from a distant province in the form of white crystalline chunks looking for all the world like washing soda. These are put into plastic Shell Rotella motor oil containers fitted with a short spout and diluted with seawater. Lighter boats are used than for dynamiting since the corals being fished are generally in shallower waters and there is no need for a compressor. Goggled swimmers hold onto the boats' outriggers and drift in the water above the corals until a suitable species is seen or a likely outcrop spotted. Then the poisoner swims down and squirts his bottle into cracks and holes. It appears that diluting the cyanide with seawater makes it less lethal and more anaesthetic in effect. By the time the poisoner has come up to exchange his bottle for a light net the first fish are beginning to reel out of the coral, moving dopily on their backs, on their sides, acting drunk. The ones that are wanted are scooped up and transferred to polythene bags of seawater in the boat. Once back in Sabay they are re-bagged according to species and twice a week are shipped up the coast for collection by an agent from Manila who generally pays the fishermen one-sixth of the price he will ask foreign dealers two days later.

Local lore has it that *kuskus* crystals are more dangerous to the humans and their families than they are to the fish, for doped fish appear to recover quickly if the dilution is correct. Unfortunately the truth of this extends only as far as the Sabayans' observation: it is what they don't see, the effects of *kuskus* on invisible plants and animals which is so disastrous. In the meantime if *kuskus* becomes temporarily unavailable there are potent alternatives, among them *bayati* and *tubli* root, both common enough plants but harder to use because more powerful even than cyanide in salt water and tending to kill the fish outright rather than just anaesthetising them. They are useful for flushing out large and dangerous prey such as big eels, however, allowing a spear-fisherman time to place his shot while less menaced by the slashing mouthful of teeth which can strip flesh off a hand like a glove. Fishermen who tackle big morays many feet down are grateful for all the help they can get; a squirt of *tubli* root slightly up-current of that swaying, fanged head can make all the difference.

Poison, like dynamite, is not something I have ever used myself nor ever shall. For one thing I am far too afraid of it. For another I hate its imprecision, its casual slaughter of micro-organisms which happen to get in the way of the pursuit of a single small aquarium fish. Besides, because I do not have a family to feed I can afford to adopt the weird and quirky view that if one chooses to engage with a large moray one should be responsible for one's temerity as for one's skill. A true hunter could never allow poison into his armoury; it is a matter of pride and good taste. Eels are not at all difficult to shoot but they are excessively hard to kill. They have terrifying strength and once they have retreated into their holes enough for half their length to have gained a firm anchorage, one may all but tear their heads off without budging them. To me it is a sad and piteous sight, a great eel with his head slashed, a spear through one eye and his lower jaw torn off, the white flesh hanging in shreds in the current, still with his muscles locked in a tetanic spasm and his blank remaining eye fixed on the nearest enemy. He can never survive in that condition but maybe he can hold on for another hour or so (for his brain is tiny and inaccessible), long enough perhaps for weary hunters to give up and move on, leaving their ruined prey. Anyone who has ever seen his own blood blossom in green stranded clouds around him in the water ought not to lack feeling for tenacious life, the proximity of death.

Meanwhile the villagers' use of sodium cyanide remains a vital part of their *similya* operation which in turn provides a significant proportion of their income.[6] It is not a form of fishing which interests me at all so no doubt its finer points of technique elude me. Sodium cyanide dissolved in seawater may indeed be an endlessly subtle poison worthy of a Renaissance venefice. But then, plenty of apologists for dynamite – Arman himself included – will argue how selective and accurate that can be. It is true these techniques have been around a long time and still there are fish in the waters of Sabay, in Tiwarik's coral reefs. But I myself have not been here long enough to know how much better fish stocks and corals were ten or more years ago. At a local level, then, knowing the people involved and knowing their lives I sometimes think they are getting by, just on the edge between destroying the marine environment on which they depend and allowing it to survive.

This may be how the particular and partial eye observes and reasons. But if that eye withdraws far enough to see Sabay as just one more tiny village whose fishing activities are not untypical, the whole archipelago presents a gloomy prospect. No matter how skilled they may be the Filipinos are steadily destroying their corals as they are their forests. Dynamiters are often little more than cowboys raiding other people's fishing grounds in powerful boats, stuffing their ice-boxes with corpses and pushing casually on, leaving behind them shattered corals, dead and dying creatures, vital colonies of micro-organisms annihilated. In its own way cyanide fishing is even more destructive because what the villagers do not see are the coral polyps themselves being poisoned, the algae on which they depend and the hidden life deep within the reef being killed.

This is a national problem since probably almost 80 per cent of the world's salt-water tropical fish come from the Philippines, a market supplied by a comparative handful of rapacious and cut-throat exporters. It is they who keep the fishermen supplied with the cyanide, buying off local coastguards and policemen in order to get the drums of poison distributed among the islands. Certain species of fish are now becoming quite scarce. Some of the larger angel fishes such as the Majestic (*Euxiphipops navarchus*), the Blue Face (*Euxiphipops xanthometopon*) and the Imperator (*Pomacanthus imperator*) have been decimated. Blue Tangs (*Paracanthurus hepatus*) are increasingly rare as are several species of butterfly and clown fishes. As stocks decrease the prices rise and competition becomes still more unscrupulous. The American and European owners of calm and bubbling tanks which sustain their mournful slivers of life as clinically as any life-support system cannot guess – or prefer not to know – the other end of that chain. The world in which those fish were taken is lawless and destructive: greedy fiefdoms protected by bribed local

officials, smuggled sacks of poison, exploited fishermen
and dying habitats. For every live specimen which survives
to expire on its life-support system in somebody's living-
room are an uncounted number of fish which die in the
process of being poisoned on the sea bed, bagged, tagged
and exported.

Many months later and far away a small incident was
poignant with recollections for me. I was in London,
intending among other things to have an ear seen to –
presumably the constant diving had affected some remote
piece of tubing. Thanks partly to a family connection I was
to be seen by a private ENT consultant. One morning I
found myself in a typical consultant's waiting-room.

From the room itself there was no way of telling whether
waiting patients were to pass through a dark red mahog-
anyesque door for new contact lenses, a hair transplant,
dental work or a gynaecological examination. They might
from the look of the place expect to be told they owed three
thousand pounds or that with a lucky remission they might
just have six months to put their affairs in order. The air
smelt of Cavendish Square. Deep carpet on the floor, a
standard lamp with a gold shade in one corner, leather
armchairs, stacks of *Vogue, Punch, Country Life, The Lady,
Autocar* on low tables. Heavy moth-coloured curtains
framed a view of what were basically eighteenth-century
rooftops misshapen with grimy aerials, asphalted water
tanks and corroded heat exchangers. On the marble
mantelpiece stood a marble clock of enormous weight and
absurdly slow tick: 'Festina lente' said the apt admonish-
ment in copperplate script near the top.

But the ordinary gloom and tension which always
pervades such fake-clublands was pricked into real
poignancy by a large aquarium which stood in the corner
opposite the lamp. In it were the usual sorts of small fish
inertly doing nothing among the little thermometers, the
thin plastic tubes emitting sprays of bubbles, the whimsies
embedded in the gravel at the bottom. The purposeful,

unreadable courses the fish would have been swimming in their natural habitat were impossible. Suddenly from behind a pirate's chest purporting to spill a cascade of jewels onto the sea bed swam an old friend: a tiny specimen of the Queen Trigger such as I had often hunted for my supper. Each species of fish has its characteristic movements and attitudes in the water. Listless and foully lost as this poor creature was it was not so denatured as to have unlearned how to face a threat from in front, in this case my affectionate fingertips on the glass at its nose. It hung there in that familiar head-on posture, dorsal and ventral fins appearing to move in contrary motion, then half-turning to back up and re-face the threat from a little further away. That was the *moment juste* for the spear, as it briefly presented a side view. Mentally I fired and heard the *pok!* of tough hide being pierced, heard alarmed drumming as I headed up through thirty feet of water (for Queen Triggers prefer a bit of depth), my prey spitted. Even as I rose to the sunlit surface I had swept the fish back along the steel rod onto the catch-line trailing below me, starting the process of re-loading before my head broke through into bright air.

'Pretty, aren't they?' I had been joined by the receptionist who had shown me into the waiting-room. 'Are you a fish fancier?'

I made some non-committal remark and asked whether they had had the Queen Trigger for long.

'About a week. Handsome little devil, isn't he? We've had several like him already. If you look very carefully you can see he isn't black at all but midnight blue. And if you look *really* close you'll notice his scales are sort of fake: they're just a diamond pattern on his skin. I don't know why, that kind never seem to last very long. Only a month or two usually.'

I wondered whether to tell her about its high first dorsal spine which locked vertically up to wedge the fish defensively into cracks and which could only be released by pressing down the lower second spine, the trigger. I didn't tell her the fish were very tasty if wrapped in a banana leaf and roast over an open fire. Instead I wondered whether this particular specimen had hatched into life as fry in the offshore swell of Tiwarik, later to be stunned by Arman's cyanide and retrieved in his net, from that moment destined to stare for the rest of its life not through thirty feet of vivid tropical sea but through a few inches of reconstituted seawater warmed by electric bulbs at a wall of glass until saprophages grew in its gills and killed it.

The receptionist ushered me away and into the presence of the doctor who within minutes told me that I had mould growing in my own left gill and wrote me up for some anti-mould drops. That infection cleared, but the trouble persists. I have never been back, though, to see if the little Queen Trigger has survived. From time to time I think of it in its pitiless exile surrounded by fake gems and living in the poop of a bogus galleon eighty feet above the streets of London.

From a dream that the sea was dead, poisoned and lifeless I awoke, expecting to smell the stench of carrion from the strand below, the hermit crabs tearing at heaps of putrefaction. Instead the lively ocean rested in its bed, washed by moon and stars, its breathing body fanned by light pulses of air from across the strait. I went and sat outside, watching the cordillera opposite skip from one side of the sky to the other like a graph. Immediately I was caught up in the universe. Off-guard with the remains of sleep I was like some careless factory-worker whose clothing is snagged by the machinery he leans over, wrenched bodily into the mechanism and swallowed up. I became as if melted into the sea. My heart beat in time with the mountains. Stars poured down into my head. Without ears, without tongue I heard myself say the words I must always have used, will always use, whose meaning is *Why, you knew all along* and *It is always here, always now* – banalities beyond translation, beyond speech. In that silence alone the universe can be heard talking in pebbles and weed, in glittering plankton and predator's brain, in the ineffable sound made by the hills as they fold and pleat themselves. *How can it ever be forgotten?* But I do forget it. I am incredulous. How can I pretend none of this is so and allow myself daily to become dragged down by foolishness?

If one were to weep for this idiocy the tears which glistened in the starlight would at least be proper tears of regret and not of pity. To forget the only thing there is seems like a crime for which there could be no redemption. The consequence would properly be that it all became dead things: the sea turned to mere water, the mountains to lumps of geology, the wind and rain became more or less inconvenient. But miraculously the cordillera across the strait is still hefting its crags and shrugging its forests. By the standards of the world's great mountain ranges it is nothing, this cordillera, a comparative South Downs. But tonight it is the loftiest imaginable perhaps because the sea lying at its feet gives no indication of scale as would a valley floor with houses and the thread of roads.

At once, sadly, angrily, comes into my head my father, who loved mountains. I give a start of surprise at finding him there, but the more I consider it the less surprised I become. It is not just the mountains; it is not even because of my memories of war over landscapes and uneasy oppositions of all kinds. It seems quite specifically because of the dream of poison from which I have just woken, but I cannot quite grasp why.

My father entered my life when I was four. Quite suddenly, this demobbed stranger came into the house claiming to be my mother's husband. What intelligent child could believe a tale like that? Husbands and fathers were supposed to be an indispensable part of family life yet my mother and sister and I had seemingly got along very nicely without one. Why then the sudden need? Four years later still I was off among the South Downs for months at a time, months which themselves stretched on for another ten or eleven years. In the holidays my father and I scarcely met. He was overworked and testy, the rushed professional who seemed to spend less and less time in the house. In such ways it is quite possible for someone to grow up never knowing his own father. As with the God one heard about at school, the obligations were always there to love and respect and fear him but the outline was dim and hazy, the features blurred. From the remoteness on the other side there came no answer excepting only that sometimes inexplicable rages played like lightning about one's head. Why then do I any longer think of him? How could this vanished stranger play any part in my present life, still less have anything to do with my being here on this island? I do not quite know. I do know he is not irrelevant, though, and that the reason is slowly becoming clearer. Therefore I will stare at the mountains across the strait and force myself to consider once more this business of poison. It is *cyanide*; and it takes me straight back to that second school.

The headmaster met me just before lunch in the corridor outside the dining hall. I stood to attention, held my hands out and turned them over for inspection. Even I could see the wrists were grey above the tide-line but he didn't so much as glance at them.

'Your father's coming this afternoon,' he said. 'I thought you might be interested.' He wasn't smiling. A school myth was that when he was wearing green, particularly a green tweed suit, he was in a mood for blood. He was at this moment in a brownish sports jacket with leather buttons but his tie was green and hairy. I didn't dare ask him why my father was coming unexpectedly. Obviously my behaviour and schoolwork had sunk below the point where the ordinary measures of fortnightly reports and informal conversations by the tea-tent on Parents' Day were any longer adequate. He had been called to take me away. No, worse: there was going to be a Parent's Caning.

Another myth at this school, more dread than that of the Second Cellars, so awesome nobody even much liked talking about it, was of an event called a Parent's Caning. This allegedly took place once every twenty years or so when a boy had done something so truly awful that no ordinary punishment could meet the case. It was the prep-school equivalent of being flogged round the Fleet. So brutal was it the boy's father had to be called in to witness it along with the school doctor who checked the victim's pulse after each stroke. The entire thing was a pack of lies, of course, mere schoolboy hysteria, but it didn't stop us believing in it and now in the corridor outside the dining hall I knew I was to be the victim. I was so frightened I didn't even bother to wonder what I had done to deserve it. And my father was a doctor, too! That clinched it.

When at the end of lunch the headmaster stood up to make an announcement I was ready to faint, in such a state I would have interpreted anything he might have said as proof of my impending execution. The news that the whole school could have a half-holiday and spend it in the swimming baths would have been utterly plausible. What more natural than that a special site was necessary for a Parent's Caning, somewhere unusual to impress the gravity of the occasion on everyone present? Actually the man merely said that we should keep clear of the top of the field beyond the junior cricket pitch and walked out. Electricity shot through me. What did that bit of waste space contain but the old oak? Of course. The Hanging Oak, as it was known for its stout horizontal limb with a scar around its bark from the days when the Hall was newly built and it had regularly been used as a gibbet for insubordinate coachmen, cocky servants, mutinous lackeys. The Hanging Oak! The perfect spot for a Parent's Caning.

It was a Saturday and so we had the afternoon off in any case. At two o'clock a few informal games of cricket convened in a leisurely manner here and there around the playing fields. Some boys were expecting their parents to arrive and pay them a visit. So was I, now, but how different was to be my father's rôle! Many of us stood about, not actually near the forbidden tree but for that matter not very far from it. Speculation ran high about what was going to happen. Somebody suggested they were going to cut the Hanging Oak down and that there would be danger to bystanders from the displaced ghosts of those who had dangled from its limb; we had been reading M. R. James under the bedclothes by torchlight. I kept quiet, not daring to tell them the truth because I knew that once I had said it everybody would recognise it as the only plausible explanation.

At two-thirty a familiar car emerged from the rhododendrons at the far end of the drive and crunched to a stop in front of the school. My father emerged carrying a clinical-looking bottle. Sal volatile, of course, to restore my vital functions. I didn't dare run to meet him. Instead the headmaster, who was already chatting to a group of parents, detached himself from them and shook my father's hand with, I thought, a smile significantly tinged with graveness and sympathy. Together they began walking up the grounds towards the junior cricket pitch and the tree.

'Do you have a stick?' I heard my father ask.

'There'll be one there,' replied the headmaster.

Since I could no longer postpone the inevitable I went to meet them, unable to feel my legs walking beneath me.

'Hullo!' my father greeted me with tasteless cordiality. 'This is unexpected, isn't it? How about this for a pretty bottle?'

The bottle he carried was indeed striking, ribbed and blue, bluer even than those milk of magnesia bottles, round and with a ground glass stopper. On the label was a red skull and crossbones. I nodded miserably.

'Cyanide,' he said.

'*Cyanide?*'

'That's right. Awfully dangerous stuff.'

'It's extremely good of your father to have come,' the headmaster said with the hypocritical expansive smile we all knew headmasters reserved for boys whose parents were nearby. 'It was poor old Pollock last night that finally did it.'

Pollock was the First XI wicket keeper who had been stung by a wasp the day before and was all swollen up in the san, instead of playing against a school in Kent which was full of wets but which had really good sausage rolls for match teas.

'So,' the headmaster went on, 'I got old Bisley to do some sleuthing and when he'd tracked it down I thought immediately of your father, being a doctor and so forth, and he very kindly nipped over to the hospital pharmacy.'

'Yes but what are you going to *do*?' I asked miserably.

'Kill a wasps' nest, what did you think?' my father asked.

'Well actually,' the Head said, 'I quite deliberately didn't tell them what we were up to. If you announce to a lot of small boys that a large wasps' nest is going to be attacked at two-thirty with the most deadly poison known to man, and they are on no account to come anywhere near it, there's not a boy in the school who won't be there. If, on the other hand, you keep it vague and casual there's just a chance . . . Hello! Over here a bit more, I think. Bisley said it was about fifteen yards from the oak and that he'd marked it. Yes, there's the stick. Good. Now stand back everyone.'

And the sun which had been vertical, molten and glary slumped several degrees and began to shine benignly in a beautiful June afternoon, on this island surrounded as yet invisibly by creeping suburbia. The trees cast their shade in which Tortoiseshells and Brimstones and Marbled Whites fluttered and in the distance white-clad figures scampered and the pock of ball against bat came flatly on the drowsy air. We boys were waved safely back while I proudly watched my father advance with a pint of the world's most deadly poison to do battle with what were clearly hornets and not wasps at all, probably the biggest and most dangerous nest ever found in the south of England.

And when his crouched figure had straightened up, slightly red in the face from holding his breath, the head-master sent someone for a spade and they covered it all up with a mound of soil leaving nothing but a faint and pleasant smell of almond essence. How far away those days now seem, not because they are in the least bit faint but because they enclosed a way of life which seems unthinkable in a modern England. What more reasonable and straightforward way to deal with a wasps' nest than to ring up a consultant neurologist and get him to trot down to Pharmacy for a pint of cyanide and come on over in the car and pour it into the school grounds? Then back to the house for a cup of tea and maybe watch the Second XI in the nets and take your coat off and chuck some nasty balls at the slip-catching machine which even Pollock couldn't have taken. And finally remember to pick up the cyanide bottle which you think you may have left in the pavilion but later, after a worried search, you discover in the boot of the car where you had put it for safety's sake, and back down the drive in a low-lifting cloud of dust and away through the rhododendrons leaving a small son ecstatic with relief and full of pride.

It was a way of life which was really a hang-over from a relaxed patrician world which had ended with the General Election of 1945. On Tiwarik the distant cries of cricketers on slumbrous June afternoons might come back as fresh as ever if I let them; but that regular pock of their play would now sound to me like the ticking of the termites in the night which slowly reduce my house's framework to dust from within.

It seems incredible now that I should ever have felt myself so terrorised as I did then, at the whim of any figure in authority. But unknown to myself it must have produced an anger in me because after all my father had won in his heroic campaign against the wasps that afternoon: he had punished me with drawn-out terror for once trying to kill him with a wasp. At one level this was only fair; at another it was horribly unfair to blame me for his not being more lovable, better loved. A defiance, a stubbornness grew in me which later resulted in my refusal to think and do as he and his paid deputies, his headmasters, so clearly wished. It had been all of a piece to deny the beauties of the English countryside and to go on failing maths 'O' level. Those two incidents were perhaps ten years apart but another twenty-five were to elapse before this simple connection occurred to me, something which to anybody else would appear as trivial as the laboured self-perceptions of others always do.

The cordillera opposite is still busy; the idea that hills are always motionless is visibly absurd. The moon, meanwhile, has slid to another corner of the sky. Its newly angled light has thrown up different aspects of the slopes and screes and ravines which now seem to be poising themselves to roar down and engulf Sabay, asleep without trace among the black line of coco-palms fringing the coast in either direction. Mountains. How predictable that I should have resisted mountains longest of all.

Among my father's books had always been, discreetly

laid flat beneath other things, an album of text and photographs done up like a book and titled *Those Kingly Days* . . . It was the record of a fortnight's climbing holiday which he, his younger brother and two friends had spent in Norway in July 1939. My uncle wrote the text, my father took the photographs, some of which are of great beauty and accomplishment. I am sorry now that my father did not write the text as well. My uncle's style, eminently readable, was still that of a very young man (he was then nineteen) and leaned slightly back towards the world of *Three Men in a Boat*, poised sometimes on the edge of the facetious without ever quite being so. In fact he adroitly counteracted this tendency by giving detailed accounts and diagrams of climbs the party made each day and in this respect *Those Kingly Days* . . . is a short and quite serious climber's journal. Of course the camaraderie was of its time; it is nearly half a century ago now. Reading between the lines one can see the holiday must have been a miraculously snatched interlude. My father was a newly qualified doctor; probably never again did he and his brother spend so long together. If there was a flavour of old times the new times were obtruding remorselessly: six weeks later Britain was at war and some seven months after that Norway was occupied by Nazi troops. But the reason I wish my father had written the book himself is that he might have given something away. All one really learns about him is that he had to go home a day or two early, to the regret of the others, although the reason is not given. In fact he went to take up his first houseman's job at UCH.

Yet this very muteness of my father's part in the story is itself eloquent. Nobody who did not possess a tender eye could have taken those photographs: they speak for him. From the text I first learned he had been there at least once before, in 1937, so much of the point of this chronicled trip must have been to re-climb peaks he had already climbed, perhaps acting partly as guide and partly as one who longed to pass on some of the pleasure he had already experienced. Fifty years on a poignancy clings to those neatly laid-out pages, those black and white pictures of pale English young men bathing naked in glacier water. For my father, at least, the sense of temporary freedom and adventure must have been overwhelming.

To understand why, it is necessary to imagine how it must have been for a child to be packed off from China half the world away to southeast London to live thereafter cut off from his parents as from the magnificent wild terrain which surrounded his birthplace in Kuling – to live out of suitcases in a succession of the suburban homes of devout and elderly relatives for most of his schooldays, like so many other sons of the Raj and the Missions. How those long terraced streets must have mocked him with their ironic and inappropriate names of Scottish scenery: Glenshiel Road, Glenesk Road, Glenlyon Road, Balcaskie Road. How that nonconformist dullness must have oppressed him. (I never remember hearing my father speak once about Christianity: his loyalty to his family was too great. But I am quite certain now he never believed a word of it.) An atmosphere of worthy impoverishment, both financial and spiritual, pervades what few accounts of his youth I ever heard, except for the brief remissions of occasional holidays in the Lake District where he walked and climbed. There he must surely have re-discovered long unstructured days of wild silence and exhilarating exercise, sublime antidote to the cramping admonitions of the Congregationalist zealots of south London whose ugly churches he had dutifully to attend.

It was sad for him when as a paterfamilias he wanted to take the family somewhere which had meant much to him, my sister and I were little enchanted by the Lake District. I was particularly scornful. To a boy already accustomed to roaming the South Downs in search of cordite a lot of rain-soaked peaks full of gloom and wet sheep was no antidote to anything except good temper. My mean querulousness ruined several of my father's holidays and probably did much to contaminate our relationship. It was one more of a short enough list of possible pleasures he was destined not to share with his only son.

I believe the Norwegian expeditions remained for him one of the high spots of his life, to judge from what I remember now of his accounts in the days when we were still talking. There were comrades and good fellowship, a certain amount of expertise and danger, breathtaking landscapes. In those days such parts of Norway were presumably not much travelled except by climbers, probably little more than Iceland was when Auden and MacNeice went there a year or two earlier. There were language problems and discomforts (great stinging clegs) and pleasures (kilos of wild strawberries). Above all, literally, there were mountains. My father returned in states of exaltation: Kolåstind . . . Vellesaeterhorn . . . Kvitegga. *The mountains.* Another high spot of his life, like that of many a young man at the time, must have been the war. What other set of circumstances could have turned a recently qualified houseman into a Major in the RAMC and taken him out to India? *The Himalayas.* It is hard to get details of exactly where he went and for how long, but I remember his accounts of climbing and his face would be transfigured by the images behind it of majestic peaks and snowfields and glaciers of savage and unearthly beauty. He had stood, if not on the very roof of the world (for he was an amateur climber and no Mallory), then at least in an upper storey and from it had gazed eastwards across Tibet to the country of his birth, to where his own father was at the moment racked with typhoid in a Japanese concentration camp. He must also have looked westwards towards where he had left a newly married wife and an infant son.

Afterwards he was very quiet about it all, becoming more so as I evinced my assertive uninterest in his boring old mountains. But along the way he had secreted his own treasures, strange and beautiful pictures taken with his Zeiss Ikon. One of the earliest, a picture of Smørskredtind taken for *Those Kingly Days* . . . he kept framed on the wall of his study for the rest of his life, which for a man of almost painful modesty must have been a token of deep private significance. Perhaps as career and family took their toll he came more and more to recognise the appropriateness of that title. For years I assumed it was a quotation from Shakespeare, a dying Falstaff dreaming of his youth, maybe. It was not until recently that I read the album properly through and on the last page found the stanza from

which the quotation comes. It is by G. W. Young, the
mountaineering poet and probably the greatest English
climber of his generation:

> What if I live no more those kingly days?
>   their night sleeps with me still.
> I dream my feet upon the starry ways;
>   my heart rests in the hill.
> I may not grudge the little left undone;
> I hold the heights, I keep the dreams I won.

But at the time all this was wasted on his son. Nor, sadly
for him, did I share his passion for ships which in those days
pre-dating mass air travel were still invested with a degree
of romance quite hard to imagine now. What complex
associations ships must have had for any expatriate who
necessarily viewed them as instruments which could unite
as well as sever families, bearing them laboriously off on
journeys across half the globe, each mile of which was
truly felt to be travelled. Like many schoolboys then he
knew all the shipping lines together with their flags and
funnel insignia. He could stand wistfully at Tilbury or
Southampton and know merely from its name and livery
more or less exactly where each ship was bound, from
where it was likely to have come. (It would not be at all the
same to stand today at Heathrow and see a Boeing of the
British Airways fleet. Not only would destination or provenance remain opaque but the aircraft itself would be identical to that of any other airline, differing only in its paint.
My father could say 'P & O' or '*Viceroy of India*' just by
glimpsing a silhouette far out to sea.)

Under those conditions the world was viewed differently
and experienced differently. Journeys meant and felt something different, the lands eventually reached were not the
same lands reached today because they occupied a different place in the traveller's imagination. A change in
transportation changes the destination. This sounds
strange but nevertheless it is so. In a trivial way this was
demonstrated one day when I knew enough about the
currents off Tiwarik to swim to Sabay, have lunch and

swim back. At that moment both places took up different positions in my mind and since then each has felt different. This is a mysterious law and it must have been well known to my father as to countless thousands of mariners and passengers who overlapped with the air age. I can visualise my father most clearly now not with his camera, with which he was so accomplished, but with his battered and treasured pair of binoculars. I think the reason is that whenever I glimpsed him with his eye pressed to his camera's viewfinder I knew that what he saw at that moment we would later see ourselves and feel obliged to admire. But when I glanced sideways and saw his face concentrated into the eyepieces of his binoculars I knew he was somewhere else and seeing things nobody would ever be privy to except when he elected to share them. One holiday when I was very young I walked with him to the top of a cliff somewhere on the southern coast of England. Down below was a small port and outside this in the roads a warship of sorts lay at anchor. My father became excited.

'By golly, look, it's the *Matapan*,' he said and trained his binoculars on it to confirm his certainty. He then handed me the glasses, taught me how to focus the individual eyepieces and then the entire instrument, and spent some time on his stomach in the grass next to me pointing out details of the ship below. I now remember only its grey paint, its small size, the circular all-weather clearview windows set in the raked panes of the bridge and, above all, its name. *Matapan.* For quite thirty years this name had associations of something sweet and bitter: 'marzipan' and 'pa', probably. Then after I had first visited the Philippines I had a vivid dream about the ship which seemed to come out of nowhere, out of the depths of memory. The ship itself wore my father's face: its face and hair were grey and it seemed to be snarling as if in terrible rage. I awoke in the grip of infantile fear. The source of this dream was one thing, but I puzzled for days to find what had made it take that particular shape. Then I thought of the new language I was learning. In Tagalog *matápang* means 'strong' and 'courageous' with, in the case of alcoholic drink, conno-tations of 'fiery' and 'fierce'. It was quite precisely my father's rages I had feared. Living with him in the school holidays had been like walking across mined territory. One never understood quite why a particular step had been false beyond the fact that it had blown one up. The explosions were terrible.

A vignette from yet another holiday is imbued for me with a piercing melancholy. I have no idea now what we were doing there but we were at a place called Allhallows in the Thames Estuary, just downstream from Tilbury. It was probably mid-September, late tea-time. The afternoon was thick with mist. I recall only a damp marshy place at the edge of a waveless stretch of disappearing water. In this half-light my father was standing, sweeping with his binoculars the bank of fog which had rolled in from the North Sea. From somewhere within this fog came a deep bass hooting which gave everything an atmosphere of utter doom. After a while he said: 'I think it's the old *Burma Star*. Quick' and handed me the binoculars. Somewhere in the grey I caught a glimpse of a greyer bulk out there before the fog swallowed it up. It might have been some prodigious mammal heading seawards to its secret burial ground. Then from behind that glooming opacity the heavy sound of a ship's engines rolled across the water. 'Yes,' said my father in satisfaction, 'that'll be the old *Star*. Ohh.' He gave a great sigh. 'Think of it: Marseilles, Genoa, Port Said, Aden, Bombay, Rangoon . . .' His litany made me want to cry.

The last memory I have of him with his binoculars did involve real tears. It was our last holiday together. I had just left Canterbury and was about to go to Oxford. I was miserably in love, crotchety, not wanting to be on a family holiday at all, not really wanting to be anywhere. My father now had less than a year to live. To this day I do not know whether he knew it. Doctors are as good as everybody else at concealing truths from themselves. We were in the south of France, had been to Avignon, had seen Arles, had passed north of Marseilles to rejoin the coast below Fréjus. At some point well inland, it might have been near Draguignan or even as far east as Grasse, we picnicked on high ground. My father trained his binoculars on the horizon. Glowering at some pâté I was only half-aware of a sound he made. Then looking up I could see from my position slightly behind and to one side of him an eye brimming with tears. I was shocked. It had not been a good day so far, nor an easy holiday. Horrid late-adolescent egotist that I was I chose to interpret his tears as disappointment with his son. Full of self-pity I slumped further.

I am now sure my father's tears were for nothing so immediate or prosaic. Most likely they came at one of those moments when anyone of a certain age can sit amid the ruins of a picnic and be suddenly unable to look through a pair of binoculars without seeing something besides what is merely imaged. Maybe from the perspective of an anxious and complicated life he was looking across eighty miles of shimmering French clarity at the southernmost tip of the Alps and feeling once more with a panging rush what mountains were to him, had always been, at a former uncontaminated vision which his every turning since had seemed only to muddy. Perhaps he knew, perhaps not, how little time he had left but at forty-six and at his professional eminence he would have known he could never again find the time or fitness to set foot on a glacier or brew tea with meltwater from Annapurna. For that matter nor would fate once more afford him such blissful circumstance that he could be invited to sit in the pilot's seat of an RAF DC-3 and, completely unqualified, fly thirty officers and men for a quarter of an hour high above Burma. In their way those, too, had been kingly days.

What is he to me now? I am at last old enough and temperate enough to be able to see what I have inherited from him. A physical likeness, certainly. Now and again I surprise a look on my face like the one he wore for his television appearance as a neurological expert in the series 'Your Life In Their Hands': part wistful, part stuffed. We are still opposites in much that I was determined we should be, but more and more I catch my own voice as out of nowhere saying 'He would have liked that,' or 'If only he could see this.' There was, finally, a part of him which escaped his parental family's urge to do good. It escaped his own doctoring and his begetting and his breadwinning, it undercut his yearning for respectable stability and could be caught gazing through binoculars at distant ranges where such things were of no account. In short there must have been times when that part of him wished me dead.

I am immeasurably cheered by this. It is a liberating realisation for a son to have because it frees him from any obligation to reciprocate that messy parental turmoil which masquerades as a simple and straightforward love. Instead I can meet him on that other level about which he could not speak and I would not have listened. For the first time I feel a certain closeness to him. Given how father and son hardly knew one another and scarcely ever talked it is strange this feeling I have that of all people it is he who would most readily understand what it is I am doing in the forests of Kansulay and among the reefs of Tiwarik, although he would have been as diffident about attempting to put it into words as I am ultimately unable. This reflection serves partly to remind me that I have no son with whom to share an experience any more than my own father had.

Now, far too late, I miss him. He is long gone.

The cordillera opposite has stilled. Behind it the dawn is coming and the strengthening light has frozen its black outline in mid-skip. The stars are dimming and night is leaving in a great turquoise sigh. I get stiffly to my feet and stretch. Down there beneath the sea across whose face the dawn wind skitters the parrotfish will be slipping out of the mucus sleeping-bags they made themselves for the night. Among the corals shifts are changing: the predators of darkness are giving place to the predators of day. Between them are a suspended twenty minutes or so of near-inactivity, a general pause as if the attention of all creatures were pre-empted by the daily miracle of growing light.

I walk down to the shore. The hermit crabs have gone; nothing moves. I cup my hand and drink several mouthfuls. It is harsh, sweet, alive. Naked I swim out and slide down the blue gulfs.

9

Something has happened to the weather. Maybe it is a foretaste of the *habagat*, the south-west monsoon. The days are comparatively windless but the moon, perhaps, is dragging the water into fretful heaps at nightfall when the tide drops unusually low. It is the season. The tops of corals emerge, whole stretches of level shelf broken by crevasses. In the water one is lurched into jags and spines: rocks approach and bang one suddenly leaving a shoulder bleeding while tensed against the receding suck. The water itself is cloudy, the agitation of the upper layer reaching down to involve pockets of silt long ago washed off the land. The tides are full of plankton and diatoms. Night fishing is no longer worthwhile, visibility being so reduced that one is diving blind into a black soup sown with the mines of sea-urchin s.

I cross in my boat from Tiwarik and visit friends on the lower slopes of the mountain behind Sabay. All among the coconuts and steep red fields of baked clods are the bleached heads of fishermen, temporarily deserting the sea to work the land. Their flexibility surprises me. At Kansulay farmers and fishermen tend to remain separate and do not swap rôles when the weather does not suit them. They sit indoors and drink instead, one occupation in which both feel at ease.

The top of one field is bounded by a low cliff whose volcanic face is pitted with various-sized holes. Arman and I walk past, instinctively and at the same moment slightly stooping to see beneath an eyebrow of rock which protects a socket of unknown depth. We notice each other at once and laugh in recognition: two displaced hunters looking for fish on dry land.

I decide to go back up the coast to Kansulay for a few

days and let the sea recover from its struggle with the
moon.

Kansulay at dawn. The crowing of Sising's cock below is
relayed to other cocks hidden among the palms, taken up
and passed on, some cracked and flawed and some arche-
typally true of note, like calls to prayer from leafy minarets
fading distantly down to the village. I am up and admiring
the bustling activity in the air, the grass, the bushes.
Everything shines: the gloss of dew and natural oils blazes
off the pale midribs of banana leaves whose elegant droops
balance themselves in the gently rising air. From day to day
it is precisely the same while like all dawns suggesting it is
the first in the history of the world. The birds are particularly riotous. It is *sound* which is a part of the scene as
much as anything, the part I most miss when living in Italy.
For there, while the house commands an astonishing view
and while the sense of isolation in rough hill-country with
its great sighing forests faithfully conveys the sight of the
seasons in their turning, the place is aurally a desert. That
disease of being unable to see a living creature without
wanting to kill it at once, preferably with an automatic
shotgun, has achieved a general muteness broken mainly
by the sound of gunfire. Another of my landscapes. Over a
quarter-century ago Rachel Carson foresaw a silent spring;
in my part of Tuscany it has finally happened. Only for a
month or two may one lie in the shade of the vines and hear
that extraordinary sound of swifts' wings cutting the air at
seventy miles an hour, a tearing rush like a glider's aerofoils
at times so sudden and so close it raises gooseflesh as from
some primordial terror of gigantic raptors.
   In Kansulay the aerial sounds of wings come principally
from the ragged-tipped crows, not unlike their English
counterparts, as they flap low over the ridge looking for
chicks following their mothers through the undergrowth
with one eye always on the sky. Another characteristic
sound is of the wings of wren-like birds, lustrous brown with
delicate curved beaks like carpet needles. As they hover

around the *lumboy* trees they produce an explosive whir of beaten air not unlike that of humming-bird hawk moths sipping nectar at dusk. Thirdly, the crispness of tight and powerful wings clatters down from golden orioles when chasing each other aerobatically or mobbing a crow back to its own territory.

The golden oriole is the Philippines' National Bird, a very handsome animal not much larger than an English blackbird but slimmer, more powerful and with a heavy pink bill. Its plumage is a dazzling yellow and black and against the green ribs of the coconut fronds up whose spires it climbs and twirls it glows like an exuberant jewel. On this particular morning there is one hanging from a string around the waist of Kado, Sising's nine-year-old son, who emerges an hour or two later into the clearing with a couple of friends. They walk towards me, smiling, competent. Little hunters, their teeth sparkle in the sun. They are all carrying catapults, all have strings from which dangle small birds by their feet, some still fluttering feebly against their shorts. I congratulate them on their skill.

'*Pulutan lamang*,' said Kado disparagingly. 'Just snacks.' But they are clearly proud. One of the boys sights at something in a nearby tree. There is a brisk snap of elastic and a stone claps against wood and hums away over the valley. The boy shakes his head and laughs. I laugh too, feeling an admiration which would be jealousy were I not myself a spear-fisherman. Anyone who can bring down the National Bird with a catapult at twenty paces knows how to live in this world. Kado now takes the splendid corpse from his game larder. Its saffron breast is streaked with crimson for its head is smashed and one eye knocked clean out. Exemplary shooting.

'Pretty,' he says, laying it out on the ground on its stomach and spreading its wings as if it were still flying high above an endless plain. One of his companions adds other little birds from the collection at his waist, finches mostly. The struggles of the living have tightened the nooses around their feet so he has difficulty in undoing the knots. He pulls impatiently and their twittering becomes strident; a bit harder and it becomes a thin tiny screaming. Their

feet come off entirely like twigs and the child adds these
forcible amputees to the row on the ground where they beat
their wings in the dust. 'Seven,' he says. 'Very good roasted.'

The sound-quality of anguish has nothing to do with its
volume. This is as true in a Mozart opera as in an interrogation centre. Presumably these birds are yelling at the top of
their lungs but the sound is not as loud in terms of decibels
as their ordinary song at dawn. It is merely high, hopeless
and unbroken. It reminds me at once of a morning when I
had to call on an Italian farmer very early and found him in
his kitchen brewing coffee and inspecting his mousetraps.
These were not sprung traps but pieces of thick paper
spread with birdlime. On this particular morning there was
a mouse stuck to a sheet of paper on the floor outside his
larder, its ineffectual scrabbles of the night clearly legible
in the dense glue surrounding it. As the farmer chatted about
what the hail had done to his vines the previous afternoon he
scrumpled up the paper, glue, mouse and all, and tossed the
ball onto the fire. I had not been paying much attention to
what he was doing and from the mouse's necessary
immobility had assumed it dead. But then from the fireplace
as the ball of paper caught there came a tiny appalling
scream. I don't believe the farmer noticed it at all: it was less
than the momentary squeak of steam from a damp log, the
breath of a lobster in a restaurant kitchen. That minute
bellow of unhelped pain still rings in my inner ear, however,
set off by the finches, a memorable commonplace which
itself prompts other commonplaces: *What casual fate is in
store for you?* and *Do fish feel less for their silence?*

For indeed not all fish are silent when speared. *Bujhong*,
the long-beaked eel fish go *aww, aww, aww* as if protesting a
monstrous unfairness. Many species of trigger fish (such as
boriri) produce a drumming sound. These are perhaps
alarm noises rather than expressions of pain: I have
occasionally heard these fish make them when threatened
but unmolested. Most species merely flap silently, mouths
working or fixed open in a rictus, *O*, in which the delicate
chitinous plates of the mouth-parts and cheeks are fully
extended and, because no longer overlapping, become
translucent and project the fish's lips spectrally in front of

its head. I am clinical, I feel remorse, I eat. But one day I know I shall eat only vegetables. It is not precisely squeamishness (I have death on my hands and they are familiar with their task) but more a weariness with squatting on the imagination, with the dejection of causing pain. At some point killing to eat is a reason, not an explanation. An explanation was given by Rilke when he said 'Killing is one of the forms of our wandering mourning.'

I have only been back in Kansulay for a few days before I discover my mountain retreat is no longer the isolate fastness it was. By night Lolang Mating's ghostly familiars no doubt still exercise their guardianship, but with the daylight full on the hill's abrupt spine children move from dense patch of shade to dense patch of shade with long-handled fishing nets. The *duhat* season has arrived.

The shade is cast by venerable *duhat* or *lumboy* trees, each with its heavy crop of purple fruit. These fruit are about the size of a rose hip with a single stone inside, the flesh watery blue, sweet-astringent with a slightly resinous flavour. I quickly tire of them but they are highly prized by others. Now the children in bright fragmentary T-shirts and torn cotton shorts festoon the branches, calling out of great cumuli of leaves, cheerful parakeet-voices, while beneath them a rain of droppings patters to the ground as fresh-sucked *duhat* stones. My hut is built directly beneath one tree. The voices overhead come from bright blue mouths. The sound of stones plopping onto the sun-crisped thatch brings me out and looking up I see branchloads of children examining each other's tongues competitively to see whose is bluest.

But there is another current of village life which intersects here as I discover when several teenage boys, one of them Lolang Mating's youngest grandson, come asking if I have an old tin they can borrow. Thinking of *duhats* I lend them an odd battered aluminium pot with a handle I once found on the seabed and which I now use for gathering wild beans. The boys thank me solemnly and disappear behind a tree. I go back to writing. Smoke drifts across the shade and up towards a palm whose head is backed by cloudless blue.

The smoke is barred and sliced by the shadow of its leaves as it slips through and disappears beyond. Eventually I go to see what they are doing.

They are cooking, somewhat earnestly, over an open fire. In the now blackened pot balanced on the flames, the contents dim behind smoke and steam, is a vegetable mess. They are making an infusion of guava leaves which is good for fresh wounds. Who, then, has been wounded? The answer is they all have. Their slightly strained manner and unnatural calm betokens pain, for just that morning they presented themselves at a hut down in the village to be circumcised.

Empathic anguish shoots through me which I conceal by offhanded cheerful concern. These are not children: the eldest is sixteen. I recommend that if the guava leaves don't work they should come back and I will give them sulphanilamide powder. They are pleased by this idea of medical back-up and borrow a pair of nail scissors to cut up a cleanish T-shirt they have brought with them. They make a quantity of circular patches and, with much mutual joshing about diameter, cut a hole in the centre. They take their pot of brew and withdraw, laughing.

I thought at first this was some peculiar hang-over from the days of the Americans, a petty-bourgeois puritan obsession with hygiene or guilt which required the mutilation of male children regardless of medical indications. It is not, however. In this province at least circumcision is a real rite, an entry into manhood. So much so, in fact, that while they remain uncircumcised boys are often referred to as *baklâ*, a word which translates approximately as an effeminate homosexual. There is an accepted social place for the genuine *baklâ* and whatever mockery he may attract it is far more tolerant amusement – even affection – than the merciless hounding which certain other cultures afford. Yet however inoffensive, it is still a taunt although one which can apparently be rendered without substance merely by recourse to a razor blade, and the reason turns out to be very simple. It is not that the boys of Kansulay really feel their sexual orientation is dependent upon submitting to an operation without anaesthetic in their early teens. There is a straightforward belief that an uncircumcised man cannot make a woman conceive. That they know this to be false is, of course, no bar to their belief any more than any other kind of knowledge has the least reference to faith. So perhaps after all it is merely an ordeal many feel attracted to and they choose the long school vacation (which happens to coincide with the *duhat* season) so they may recover at leisure.

The boys return to the mountain daily to brew up fresh leaves and anoint their wounded members. I ask slightly gruffly how they are: the truth is they are quite unembarrassed and I am extremely so. I refuse to look at anything; I keep insisting I am not a doctor. I am appalled at the thought of my hut being turned into a sinister clinic of the woods. Already I see it in English Sunday-tabloid terms. *Who is this mysterious foreigner posing as a doctor at whose isolated house a constant stream of adolescent boys submits to intimate examinations?* After several days when it is clear from the boys' remarks that guava leaves cure but slowly (not surprising when one sees the dark brown liquid with its flimsy silvery scum like a pot of cold tea) I give them orange paper sachets of sulphanilamide powder, instructing them to use it sparingly on clean dry dressings. No infusions, no washing, no wet for a couple of days at least and then come back for some more if the wound still isn't drying. I am a school matron dealing with the rugger team's *tinea cruris*.

They all return for a second sachet and naturally it occurs to me they may be selling them back to the chemist where I bought them and relying on time-honoured guava leaves with which, after all, everybody else seems to recover. On the other hand the chemist is a long way off in town and after a couple of weeks the boys greet me in the village, calling from their houses that they have recovered now.

'You're still *baklâ* though,' retorts a mischievous sister. Laughter on all sides from among the bananas and coconuts, laughter in which the boy himself joins. Good-natured whoops startle the chickens and the pigs.

At night, however, my place on the hill is still as deserted of humans as I wish it to be. Lolang Mating keeps all casual visitors at bay, the glowing timbers of her collapsed shack a demarcation beyond which none dare set foot unescorted. Not even Sising would come up alone. Instead my hut is the nexus for non-human visitors of a kind which would reinforce the worst fears of the superstitious. The *lumboy* trees become thick with big fruit-eating bats fighting and squabbling, the air loud with their leather wings. Some have bodies the size of cats with wings of well over a metre span. At dusk a cloud of lesser bats fumes up from the forest into the purple sky, but only with the coming of real darkness do these fruit bats unfold themselves and row across from the forest top, pulling up at the tree above my hut with a noise like wet mackintosh being shaken. All night they clatter in the branches while twigs and *lumboy* stones rain on the thatch. Now and again one of the smaller bats may fly straight through the hut from one open window to the other, passing only a foot or so above where I lie on a mat on the floor, naked body fanned by their whirring passage.

One night the bats seem particularly noisy: my sleep is broken by an insistent thin mewling, a lost and hopeless wail. When dawn comes I have forgotten it but soon afterwards another group of boys arrives and makes triumphant noises beneath an adjacent *lumboy*. I discover they have set a trap the previous day consisting of a single nylon thread high in the air from which dangle fish-hooks. One of the fruit bats is caught on two of these hooks, hopelessly entangled, and has been hanging there all night.

A boy climbs up and a good deal of shouting ensues, instructions and cautions mainly for the bat is still very much alive and has a jaw the size of a small cat but narrower and with needle-sharp canines. After some wrestling up among the leaves during which the bat screams twice it comes thumping through the branches to the ground where it heaves impotently, for the boy has broken its wings halfway along thus immobilising them and its fine little hands. The splintered ends of bones now poke through the reddish fur of both forearms. Its head swivels to meet menace, eyes huge and black and perfectly spherical like beads of ink. I am shaken by its vulnerability which seems caused as much by its being caught out of its proper medium as by hooks and broken bones. It is a victim of daylight, a fish taken from water, deserted by all the skills which ordinarily make it so powerful. The boys tie its wings outstretched to a length of cane; crucified, the bat looks from one of us to the other.

'Take it away and kill it quickly,' I say brusquely. The boys are baffled by my anger; they do not know my hut has been violated by their casual brutality. I make them take down their fish-hooks and forbid them to put them up anywhere in the vicinity. At the same time my annoyance is increased by having to listen to myself giving these tetchy orders. Who am I to forbid people to trap their food? I am no campaigner for animal rights (how could I be without hypocrisy?) and still less do I own so much as a single square foot of their home territory. But life would become impossible, I try to explain; I would be unable to sleep for listening if I knew there were traps set nearby.

They affect to understand and agree to set them far away, a compromise I accept. That is how Arcadia is. Later in the day I pass the house of one of them and find the bat still alive on its cross though now visibly weakened by injuries and thirst. My look attempts to convey something to the young man leaning out of the window above it but he just smiles. No electricity, no refrigerator, no quick and early death, he might have said. But he wouldn't: it just means nothing to him.

Amid all this my hut is calm and expressionless. It lives as I do, as we all do, exposed to all sorts of animal and vegetable activity. In some senses the life is that of endless camping except that being able to stand beneath one's own roof is a luxury whereas crawling into canvas makes me low-spirited. The gathering and drying of firewood, the daily fetching of water from the pump at Bini and Sising's, such are ordinary enough chores which become notice-able only when the weather is bad. Things of this sort become mere habit. I had more difficulty adjusting to the persistent discomfort of a cushionless world: right-angled chairs made of bamboo, benches made of two poles lashed across trestles, seats of split logs. The body touches the ground at the soles of the feet; all the rest touches hard wood polished by thin bottoms and bony limbs. I look around for somewhere – anywhere – comfortable to sit. I dream about my study at school, about the JCR at university, about libraries and clubs. I come from a sitting culture where speculative conversations are conducted from deep armchairs in book-lined rooms. I am (I tell myself) a bachelor of the Victorian, Holmesian model. I crave a favourite dog-eared smoking jacket, chairs over whose plump buttoned arms I can swing my legs, a glass of good brandy 'to aid lucubration'. There is no such thing in Filipino life as a three-pipe problem, as smoke-hazed chambers of conceptual thinking, as quiet rooms designed for the unhindered life of the mind . . .

And on the brink of this port-stained nonsense something gives in another direction and I am through to the far side of discomfort. Suddenly the slat floor on which I sleep seems better designed for the body, the breeze filtering up through it delightfully cool. Life becomes not luxurious but eminently possible again, the craving for softness has gone. What better than that one write standing up, like so many Victorians? I have some idea Dodgson wrote much of *Alice* standing; Edward FitzGerald wrote the *Rubaiyat* on his feet; solid Anglican favourites like 'Onward, Christian Soldiers' and 'Through the night of doubt and sorrow' flowed from the Rev. Sabine Baring-Gould's pen as he stood thoughtfully at his desk. I buy nails, I borrow a saw, I cut some bamboo. Now outside my hut in the shade of the *lumboy* tree stands a makeshift bamboo lectern at which I write. The children are bewildered by such behaviour. Ever-new standards for the bizarre are being set. Writing is weird but writing standing up on a mountain surrounded by forest and palm trees is beyond-weird fit to set a fashion.

Other adjustments, too, are necessary. One evening a speckle rain begins. Later that night I am woken by water falling on my ribs. Outside is a steady downpour which the roofing of last year's fronds cannot entirely shed. Another repair in the morning, I think: cut some palm branches, weave some new sections of *sulirap*. It is early yet for the rainy season but nevertheless time to prepare for the arrival of real monsoon deluges. I roll on the floor in search of a dry patch. In that half-awake state when one's eyes open onto black I wonder how many of my ex-classmates – now all in their forties – have to roll on the floor at night to avoid a leaking roof. What evidence of abject failure that would have seemed in those days had I known what the future held for me. I would have been at a complete loss to understand what kind of a calamity could have overtaken me to bring about the forfeiture of my birthright to become a respectable and affluent middle-class Englishman. I should probably have been forced to conclude that somewhere along the line I had fallen prey to missionary zeal: that from deep in my blood The Call had inexorably come, something genetic asserting itself and condemning me to good works in the outback.

At that time a far simpler likelihood would never have occurred to me as I sat in class and considered a career, that I might instead have been overtaken by something far more voluntary, altogether more reasonable: an utter boredom with all I was supposed to become. For I never suspected then I would one day be foxed by that over-prosaic world we were earnestly envisaging for ourselves, or baffled by how so many people successfully ignore the fallings-away and blatant constructedness of such a world. My juvenile self never foresaw my astonishment at how huge numbers of individuals remain steadfastly immune to distraction, to effusions of light and scent and sound, to ravishing disorder, to the discreet pleasure of living chancily in the cracks of a universe so clearly and so sublimely never designed for human beings at all. How could I ever have contemplated sitting in a traffic jam morning and evening on the South Circular Road listening to the radio and cursing, still less have agreed to that as a reasonable price to pay? (*O time too swift, O Swiftnesse never ceasing.*) I am flawed in some way and it is incurable. The flaw does not make me yearn to have been Burton or Speke but it does require me to acknowledge that exploring always carries with it an element of the desire to become lost.

And lost I am: eyes sightlessly open in a hut on a hill in a forest, hard to imagine on any particular map. It is scarcely a place, even, more a locus for sleepy speculation like that with which the fitfully dozing airline passenger looks out of the window at the dark earth below, sees a fragile cluster of lights and wonders idly where it is and what it is called, an unnamed island in an unknown sea. Then, headphones back on, he naps again and slips below the horizon. Many times I have looked up at night from among wave-tops, from a desert or a forest, have watched the winking lights of his passing and listened to his diminishing thunder.

I am walking down early from the forest to the village in order to meet a local government official from the regional water authority or something. He might be bossy because he has authority in such matters and I have none. On the other hand he might be deferential, obsequious even, because I have a rumoured access to money and he and his council certainly haven't. (In the event he is charming and useless with a San Miguel beer pot pushing out his bogus Lacoste sports shirt like a tumour.)

As I walk towards the village the first butterflies of the day float out of the shade into the sun as spangled membranes before lurching out of the light once more and turning back into large insects. I begin to meet the first villagers making their way into the forest to patches of ground they till or to the huts where they keep pigs, goats, chickens and which they often use as temporary bases during the day. If they have chicks not yet old enough to roost up a couple of members of the family might spend the nights there as well in order to chase off snakes, wildcats and crows. When copra-making takes place far from the village and especially when the landowner wants his workers to do overtime in order to catch a particular boat or a favourable market price these huts often become crammed dormitories and scenes of convivial labour by night. Then the light from the cooking fires supplements that of the *tapahan* fire smouldering in its pit beneath the stacked coconut halves and makes even more intense and threatening the blackness of the forest which surrounds them.

We meet each other with that characteristic Tagalog greeting which so irritates certain foreigners when they discover what it means: 'Where are you going?' I was once told of an Australian who had actually bothered to learn the phrase for 'Mind your own business' expressly to reply to this greeting. This was seemingly the only Tagalog he knew and he was probably unaware of the effect it had. Had he been at all reflective it might have struck him that seen from neutral territory it was no more intrusive to ask someone where they were going than to ask how they were feeling, as in 'How you doing, sport?', especially as both conventions require only the most noncommittal answers. 'Fine.' 'Okay.' 'Not bad.' are merely the Western equivalents of the replies I now give to those who greet me on the road to Kansulay: 'There'. 'Down'. Sometimes in response to my own greeting the people I know offer a bit of explanation: 'To the forest'. 'To feed the pigs'. – hefting an old plastic container half full of swill. Or they may with equal courtesy not reply verbally at all but make a gesture I thought in my ignorance peculiarly Filipino until I came upon this passage in an eighteenth-century Chinese novel, Cao Xueqin's classic *The Story of the Stone*:

> Golden realised that Zhou Rui's wife must have come with a message for Lady Wang and indicated that her mistress was inside by turning her chin towards the house and shooting out her lips.

That is it exactly – pointing with the pursed mouth rather than with a finger. To gesture with the organ of speech instead of speaking with it strikes me as oddly expressive.

Who else is coming along the path towards me? Several children going to their family's huts with provisions or merely carrying large knives. Boys are seldom without their catapults. Soon I encounter the carpenter's son Nilo and his friend Yor (whose nickname derives laboriously, by inversion, from the word for 'Ouch!' dating from the day he found a bees' nest). Nilo is carrying a pole with a crossbar on top. On one of the limbs sits a disgruntled-looking dove tethered by its leg to a little bamboo drinking cup; the other limb is wound about with what looks like browning chewing-gum, an extremely sticky birdlime made of various resins. As they walk Yor is practising his *komokon* calls: the dove's characteristic hollow coo on one note repeated *accelerando*. He does this with cupped hands as any European country child imitates an owl. All three of them face a long morning sitting up in the hills trying to induce another *komokon* to perch beside the decoy.

Nilo himself is a born woodsman with an amazing repertoire of bird and animal cries, whistles, grunts and screams. I have watched him call golden orioles to a palm tree, standing invisibly in the dappled shade with odd pieces of brown skin showing through his tattered shorts and T-shirt. He is a true Filipino Papageno with no need to dress up in feathers to make the point. But something awful is happening to this gifted bird-catcher: his voice is breaking and he can no longer do some of his best calls. Either he will have to re-learn everything using falsetto or employ mechanical assistance. (Perhaps that was why Papageno had a flute, to make up for the real magic he lost at puberty.) Nilo is resigned to becoming a less good bird-catcher, however temporarily. But no matter how pleased to be growing up he is quite sad to be losing his undisputed position as Kansulay's number one bird-boy. It is amusing to imagine him in a quite different milieu dressed in white linen amid cool grey Gothic, suffering the erotic melancholy of being unable ever again to sing the treble solo in 'O for the wings of a dove'.

As I approach Kansulay the huts scattered among the vegetation on either side grow more numerous. Everywhere people are busy scattering *yamas* for the chickens, going to the stream with bowls of dirty washing, hawking vegetables or last night's catch. Nilo's father the carpenter is outside his house splitting fat green bamboos into inch-wide laths for flooring or rafters or maybe to make somebody a couch.

'Where are you going?' he calls.

'To buy rice.'

He smiles. (The implication that one has no more rice has delicate overtones of misfortune. The smile is also an acknowledgement that my life is governed by the same laws as his.) 'What is your food?'

'Dried fish. I'll have to go fishing tonight, maybe. If the weather's right.'

'Ah. No work, no food,' he says sententiously. He doesn't consider writing to be proper work at all, of course, but I have often given him fish and he takes me perfectly seriously as a fisherman. He gives a cheerful wave and goes back to his splitting. On the other side of the path almost opposite his house is a small clearing in which two sawyers have set up their cradles bearing a bright pink de-barked palm trunk. They have just twanged a charcoaled cord against its flank to mark the first cut and are tightening up their saw before beginning the laborious task whose steady rhythm will send a regular chuffing through the groves like an old-fashioned steam locomotive at a gentle pace heard from afar.

I suddenly understand something about this community and others like it. There is nothing hidden in the way it works; one can see its mechanism. The literal redundancy of people's greetings is that everybody knows exactly where everyone else is going and more or less how they will spend each hour of the day. I might for instance have encountered old Toly in the forest who *en passant* said he wasn't going to bother coming all the way back for lunch. This news would be greeted with real interest by his cousin a kilometre away down in Kansulay.

'Not coming back? Did he have rice?'

'I didn't ask.'

'Was he carrying his rush bag or the cement-bag one?'

'I honestly can't remember.'

The cousin looks knowingly at her companion. 'He'll boil some bananas to eat, then,' she says. 'That's what he'll do,' agrees the companion. 'He always does.'

To urbanites this inquisitiveness of a world privy as by right to one's least doing would be intolerable, suffocating.

They invoke the blessed anonymity of the city, the great freedom to disappear unobserved into a life of one's own contriving. On the other hand the life of a village like Kansulay does at least make a visible, coherent sense day after day. The cause is work, the effect is food. Anybody can see the system functioning out there in the open, there is no mystery to it.

Well, the world's increasing urbanisation is not going to be reversed and very likely that precise advantage of living a comprehensible life cannot be appreciated until the displaced villager finds himself for the first time having to cope with real anxiety, for that seems to be the price of his progress. I am a spectator of this crazed whirligig: watching the young men and women of Kansulay yearn to go to Manila to be subjected to squalor and over-work such as they have never known, each nurturing that ultimate dream of a passport and a work visa abroad – anywhere, anything. Meanwhile here am I, a refugee from that developed world, not rejecting its values so much as at a loss and bored by so many of them, equally incomprehensible to the villagers I live among.

I am a primitive, I think. For me living and writing are not separable but at some level I do share the view of Nilo's father that writing isn't proper work even though it is a perfectly proper way to spend a life. It has been a revelation to me that in my forties I can earn a real living with my spear gun. This belated discovery has afforded me extreme pleasure, even an unsuspected self-confidence. Day after day I can feed myself, could feed a family if I had one. And because so few people in Kansulay like fishing at all, still less are particularly good at it, this strangely enough gives me a place in the village – a place in its economy clearly recognised and understood even as they ask me every time they see me:

'Where are you going?'

Where I am going, a week or so later, is to a meeting of the *baranggay* Water Committee which I have requested ostensibly to find out how everyone thinks the project is going but actually to ginger them up a bit. Since I went to live on Tiwarik the whole thing seems to have become as stagnant as the water it is designed to replace. Already an indomitable spirit has shown itself, that lethargic determination to make do with things as they are. Secretly I am on the verge of applauding this but I am resolved to be brisk. I am not a meliorist. The idea of Progress strikes me as one of humanity's drearier self-deceptions, but I still think it ought to be possible to save Kansulay's infants a certain amount of death and a great deal of gastroenteritis without much effort. Besides, I tell myself as I walk down the track, nobody in Kansulay will have to pay a single penny. There will be no charge for the water, unlike in *baranggay* Balimbing where after five years' efforts they finally got a water system constructed by provincial government contractors with central government funds only to discover that the grant for the project was really a long-term loan which the people of the barrio were obliged to pay back at the monthly rate of ₱7.00 per household tap. At least the Kansulay project was not going to saddle the already impoverished with either an endless debt or an invidious choice between free dirty creek water and clean expensive tapwater.

Having worked myself into the appropriate mood I march into the Captain's house. And there among the familiar faces of the village officials is one I certainly had not expected to see, the old Judge's son Cads Soriano. What on earth is *he* doing here? He is no more a *baranggay* official than I am.

After the greetings I enquire very amiably about Cads' presence. Cads smiles at the table and sucks his fraternity ring while the Captain explains he thought it better if all interested parties were present at the meeting, and since the water source is on Soriano land the Soriano family clearly have an interest. A certain foreboding settles on me at this news. Something is going on but what it is and how many other people in the room know about it is anybody's guess. The self-righteousness I have brought with me begins to intensify. The last thing I wish to be is a philanthropist but I see no reason to be a dupe instead. Why should this perfectly straightforward project become bogged down so quickly? Is it not possible to do anything in this country without endless intrigues? (And more in the same vein.)

Clearly Cads is not going to explain his presence any more fully for the moment. He makes a great fuss about pouring me a glass of ESQ rum (at eight in the morning) which I refuse on the fictitious grounds of 'LBM'. Everyone laughs hugely at this, the very idea of loose bowel movements being pretty uproarious really, except that of course the laughter is sympathy or something I can't be too bothered about since I am not suffering. The Captain then reminds everybody that it is I who have requested this meeting and courteously gives me the floor.

I briefly review the agreement we reached several months ago about Kansulay's water problem, its solution, the test well we have dug and my friend's professional assessment that there is water enough only for drinking purposes. None of this is news but everybody smokes hard and looks grave. I then change gear slightly and say I am becoming a little Concerned about the Time Factor. Could it be, perhaps, that the Captain is experiencing difficulty in organising teams of men prepared to give their labour free? In case this gives the wrong impression I add that I realise how difficult it is to expect people to do anything *bayanihan* now that the rains are due when villagers will shortly be preoccupied with planting rice and vegetables, a critical agricultural moment.

'Well of course James is quite right,' the Captain looks at his committee. Everyone nods. A bottle clinks on a glass. 'It will be a very busy time for all of us.' His wife comes in with a plate of little white riceflour cakes as *pulutan*. 'I believe when we discussed this we agreed it might be necessary to provide the workers with *merienda, tuba,* cigarettes and things like that to keep their spirits up. Oh, James, have a *puto.*' He pushes the plate towards me. 'Very good for LBM.' More laughter. 'Well, I have to tell you the money you so kindly gave me for that purpose is now exhausted.'

Exhausted? I can't believe it. I gave him ₱5,000 to buy a carefully itemised list of materials for building the spring box up in the woods. My engineering friend and I also calculated a decent margin for providing the workers with food and drink. Surely he couldn't have blown the entire five thousand with nothing to show for it and now be working up to demanding more?

'There is no money left at all?'

'None, I'm afraid,' the Captain says. 'You calculated very well. Only the carpenter has still to be paid for making the *kwan? porma*. He worked very hard. Naldo's a good man.'

Belatedly, only just in time, I grasp what he is saying. They have probably already built the spring box. Having heard nothing I took it for granted nothing had happened. I had not thought to go up to look again at that slimy hip-bath we excavated in the territory of the demons so long ago. How could I have been so inefficient and lackadaisical? So accusing? I hastily say that I also requested this meeting so as to bring myself up to date with developments since I had recently spent a lot of time down at Sabay and had regrettably got out of touch with what was going on here. I assure them that the extra money will be no problem.

'Well, I know we all appreciate that very much,' says the Captain. 'You have already visited the spring box? Are you satisfied with it?'

Probably at any time up to my fortieth birthday I would have said yes, indeed, it's a beautiful spring box and have trusted to luck that I had correctly read the thing's existence. However in the last five years I seem to have been overtaken by a kind of reckless truthfulness.

'No, I'm afraid I haven't yet been there.'

'Oh, never mind,' says the Captain, and it is plain that indeed nobody minds at all.

'I shall go and look at it just as soon as this meeting's over,' I tell them.

'We'll all go. We can take, you know, some refreshments along.'

The price of my sloth is to be a drinking session in the woods. So be it.

'Now, about Phase Two of the project,' says the Captain. 'Phase Two is of course the installation of the pipe leading from the spring box down to the village here. This is the most expensive part. The distance is, er,' he looks for a sheet of paper, 'one thousand eight hundred twenty metres. Now according to our canvass of prices . . .'

A discussion ensues about the relative merits of polythene and galvanised iron, of the discounts offered by Sasco Trading, Tomas Tan, Rey Ong, Fortune Enterprises and other hardware dealers in the provincial capital.

'. . . whatever our choice we must remember we still have P2,500 left over from Phase One,' the Captain is saying at one point, jerking my attention back from his bodyguard/factotum who has just come in with fresh supplies of ESQ.

'Sorry, I didn't quite get that?' I interrupt. 'I thought you said we needed more money for labour?'

'Correct, James. You stipulated you wanted materials and labour itemised separately. As regards labour alone we are in deficit.'

'But as regards materials we are in surplus of two thousand five hundred pesos?'

'Exactly.'

'You mean to say you've built that spring box at a cost of only half our estimated price?' Good God what corners had they cut? Was it half size? Made of wattle and daub but with a cement lid? Why the hell had they built the thing while I was away? Why the hell had I been away when they built the thing?

'Of course not. But with the generous contribution of Mr Soriano here we are in surplus as regards to your own generous funding.'

I look at Cads. 'I'm very sorry once again; I'm obviously badly out of touch. I hadn't realised there was another source of money.'

'Oh yes,' the Captain explains. 'I thought you were here then. We had just started building the spring box when Cads offered to match you for half the cost.'

'Of the entire project?'

'No, I fear I could not afford that,' the lawyer says, speaking for the first time. 'Half the cost of the spring box. Two thousand five hundred pesos. Too little, I'm afraid, but I did want to contribute in my small way to such an important project. I hope you don't mind, Mr James?'

'Mind?' How can I mind? I am unnerved, anxious even, but how can I possibly mind? 'Of course not. I think it's most generous of you. Now we can afford to pay for labour when we install the pipe. If we opt for polythene we will have to bury it and digging a trench nearly two kilometres long is an enormous job even if we get every man, woman and child in the barrio to dig.'

'*And* Janding.' More laughter. Alejandro is the village *baklâ* who, in partnership with a friend, makes rather a decent living in a home-made beauty parlour among the coconuts where they cut hair and give manicures and pedicures to the women of the area, some of whom come many miles. Janding has often cut my hair for me and shortly after the last time appeared at my hut a bit breathless and dishevelled with a coconut shell piled full of truly awful objects. They looked like wrinkled black breasts amputated because of a fulminating growth which had broken through the skin and formed a flattish pink ulcer. They were clammy and cold to the touch and the exact consistency of a silicone implant.

'*Ungus baboy*,' Janding said. *Pigs' snouts?* Now I came gingerly to turn them over they might perhaps have looked a bit snoutish. Re-orientated, the ulcer part became the flat end of the snout, the general contours less breast- than muzzle-shaped.

'What on earth are they, Janding?'

'Fungi.'

'You mean, you *eat* these?'

'Of course not, silly. They're for your hair. They cure baldness.' He explained how they were full of a colourless, odourless jelly which had to be massaged into the scalp each night. 'I'll show you. Look.'

Unable to refuse I let him break open a snout and rub in its surprisingly chill contents, leaving my scalp covered with candlewicks of hair plus a certain amount of earth and twig fragments.

'If it works,' I told him, 'you'll make your fortune, I hope you realise.'

'I will?'

'Of course. The whole world will come to the Philippines

looking for you and your pigs' snouts. I'm not joking, Janding; you'll be a millionaire. You won't know what to do with all your money.' I caught sight of myself in my shaving mirror. It didn't look like the beginning of anybody's fortune but one never could tell.

'I know already. I shall go to Hollywood.'

I was touched by the thought of Janding grubbing about in the forest in the hopes of repairing a defect presumably already present in my father's genes. And now, sitting in the Captain's house, I am as hard put as anyone else in the room to imagine him with his highly polished pink nails and tight white trousers wielding a pick and shovel.

I watch Cads covertly. He has plumped up in the last two years but in a way he looks rather younger than when I first met him. Obviously in those days the strain of life in Manila had kept him careworn, plus of course his father had recently died. Now there is something piggy and placid about him, not disagreeable but he is after all his mother's son as well as his father's and I badly want to know what is going on. What is that monster Mrs Soriano up to? How can buying his way into a non-profitmaking scheme help her? And suddenly I think I know. He could have the spring box legally declared a co-operative venture and with a fifty-fifty stake in it later demand consumers pay for their water after all, once I am safely out of the way. Surely he can't do that? But perhaps he can if he claimed it was rent for the land on which the spring box stands. Who the hell can I ask? I decide to have it out with the Captain as soon as possible. Meanwhile the morning proceeds. The body-guard/factotum goes off to fetch my engineer friend who recommends polythene rather than GI pipe not just because it won't rust but because he has contacts in Fortune Enterprises and may be able to get us a good reduction on a bulk order.

Slowly – some of us rather drunkenly – we set off on foot for the woods to look at the spring box. On the way I aggrievedly tax my friend with not having told me the thing had been built but he has no idea I did not know. I have been away so much, he explains, and this is true enough for it not to be worth pursuing. I should have gone and looked for myself and there it is. When we reach the spring box we all gaze at it as proudly as if we had built it with our own hands. It stands in a trodden-down mush of undergrowth at the foot of the hill, gleaming in its grey newness like a freshly consecrated shrine. My friend thumps the top as if to demonstrate the stoutness of its construction; Cads proprietorially straightens a meaningless sapling nearby and bounces his weight on the ground at its root. I cannot think what I am doing here nor why I had a major hand in bringing into existence this small but ugly concrete tank in the middle of the woods. I am not at all convinced anybody in Kansulay really cares very much about water, it is merely one of the appropriate things for a *baranggay* captain to make noises about. Over the centuries the villagers· have learned to accommodate sickness and death; why upset the pattern? It is a social order which works. I am filled with remorse for my unclear motives, for an amateurish health-improvement notion which is all that is left of the pure medical zeal of my grandfather in China. That gene, too, is weak and defective. I am further depressed by how little I really understand about how things are here.

I excuse myself from the alcoholic conviviality now breaking out around the offending structure which more and more looks like a monument to an outsider's folly. My engineering friend walks back with me along the track. I ask him what he thinks Cads is really up to.

'I don't know,' he replies neutrally in that way which Filipinos often have of appearing genuinely not to know something while at the same time being incredibly discreet and diplomatic. 'Should I go ahead and order the pipe?'

I can't think what to do. I know so many people but all of a sudden none feels like a possible adviser. My friend is looking expectantly at me.

'Well, I suppose . . . But why did he suddenly decide to fork up twenty-five hundred pesos? Cads? Why should he? That's quite a lot of money.'

'Maybe you could ask Ate Bibyan.'

Who is this Vivian? I've never heard of her. I say so, gruffly.

'The sister of the *kapitana*.'

'Why her?'

'Because she is married to the younger brother of Soriano.'

I halt in the middle of the track. 'Let me get this straight. The sister of the Captain's wife is married to Cads's brother? You mean the Captain is related by marriage to the Sorianos?'

'Of course, James. You did not know?'

'Certainly I didn't know. I don't go round asking for a complete list of everybody's relatives.'

And as soon as I hear myself say it I perceive my own naivety, yet further compounded by pretending a thing as straightforward as installing a simple water supply need have nothing to do with family ties or messy intrigues or anything else. *You want it? Here's the money. Do it.* What kind of foolishness was that? Why couldn't I stick to killing fish? Stuff my ears with the sea and listen only to the *aww, aww, aww* of some other creature's desolate complaint? Overtaken by weariness I tell my friends of course to go ahead and order the pipe. I shall do my bit and keep my word. If then some fast trick is pulled which forces the villagers to pay for their water they will just have to fight it out among themselves while I go through my silly ritual of pretending I can expose Cads and his family to the contempt of the civilised world.

Back on my hill-top it occurs to me to re-phrase that old Western determinant of social forces with its bleak verticality *Who-whom?* into an Eastern, horizontal *Who-whose?* Whose man is he? Whose family interests is he upholding or threatening? I become prey to jejune reflections on administrations which depend on intrigue; on systems of government where a president can install his own men so that with each new dynasty the entire management of a country has to collapse and be once more built up with a fresh set of yes-men. For the first time I begin to admire the theoretical value of the British system which has civil servants, policemen and the armed forces pledging allegiance to the Crown – that mystical entity which is higher even than the family of *lumpen*-monarchs currently wearing it. Independent judiciary ... impartial bureaucracy ... rogue-proof administration ... I stride up and down for quite half an hour discharging my self-annoyance, like a Sixth-former full of *ab initio* insights. Then I lose interest (very like a Sixth-former) and slump over my lectern which I notice is getting mossy in the shade of the *lumboy*, staring seawards towards where Tiwarik lies, immensely full of gloom. Not even the sight of young Kado and friends crossing the clearing with their catapults on another hunting expedition cheers me up. I merely incline my head sombrely like a bishop with a spasm of gas. LBM of the soul. So much for my lofty notion of the simple village mechanism. The hubris of it.

Daily now I crave Tiwarik and the sea. I carry my lectern over to the shade of a neighbouring tree from where I can see the blue funnel of water framed by a valley of palms. I look up and gaze at it between sentences, at the far catspaws and the skeins of shadow crossing its surface. The wind has swung, the current has changed. I think the moon is weakening. I have become a landlubber, estranged. My skin aches to be in live water, my soles to tread on fathoms. This amusing life of fruit trees and circumcision and water projects and scribbling is all very well but I am a hunter, a lover. I fear for my skills and my passion, I fear rust and inertia.

All at once the great sea sends me a message. For weeks its distant roar has carried up the valley, through the tree-lined megaphone, telling me of its preoccupation, its busy-ness with other things. I have listened to it from the darkness of my hut, jilted and forced to overhear a beloved voice in animated conversation with a stranger. Tonight, however, there is nothing to hear. By means of its silence the sea tells me I may return.

I pack a canvas bag, nail up the door and go back to Tiwarik.

10

However, I am wrong. The sea has not deluded me so much as that in my eagerness I have misread it. It has not yet returned to its former clear condition and my pleasure at being back on Tiwarik is soon undercut a little by its uneasy state. This leaves my days with a certain hanging feeling when it no longer seems quite obvious how the time might be filled. This is of course also partly due to having spent just long enough in Kansulay to have adopted a dry-land routine. For a day or two, therefore, I mope about rather and allow myself to be dragged down. Embedded in the back of my mind is a fresh lump which I bump up against when thinking of other things, a bulk I would rather not consider and which in consequence insists on reminding me of its presence. If I can bring myself to look squarely at it I can see what I already know, that it is labelled 'Water Project'. I am full of remorse at the foolishness of having allowed an officious public self to get away from me and start living a bossy sort of life on its own. I can't imagine what I thought was wrong with living as I always had, giving and receiving small favours, none of them amounting to much but in time building into friendships such as that with Sising and Bini. Small acts of mutual regard were one thing. But *projects*, the expression of a diffuse and self-regarding concern – how could they lead to anything but trouble?

I become restless in a search for something comforting. I carry my *bangka* down to the water, retrieve the paddle from the roof of the hut and go across to Sabay to see if there is anything nice to be had in the village shop. I know the answer but making the journey is an occupation.

The shop in Sabay is really no more than a counter set into the side of somebody's house. When it is fully stocked one might be able to find ESQ rum, soap, shampoo with an anti-lice ingredient, Birch Tree evaporated milk, fish-hooks, soy sauce, kerosene, cooking oil, nylon line, sugar, things of that sort. Cigarettes come singly: as in any *sari-sari* store in the country there is always an opened pack behind the counter and often a courtesy box of matches dangling on a string. (Even in Manila cigarette sellers weave in and out of the traffic offering individual smokes or sticks of gum to drivers, just as pavement vendors peddle single sweets to passers-by. In England before the First World War it was similarly possible to buy cigarettes individually, as well as Woodbines in little packets of five.)

Also on the counter at Sabay is a cardboard box of assorted medicines, a jumble of old pills and capsules. Here can be found the tail-end of somebody's course of anti-biotics, pain-killers, home-made remedies, steroids, ant-acid pills, some saccharine tablets which have got in by mistake. It is a grab-bag of wrapped and unwrapped, named and anonymous, white and multicoloured from which people select what they feel looks most inimical to their symptoms. This system of self-medication appears to be quite successful and the notion that the patient plays the leading rôle in deciding his own fate is an excellent piece of psychology. Pharmaceutical roulette is an idea I should very much like to see introduced into the high-street chemists of Britain. A large drum like a bran tub inside the door with a cordial invitation to take a real gamble on getting better would suffice. Here at Sabay people buying pills fall into two categories: those who want proprietary brands for colds and 'flu, and the rest. (Colds are very common, maybe because fishing is the main occupation.)[7]

This morning I meet Intoy at the shop. He has been sent by his mother with an empty *lapad* which she wants half filled with coconut oil. He is clearly pleased to see me back again, but remarks that I have become thinner and that I must have been leading an unhappy and unhealthy life at Kansulay.

'It's better here at Sabay,' he says. 'Here you will become happy and fat.'[8] He is not familiar with the concept of comfort-eating under which regimen millions of unhappy people become very fat indeed and stay unhappy. Looking around the shelves of the village shop I cannot truthfully see much likelihood of that here. I send him back to his mother with several additional small things and he tells me he will start sleeping on Tiwarik again even though the sea is wrong for fishing.

But when I return to the island with my few basic purchases it still seems very unmagical. While I have been over in Sabay some fisherman has baled out his bilges offshore and a film of diesel fuel coats the wavelets, blunting their sparkle. Before dispersing it wafts its stench to my hut. It is a perfectly reasonable thing to have done but all of a sudden I feel prey to a kind of crudity. I long for uneasier people.

A couple of dull days later I decide to go to Bulangan, still in search of a comfort, a pleasure, something nice. Anything nice: it may be a tin of food or a drug, I shall know it when I see it. I am made of glass, deep black and very frangible. The jeep gets as far as Malubog when, too full of inertia to go any further, I get out to see what the smaller town can offer. Then, just before it is too late, I get back in again. Nobody finds this odd but it is exactly the sort of dithering which gets me down further.

Once in Bulangan I wander about, unable to find in any shop a single thing I wish to own or eat. Even the bakery, whose smell is normally enticing, nauseates me. The Filipinos put sugar in their bread, American-style, which as far as I am concerned makes it all but inedible. Even the *pandesal* has had its Spanishness vitiated. I buy a two-day-old newspaper and sit down in a cafe where it seems they have run out of everything but warm soft drinks and beer. My resistance is low; I call for a Coca-Cola although I detest the stuff.

I have no sooner opened the newspaper than somebody kicks back the metal chair on the other side of the table and bawls 'Hi Joe!', sitting down. I freeze and look at him over the top of the paper like an elderly Tory disturbed in his club. I know it is a waste of time. The ones that come on like that are unstoppable in every culture.

'You know how to speaking Tagalog?' he says. 'I hear you

talk to the girl. You are with the Peace Corps? What is your name? How old are you? Where are you living?'
This morning I put down the newspaper and say in Tagalog, 'Kindly go away.'
'We will make happy-happy.' He ignores me completely, calling for two *grande* of San Miguel beer.

I am under no obligation to pass the time of day with this boor, still less to have a drink with him – or at least I wasn't until by sheer misfortune someone I know slightly comes into the cafe at that moment and greets me. Worse, it turns out he is related to my persecutor so there is no easy way of simply getting up and going out without being rude to him. Besides, I have been meaning to ask him a question about bacteria in well-water. I slump back with not the best grace and stare at my drink while they get down to the beer and the questioning.

The questions. Where is your wife? Why are you not married? Where is your companion? Why are you alone . . .? Since these are the very questions one was brought up to regard as the depths of intimacy, hence otherwise the height of rudeness, how could they fail to provoke? Childhood training can be overlooked in the cause of social expediency, it may even be flouted completely in the pursuit of pleasure, but it can never be forgotten. Nowadays I have no difficulty in telling a stranger my age, how much I earn, how many brothers and sisters I have; it is of no consequence to me. On the other hand I have little incentive to ask the same questions back, which is not playing the game. Maybe this explains why the Filipino way with foreigners can sometimes be of belligerent curiosity. *What is in your bag? How much did your watch cost?* Such a person may think nothing of walking into your house, sitting down and going through your books, fiddling with your radio, a penknife, anything which catches his eye. With stoicism I sit it out, with good grace and a fixed smile. I owe that much to the millions of other Filipinos who behave with the ordinary courtesy which crosses all cultural boundaries. The international bad manners of this uninvited creature now swilling beer at my table are compounded by his shouting his questions with any interrogator's lack of charm. This unfortunately is a Filipino characteristic, that of addressing somebody two feet away as if he were a buffalo on the other side of a paddy-field. Lord how I loathe extroverts, especially this morning.

Now I match his aggression by answering all his questions with perfect candour except the one about why I am unmarried. Finally, of course, this is the only thing he really wants to know. Very likely it is the only thing anybody ever wants to know about someone else in a cafe: *Who or what do you screw?* Once this is clear the stranger has acquired a handle and all else can become part of the larger narrative. All those details about his age and salary can join up a few more dots but already the broad outline of the beast has been discerned, already that tedious Latin polarity is clear: *very well hung* or *very long ears.* Well, boyo, stud or cuckold?

I sit not looking at my questioner, my hands folded on my unread newspaper, far-off and waiting for him only to stop as the interrogation goes on and on, sometimes emphasised by an insistent nudging of the back of my hand. Where is your companion? Har-har what about chicks?

This last word brings down upon me such a pall of blank misery I come close to standing up and saying very firmly and quietly: 'Sir, I am quite twenty-five years your senior. I consider you grossly impertinent and do not wish to hear another word. Good day to you.' Instead of which, drained of all energy, I merely hunch down and wait for it all to go away. That one word, heard so often here, lowers me and my surroundings so that suddenly the whole of the Philippines and I are sitting in something like a truckers' cafe in Tulsa about thirty years ago. While still maintaining my thousand-yard stare I shoot it through this appalling little oik who I now notice is wearing a fraternity ring. The worst ones always seem to. Why on earth is he speaking sub-working-class American slang far older than he is? It will be dolls and dames next.

Of course it is aggressive of me too. By not answering I am rocking his cultural boat. I am a *'kano* who won't conform to his stereotype, who apparently doesn't like drinking much and 'chicks' at all. Nor does he seem interested in beach resorts and disco clubs, in tourist sites and duty-free hardware. That is unsettling. But my not being married and expressing neither contrition nor belated intent, that is a threat. It throws one of the eternal verities of Filipino life into doubt. *Good.* Eventually he stops. He is getting nowhere. Even the staff of the restaurant are giggling with embarrassment while my acquaintance cannot find anything comfortable on which to rest his gaze. Sadly he leans it on the sloping shoulders of the beer bottle but time and again it slips off and drops to the formica table top. My interrogator shrugs and goes off, slapping a handful of peanuts into his open mouth, thinking it is maybe a language problem and little guessing how right he is.

Once in another province I was introduced to a venerable old man, the grandfather of a friend, ninety-two and eminently coherent. He was famous throughout the region for having fathered a quite unbelievable number of children (his last son was then rising five) and for being a stubborn Filipino patriot and nationalist. His family had emigrated to the United States before the Second World War, he alone refusing to join them. He had resisted the Americans, the Japanese, the Americans again; had mocked Quirino, welcomed Magsaysay, had fervently embraced Marcos. With the respect due to his age and querulous intransigence a silence fell whenever he spoke but I never heard him say anything at all interesting except once when he listed the cigarette brands available in Manila in the 1920s. If there was still heat and clarity in his old brain it came from the flame of a monumental ego still burning away in that hairless skull. It banished all the shadows, the flickers and half-lights of observation which might have been engaging, leaving only itself illuminating itself like a candle in a pumpkin.

People (all relatives of one sort or another, I judged) came and went in the room, ministering to the old tyrant in various ways and with a variety of honorifics as he sat in a high-backed chair whose motheaten velour seat was covered in plastic, calling for cold drinks, hot tea, authorising a chicken's death and a fresh sack of charcoal for the kitchen.

I came by to see my friend a couple of days later and found his grandfather de-throned and transformed in a very Eastern manner into a little bent old twig in tattered underwear squatting under the pump in the back yard and soaping himself with a bar of Camay.

'Pump!' he was roaring in his monkey-voice which scarcely carried above the squeak of iron and rhythmic gush of water as a teenage girl moved the handle up and down, up and down, while her eyes watched the to and fro of heads in the street beyond the top of the wall. 'Pump! *Putang ina . . .!*' as the soap got in his eyes.

I can't think why this ordinary domestic scene entranced me but when the old man got up and began trundling the soap around beneath his underpants I was glad it had. The gaunt, veined shanks and hanging flesh of his ancient body were scarcely a surprise, but the tattooes were something else. I had not expected a ninety-two-year-old local sage to have deep blue – almost black – etchings of naked girls on both arms and extending beyond his withered biceps out across his rib-cage as if with time the ink had bled along the fibres of his skin. Yet they were not at all the fading, spidery traces of a former youth scrawled across a parchment whose own message was loud and clear. They were more like the lines marking out an ice-hockey pitch, thick, ineradicable and of indeterminate depth.

Bizarre, gross – the adjectives suggested themselves but lapsed. Once again what was being expressed was that old announcement of an extraordinary hubris. But why, when the human ego decided to advertise itself, did it choose something about as subtle as cockcrow which told of anything but individuality? Such tribal markings the world over, the nude women, were they to remind the wearer of his own sexual preference in case of a moment of beery amnesia? Or to convince others? Or were they simply a ploy, a charm against ageing just because it was so unimaginable that the array of a sappy twenty-year-old should still be clearly legible seventy years later?

This bedraggled creature now rootling round his crotch

with Camay suds under the broad leaves of a *talisay* was not at all sad for those particular slants on mortality. In fact there was nothing sad about him.

There was only an echo of that awful old cockcrow, that perpetual cry of the human male from its dunghill as it proclaims its uniqueness in the sparkling light of a new day while merely sounding indistinguishable from all other cocks that have ever crowed, a facile metaphor for self-betrayal.

It is this crudity the traveller remarks, surprised at finding the world so full of it. Not the crudity of imagery (what do they matter, the outline drawings of genitalia, the graffiti scribbled on skin?) but the sheer relentless uniformity of it. He is always meeting myrmidons, usually when feeling at his least defended, of the unending army of those who sit down opposite and grab him by the arm and ask questions, the hordes upon hordes who rise over his skyline like the eponymous heroes in *Zulu!* roaring 'Chicks! Chicks! Chicks!' or stencilling it in crimson letters on the jeeps he rides in: *Chix, Chix, Chix*. There are times when the most amused and phlegmatic traveller in the Philippines (and elsewhere) yearns for a country of deep reserve and formality where everyone calls each other 'Sir' and 'Madam' and wishes to know no personal fact of any kind. This country, it is true, sounds like a cross between Claridges and Ladakh. In such a place, he feels, he might encounter that silence alone in which things may be learned. Perhaps it does exist after all, somewhere near Thailand or Burma . . . Tibet? Or deep in Amazonia? Or maybe the crotchety traveller is once more blaming a country for not being his imagined land, his own egoic mirror.

I leave the cafe in Bulangan and wander down to the aromatic sheds which form the market by the shore. And there, at last, two things catch my eye. First a young girl walks past selling necklaces of strung *sampagita* flowers whose scent, though a little unelusive, is wonderfully fresh and cheering. I buy one, gladly overpaying her, and amble with it threaded loosely round the fingers of one hand like Islamic prayer beads, sniffing it from time to time. Next I come to a stall of caged birds manned by someone who could be Nilo in thirty years' time, a retired bird-catcher

who has finally hung up his *komokon*-perch and birdlime
and instead buys and sells the birds which other people
catch. He has the air of somebody who has spent a lot of
time staring at the sky, a little vacant, sometimes pursing
his lips absently to send a warble to cheer the spirits of his
drooping wares. From him I buy a small cage made of fine
cane containing two greenish finches which seem not yet
completely got down by their captivity.

Leaving the market with my still-unread newspaper
draped over the cage to protect the birds from the sun I am
hailed from across the street by Arman. It is a pleasure and
surprise to see him: running into people away from their
home territory often makes me feel how lucky I am to know
them at all and my recent ordeal in the cafe only increases
this feeling. He promptly offers me a lift home in the *Jhon-
Jhon*, for today he has come by boat. I accept with
gratitude and for the next hour sit in the prow well forward
of the unsilenced exhaust, my finches at my feet, sniffing at
the *sampagita* flowers as we skim over the water and the low
shoreline unrolls to our left. Soon from around a headland
Tiwarik appears in the distance, its strangely unstable
appearance increased by our angle of approach from the
sea so that for a moment, forgetting all the other possible
reasons, I decide this must be the real origin of its name. I
feel a sudden burst of affection for its singularity.

Arman very kindly drops me off at the island and says he
will tell Intoy to bring my *bangka* back from Sabay when he
comes. I wave him off from the shore and watch the boat
head across the strait carving its evanescent threefold
wake. When I am sure it is far enough away I open the cage
and release the finches. They fly a bit stiffly, unbelievingly,
into the nearest tree. Then simultaneously, as of one mind,
they go looping steeply upwards, whirring flitches of green,
towards the invisible top of the island. My spirits lift with
them.

I do not know what has happened to the weather. The sea
clears for a day or two, then clouds up again. The rains are

overdue, the heat intense. I seem to have no appetite for food
and often do not bother to take my spear gun into the water
with me. Off and on I catch Intoy looking at me with
concern and he comes over from Sabay with *suman* his
mother has made, with *niyubak* and *bukayo* to fatten me up.
I send him back with fish.

The soil of Tiwarik is baked, the grassfield is stiff and
harsh against my bare legs as I wade up into the sky each
day to look at the trees. From the way this expanse of *cogon*
is divided by rocky outcrops as it ascends towards the
miniature forest I have come to think of it more as three
separate fields and named according to the plants growing
there. These are: The Field of Chillies, The Field of Guavas
and The Field of Pineapples – for quite recently I discovered
two of the small 'native' pineapples which have somehow
seeded themselves. They are like little green hand-grenades:
proportionally slenderer than the usual Hawaiian variety,
their flavour is to those great yellow bombs of juice and
sugar as that of wild strawberries is to the contents of
glass dishes at Ascot and Wimbledon. Although I do not
know it at this moment I am about to re-name The Field of
Chillies.

The heat is solid. On all sides the ocean slumps in its bed,
the fish are sluggish. Only at dusk a light breeze may come
wafting off this immensity of water with a summery smell of
ozone and send a cooling drift of air through the walls of my
hut. This heat intensifies the smells of sea and land.
Sometimes the wind comes across from the mainland
bringing with it the steamy rot of forest, exotic resins
leached in their fractions from different layers of vegetation and boiled away by the heat. This same mysterious
perfume may often be smelt far out to sea with no view in
any direction but of water, from smacking bamboo outriggers to the furthest horizon. Then suddenly this olfactory
mirage born who knows how long before and on what
brooding shore: oils of pepper, boxes of cigars, compost
heaps, damp bath-towels. Strange quays come to mind
with barrelled produce standing in the sun, salted fish,
coconut oil, sacks of copra, tarred rope. Behind the quays
rise the hills of the interior brewing their monstrous

chlorophylls, their stagnant muds and dappled glades where pods crack and strew the earth beneath with yet more seeds. This unknown shore breathes out its rancid soul into the hearts of its lovers so that for a moment in mid-ocean their back hair lifts in pleasure and they stare at the bilges around their feet with blurring eyes. Countless voyagers from colder climates have been intoxicated by this scent. The most prosaic of men have dreamed under its influence, the sternest or dullest have felt the stirrings of unformed desire. Conrad sniffed it and was lost. And now this same tropic opiate fills my lungs and heart and awakens memories of things which have never happened and foretelling things which will never be.

Often the nights are lit with prodigious lightning but over Tiwarik at least no sound yet shakes down from the sky, nor the least drop of rain. Up the coast on the mainland it is a different matter. Far away a storm is in progress; its lightnings are very slow. Thirty miles off, electricity crawls low in the sky above Kansulay. In every corner are flickerings, pinkish blazes dying slowly in distant cloud banks, but the night above Tiwarik remains clear and still.

Then one night I am violently woken by a huge explosion and with the memory of a searing flash across some internal retina. Even as I sit up to look through the open door the echoes of a great clap of thunder are rolling back from the rocks, from the far side of the strait, from the low underside of the cloud layer. Perhaps two hundred yards away a flame is dancing in The Field of Chillies. It swells, grows rapidly taller. In alarm I suddenly appreciate how vulnerable the island is. Unhindered, a fire might sweep it practically bare. While I am indulging visions of a cindery rock where once was a miniature land the fire spreads rapidly. I shuffle into a pair of rubber sandals, grab the *bolo* as much for comfort as for utility and hurry up the path. In doing so I glare at the sky. Why for Christ's sake won't it rain? For only heavy rain could now control the grass-fire I shortly come upon: a ragged orange wall advancing with horrid speed up towards the forest. A local wind tugs at it, the fire's own need for oxygen whipping momentum from the air.

In despair I make impotent sallies into areas which are

already no more than bare char wormed with dying red, whacking at the sparking earth with the flat of my blade. I shout. I curse. I blaspheme with abnormal inventiveness. Clearly this is most efficacious for almost immediately the rain, as if it had been holding itself in until the last most pleasurable and exasperating moment, drops in raw tonnage from the sky. The fire still burns, however. It has run the length and breadth of The Field of Chillies, has somehow crossed a promontory of rocks and is – as near as I can judge – a third of the way through The Field of Pineapples. It has even spawned an offshoot, a tentacle which reaches way up beyond The Field of Chillies into the fringes of the forest itself.

But the rain is immense. It is not, as I discover the following day, rain at all but finally, at long last, The Rains. Within ten minutes I can stare upwards at the bulk of Tiwarik and see not a speck of light anywhere. The fire is drowned. Already water is beginning to run down the path, as yet unable to penetrate the baked surface. I return to the hut drenched, rinsing off the charcoal smears from arms and legs in the smiting downpour. My roof is leaking but I do not care. I roll up the sodden mat and lie naked instead upon the bare slats, panting. Sweat or rain runs from my hair as I listen, enclosed within this ecstatic sound. Everything is all right now. The fire is out, the monsoon surely has arrived. Tomorrow over at Sabay everybody will desert the sea and go to work the softening land: planting rice, planting cassava, planting vegetables. Their huge delicate buffaloes which for so long have stood comparatively idle, grazing in the shade, will be harnessed once more, glistening with grey mud, then resting in baths of slime in their newly reconstituted wallows. Even I might plant something.

In the morning I rise late, something to do with the night's exertions or with the incessant noise of heavy rain arousing memories of a time and a place of soft beds and winter storms, of bedclothes pulled a little higher. Improvidently I have let much of my firewood get wet; I am not an instinctive camper. Coffeeless I hurry off through the rain to inspect the damage.

At first sight The Field of Chillies is desolating: hundreds of square metres of charred stubble, a sodden black desert tufted with black and dotted with white and pinkish stones. I walk up it with the pungency of quenched bonfire in my nose. I find to my relief that only a tiny inroad has been made into the fringes of the jungle: a couple of trees will have been killed, a couple more partially so, still others merely scorched. I cheer myself further by remembering that grass fires are usually too quick, too lightly fuelled to generate enough heat to kill roots. The *cogon* will sprout again. My elaborate blasphemies clearly struck the right note at exactly the right moment. Mere prayers and entreaties would have had no effect and had I relied on them I would undoubtedly now be surveying the cinders of a magic isle. But my invocation of the anatomical details of the Trinity's constituent members obviously jolted the rain from the skies. Immoderately pleased I stand there, streaming, making facetious plans to circulate my efficacious spells to leading African churchmen, Baptist ministers in Wyoming, Marxist agronomists in Ethiopia, the FAO. I descend the mountain like Moses bearing revised laws.

And now, re-crossing the ashes of The Field of Chillies, I make a discovery. The pink and white stones scattered among the blackened stubble are not stones at all. They are crabs. Nor are they hermit crabs, either, like those whose stealthy clinkings come at night from high up the beach as they scavenge the fish-hunters' guttings and leavings. They are proper crabs with square bodies two or three inches across. Their fat fighting claws are sprawled unmoving amongst the char. They all seem to be facing uphill, more or less in the same direction, as if having found they could not grapple with this enemy they had tried to outrun it. The white ones are calcined: their bodies are mere shells containing rattling shards and chitins. The pink ones are cooked, done to a turn. And so, unbreakfasted and now breakfasting, I slowly browse through The Field of Crabs, sucking at legs, scooping out meat, crunching claws. Their flavour is delicate with the faintest trace of the grasses in which they were broiled, the rain rinses off the dirt. Standing there surrounded by opacities of falling water it is not hard to imagine myself on an ocean bed with sparse clumps of black weed thrusting up in stiff bunches from the silt, marine creatures scattered among them. It is yet another example of the way Tiwarik inverts the normal world. I ought not to be able to return elated and full to the hut I left empty and apprehensive, but I do. I am resolved to plant *ampalayá*, aubergines, calabashes. Who knows what may come up on an island where lightning can provide one with breakfast?

But I am now quite definitely out of sorts, I cannot go on pretending otherwise. The downhearted spells recur, everything grates. For what seems like weeks I have been nauseated by food. The very thought of my repetitive diet *fish-and-rice, rice-and-fish* is intolerable. On the other hand I find myself thinking obsessively about other kinds of food, entertaining fantasies of the most refined cuisines. In my imagination I prepare dishes which in real life I have never cooked and would probably be scarcely able to except that my memories of leafing through other people's cook-books now come back almost photographically. I start making mental *oeufs en meurette*, sautéeing button mushrooms in butter and oil, poaching eggs in the rich liquid from blanched bacon strips, onions, garlic and stock . . . But no, not eggs. Better would be the more ascetic subtleties of *volaille du Roy Henry truffée au gros sel*: the bird served with a bowl of rock salt and pickled gherkins, the fragments of truffle visible beneath its skin . . . Again I lose interest, am sidetracked by the agonisingly delicious promise of a Marmite sandwich, a cheese soufflé . . . No again. What I really want is *bruschetta*, that peasant delicacy they eat around the fire in Tuscany, up in the wintry mountains. Thick slices of tough Italian bread toasted on both sides and a piece of garlic rubbed in until worn down to tatters of aromatic skin between the fingertips. Then rich green olive oil poured on from a little slippery oil can and a sprinkling of salt. Probably the simplest and most delicious thing ever invented by man . . .

These fantasies are at once cut short by tearing gripes which drive me out among the rocks of the hillside. It is raining hard. Grey curtains hang drifting across the strait, opening and closing on blurred views of Sabay. Around the unseen peaks of the cordillera behind it purplish lightnings blaze. In the inadequate shade of a *madrekakaw* sapling I squat and think that I have indeed become rather thin. My rich diet of imagined cuisines seems unable to sustain my body and it certainly bores the mind. I wonder vaguely what, then, is being fed that keeps the interest going.

Later that day Intoy comes over with a bottle of ESQ from Arman to warm me up. The rain makes him merry, as it does many Filipinos, since it has a cultural significance quite different to that in England. His hair is stuck flat, his clothes plastered to his body. It is a kind thought and indeed the rum does seem to glow and settle in my stomach.

'I bet you've got *bulate*,' he says when I describe my symptoms.

'Worms?' I know they are endemic but I feel I should be exempt, being a foreigner, maybe immune.

'I'll bring you pills from the shop tomorrow. They really work.' Intoy goes to inspect the arrangement I have made with polythene sheeting and a plastic dustbin to catch the rainwater. 'No more problems with water now,' he says and paddles cheerfully off into the downpour. His boat disappears behind a shroud of falling water. The sea around him is flat calm, only its surface being lashed into froth by the rain's intensity.

The next morning he returns with a screw of paper containing two pinkish pills.

'"Combantrin",' he says.

'How can you tell?' I ask, thinking of the pharmaceutical grab-bag on the shelf in the village shop. These have 'Pfizer' written on them; beyond that, nothing. But that familiar nausea rinses through me and I don't much care. The conviction comes that I shall soon be cured whatever I take so I swallow them both with a gulp or two of ESQ. Intoy eyes the bottle with glee.

'Ha, you've drunk all that since yesterday. Wow, you must have been pretty *lasing* last night.'

'I was no such thing,' I tell him sternly. 'This is medicine. You can't get drunk on medicine.'

'My father can. He swallows enough of it and he never seems to get any better.'

These simple pleasantries cheer me up. Intoy, who is supposed to be helping his father at this very moment in the fields, has to leave and once more I see him off into the downpour. Then in the early afternoon I am driven out onto the hillside. The rain has redoubled its force and I am soaked at once. My jaw shivers of its own accord and cannot be stopped as I lower myself weakly into a squat and deliver myself of what looks like a foot-long earthworm. I stare at it in amazement. Surely this can't be right? I remember all the animals I have wormed and none of their tapeworms or pinworms or roundworms looked like this. It is a pinkish grey and apparently not yet quite dead for it makes a slight, stiff movement.

Suddenly I begin to laugh helplessly at the streaming ground. I laugh like a fool, in celebration of this fool crouched in the rain on a sullen isle. Consider his childish determination to defy and invert all the values to which he was heir. It cannot be an accident which brings a middle-class Englishman from a family of doctors to be squatting on an uninhabited island and watching his own intestinal parasites flop out around his ankles while the tropical rain drums upon his back. I consider this, still laughing. No, it isn't defiance which has brought him to this absurd state. It is *writing*. Writing, that fatuous *pis aller* which has so little to do with making marks on paper and even less to do with being read by casual strangers. What but such a pointless pursuit could so effectively have stood this fool's life on its head, could have caused whole years to vanish, could have imagined the worst and deftly magicked it into nasty reality? In short what else on this sketch of an island could have written the worm out of this fool's rectum and now be unable to write it back in again? There it lies, as large as life, craning blindly in a broth of mucus for the warmth it misses. It is all too real and the fool is held in his squat over it by gripes and giggles. Shaking with laughter he castigates himself for all the normal life he has written off. *Fool*: the years gone. *Fool*: the friend, the companion of days. *Fool*: the man of moderate success. *Fool*: the comfortable citizen. What else could they think but *fool* in Sabay and Kansulay?

The mud squidges up between my toes. It is pleasant. The gripes are over. That is sweet. The worm is out and now seems dead. That is good. The rain will make the *cogon* grow again and cover the burnt baldness of The Field of Crabs. Already the char is pouring past me in a black slurry. The promise of bright new grass is infinitely cheering. I stand up, wipe the water from my face and drop a large rock on top of the worm. Then I walk down to the sea to swim. One has these low spots.

Months go by. The rains stop. The conventional calendar has long since become a redundant fiction. Time passes in new ways. The phases of the moon control my hunting, dominate the one-man economic system of Tiwarik. My life enters and leaves its own phases according to a never-ending succession of wounds and their healing: the fortnight when I could not wear a plywood flipper on my left foot because of the open sore, the coral-grazed knee which turned septic and stuck to the mat when I lay on my left side. They slowly healed and were replaced by others, by a recurrently aching ear, by sinus trouble, by minor infirmities of the soul. Overriding everything is the constant working for daily food and the constant watching of the island in its detail. In such elemental ways a life could be, is being, spent.

Sometimes the straits appear to have widened so that walking up to my hut at dusk or in the morning's heavy heat I might be surprised by how far away Sabay has receded, its own huts invisible and its fissured mountain a numb bulk such as appears on the horizon at the end of a long sea voyage. I wonder whether Tiwarik might not stealthily have detached itself and even now be drifting out to sea. Even the mainland's occasional sounds fall fainter, the cocks remote, the dogs heard from another world. At such moments I can be overwhelmed by exhilaration and sadness: the confidence of recognising all there is, the melancholy of acknowledging all it is.

Christmas approaches, is in progress, passes. Daily the sea-eagles soar from their jungle top and drift above the ocean surface watching for shoals of *dalagang bukid*, for the unwary dallier with upper brightness, then unleashing their clawed bombs in a flurry of spray and climbing back up with crimson and silver in their feet. It is a villainous isle full of watchers without mercy who care nothing for a year's decline, unknown tomorrows.

But one night the sound of feet and cheerful voices from the shore:

'Happy New Year!'

'Happy New Year!'

Captain Sanso and Arman between them staggering with the weight of an iron torpedo. Wives and girls with baskets, boys with mysterious bundles, youths with lengths of thick bamboo on their shoulders. Taken by surprise I am bemused, wander dazedly in their wake, now following the women as they invade my lean-to kitchen and kindle a fire, now Intoy and Arman as they begin disposing the bamboo tubes among the rocks, muzzles pointing out across the straits to lightless Sabay.

'*Kanyon*,' explains Arman. 'This place needs livening up. You can't let an old year pass in silence as if you're ashamed of it and you can't welcome a new year in as if you're afraid of it. You're *malungkot*. Why do you always want to be so *malungkot*, James?'

I don't think I do.

'Of course you do. Why else would you cut yourself off in a place like this without a wife, without a companion, without even so much as a cat? Always fishing and fishing as if you had no other way of staying alive and always writing and writing as if you had nothing else to fill up the time. Always alone. Always miserable. *Ay, kawawa!*'

He is a little drunk. Everyone laughs and applauds since they are, too. Because there is no way of replying to such undeniable charges I pour myself a glass of *tuba* from a Clorox container and resolve to join them. I crouch beside Arman's brother as he heaps boulders over one end of a bamboo.

'What's that horrible smell?'

'*Kalburo*.' He hefts a carrier bag full of what seems to be

chips of greyish rock. I suddenly recognise the stench of
acetylene and deduce *kalburo* to be carbide. I have some
vague memory they use it for speeding up the ripening
process of fruit, in particular bananas and mangoes. The
artificer in me surfaces once more.

'Cannons!' I cry. 'Of course. You've knocked the bamboos through.'

'All except the last two compartments this end. See?
We've made a touch-hole just before the joint.'

And now all over the hillside the bamboos are deployed. It
is evident that the pyrotechnicians of Sabay are as studious
as Howard and I had ever been and that years of experiment
have gone into producing known effects. Some tubes are fat
and long, others thinner and shorter. Some have their
muzzles bound with rope or rattan, others are smooth and
unadorned. Excitement drifts over the scene with the
evaporating acetylene. A fire has now been lit outside my
hut and woks are sizzling over it. Yet another is lit beside it
and a great fish laid over a griddle of green sticks. Children
pour up from the beach, eddying among the rocks and
whooping as one by one newcomers' boats ground on the
shore below. If there were moon or stars tonight the strait
would seem a silver pond bearing a flotilla of tiny sticks
slowly across to Tiwarik with phosphorescent pocks of
paddle-strokes.

Four chickens die protestingly, their still-flapping bodies
dunked in the woks of boiling water so their feathers will
come out in easy, sodden handfuls. An enamel bowl full of
the thick slops of their lifeblood is carried off to the
kitchen. The women slaughterers exchange their knives for
glasses of ESQ and fizzy orange which has been mixed in
the plastic bowl I use for marinading fish. The children are
tipsy with excitement and in the case of one or two twelve-
year-olds with rum and cigarettes as well. And suddenly in
the middle of all this the first *kanyon* fires with a deep
explosive *chug!* which reminds me uncomfortably of a
mortar round being launched into its high parabola.
Outgoing.

'Not quite right.' Arman is in an exalted frenzy, tuning his
thunder machine. 'It hasn't got hot yet.' A wisp of sap-steam

floats from its muzzle. He pours a trickle of water down through the touch-hole onto the grains of carbide, leans forward and gives a light puff to the hole, wafting the acetylene vapours the length of the barrel, then puts a taper to the hole. This time the blast is ear-splitting. An exclamation of flame spurts from the muzzle which in turn leaps from its bed of rock. The explosion crosses the dark strait, whacks the side of the distant mountain and twenty seconds later its echo comes back to Tiwarik where it is welcomed like a returning traveller. Arman smiles proudly but critically, head on one side. He drops a small nugget of carbide into the breech, adds water, blows, ignites. Again the noise batters our ears and slams away across the sea, this time being joined almost immediately by a tenor crack from one of the smaller bamboos in its emplacement up by the rocks and undergrowth behind the hut. Soon all six bamboos are in use, the barrage continuous, the night lit by stabs of flame and cooking fires. For once the sea beneath us is empty of human hunters. Tonight the fish can prey on each other uninterruptedly as the bombers deploy their explosions on a higher plane.

'Why don't you fire stones from the *kanyon*?' I ask. 'They must easily be powerful enough.'

'They are. But if you do that the bamboo won't last. I think if you block up the muzzle with something, however loosely, it increases the pressure in the barrel and sooner or later it splits. That's why we've bound it with *abaka*. Sometimes when it splits – *ay*, very dangerous.' Arman is delighted and puts half a coconut shell over the muzzle of his own mortar. It vanishes like the lid of a skull into the night sky.

'When is it midnight?' But no-one is wearing a watch; almost no-one has a watch to wear. I look for mine, having some vague memory of leaving it in one of my shoes which are tucked up into the roof. I wear them only for infrequent trips to Manila when after months of barefoot living they cause an anguish of pinching and rubbing. In the lamplight they are now seen to be blue with delicate moulds. In one of them is a jewelled spider holding its eggs in a silk disc beneath its body, in the other the white pearl of a house-

lizard's egg and my watch. Despite my having ignored it, it
has a life of its own and has ticked on unconsulted. Now it
tells me the month has twice changed since last I looked,
that today is Monday and that it is eleven forty at night.
'Time to get the *labintador* ready.'
'You mean you've brought fireworks as well?'
'Home-made only.' Arman searches around in the dark
until he trips over the torpedo. In the light of a *lapad* of
paraffin with a rag wick I can see it is not a torpedo at all
but a large gas cylinder from an oxy-acetylene welding set.
Generally it lies half buried in rubbish just above the tide-
line on the beach at Sabay, so rusty its colour coding has
long vanished.
'*Oksiheno.*'
I had always supposed the cylinder empty. Now willing
hands drag it to a convenient spot, a decrepit spanner is
found down below in someone's boat, a length of firewood
whacks the spanner. There is a sharp hiss and everyone
exclaims in delight. Two boys are dispatched to the beach
to siphon off a few cupfuls of petrol from a boat engine. The
teenage pyrotechnician within me has his ears pricked: the
proceedings are new to him.
'I remember we did this ten, twelve years ago,' says
Arman. 'I was a boy then but I can remember it very clearly.
We had a party on the beach over at Sirao.' He gestures with
his chin, pursing his lips towards the invisible headland a
mile up the coast from Sabay. 'After an hour of our *labintador* there is a noise like an aeroplane coming from the sea.
A searchlight comes on. Soldiers with M-16s are suddenly
running all over us. Ha, we were only kids: we'd forgotten
that Martial Law had been declared' (this must have been
shortly after 1972) 'and they could hear the explosions all
the way from Malubog and even Bulangan.'
This was impressive for Bulangan is many miles away, far
closer to Kansulay than to Tiwarik. It is an odd possibility
that in special circumstances Tiwarik and Kansulay
might just be audible to each other.
'The Mayor of Bulangan thought there was a civil war in
Malubog and called out the garrison. The *komandante* there
thought the NPA had at last set up heavy artillery in the

mountains here and were shelling the town as a prelude to an all-out attack. *Ay!*' Everybody is laughing helplessly, those who can remember the incident and those who can't. The children who are now as old as Arman was then are in fits with drink and mischief. The delicious chaos! Turning out one lot of troops to fight supposed rebels who themselves believed they were under bombardment despite a complete absence of falling shells! And all because of a lot of boys on a beach playing with *labintador*.

'*Ay, 'sus,* Mandoy, we were lucky.' Silo had also been there. 'Those troops were scared. They might easily have shot up the beach first as they usually do. But nobody got worse than a thick ear that night. I still think what saved us was the fire we had going. They must have been able to see us from their patrol boat.'

Fresh laughter at the thought of a tense commander surveying through his binoculars a beach party of cavorting children in the middle of what he assumed to be a war zone. By now the boys are back with a *lapad* full of petrol. There is some rummaging in bundles and several of the large plastic sacks normally used for transporting *similya* are found.

'Come on, hurry up. It must be nearly twelve.' Arman impatiently seizes a bag and into it pours about a tablespoonful of petrol. Then he gathers up its neck loosely and, holding it to the rust-corroded valve of the oxygen cylinder, inflates it. He knots the neck and shakes the taut bag, coating the inside of the membrane with petrol until it must largely have evaporated for there is soon only the faintest patter of drops from within. He hands the bag to his younger brother. 'Not yet,' he enjoins sternly and makes five more plastic balloons in quick succession. I am a little sceptical: a polythene bag hardly offers much resistance to an explosion and I expect no more than a pleasing fireball blooming momentarily in the night. What I am leaving out of the equation is pure oxygen. 'Well?' asks Arman, tapping his wrist and looking up from where he squats.

'It's twelve.'

'*Ay. Maligayang Bagong Taon sa inyong lahat.* Happy New Year everyone.' He plucks one of the balloons from his brother's hands, goes to the nearest fire and from a couple of paces tosses it towards the flames while backing smartly away. For an instant the plastic bladder hesitates between falling and ascending in the column of heat and then there is a stupendous blast which sends live firebrands whirling like tracer through the air. Everyone has been too close for comfort, everyone screams with delight. How the noise can exceed that of the bamboo cannons I have no idea but it does. In the confusion somebody sneaks off with a balloon and finds an ember in the scrub behind the hut. Another chrysanthemum of flame, another prodigious detonation as much felt in the intestines as heard. I jump involuntarily. *Incoming*.

Now the making of balloons becomes a feverish activity. The cannonaders are running out of carbide but their bamboos – several now splitting around the muzzles – are so hot that ordinary paraffin can be substituted with practically no loss of power so well does it vaporise. *Pour, puff, ignite. Pour, puff, ignite.* The ballooners are introducing granules of fertiliser into their petrol/oxygen mixture. Tiwarik leaps in the dark, tilts in flashes of flame, thumps our feet. Its percussive breezes box the ears. I am drunk. I am drunk with explosions, too. I am no longer a hunter, being deafened and blinded. I do not care. To hell with the sea. I go and squat beside Intoy as he deftly purses the plastic bags and fills them with a tearing screech of gas. In the firelight, the oil lamps, the intermittent flashes, it is not his hands I watch but the shadows of his cheek, the outline of an ear, a burnished shoulder. I am amazed by the slenderness of his elbows, the fineness of his wrists, at the delicacy of his chest as he turns to pass the filled balloons back to eager hands which knot and shake them. Petrol fumes hang about his hair. How can anything so fragile be as accomplished under water as he is, so competent in the face of the sea's brutal energies? It is a miracle of sorts.

By now my co-celebrants, my fellow-orgiasts, my friends all have about them the aura of miracle as we drown ourselves in violent sound. We stumble into each other in the dark: glasses of *tuba* slop and clash, the necks of rum bottles saw unsteadily against beaker rims.

Indiscriminately we embrace, are embraced in turn by, children, men, women, chins glinting with chicken fat, while all around the petrol, the oxygen, the carbide, the paraffin blaze and blow away our words, reducing us to gesture.

'*Ay*, last year . . .'

'A bad year, that . . .'

'Shitty.'

We all know who died, who lost a boat, whose children never went to school. We all know the slow attrition caused by endless petty economies: the wounds left unplastered, the jeep fares saved by two hours' hike to town, the nights made interminable by keeping lamp oil for an emergency. We all know pretty much what everyone has in their largely cupboardless bamboo houses whose walls are stuffed with hoarded pieces of paper, plastic bags, half-used biros, perished scraps of spear gun elastic. We have seen behind the curtain made of rice sacks and have admired the wedding-dress being carefully kept for the eldest daughter just as we have admired the yellowing laminated plaques on the walls, plaques awarded by anonymous or defunct institutions and colleges certifying in copperplate a long-ago graduation, a course attendance, an honourable membership.

A shitty year. So what better than to stand it on its head here in Tiwarik and welcome in the new with a prodigal overturning of normality? The precious petrol blossoms skywards and its thunders run up and down the dark coast, chased by those of misered paraffin. The release is boundless. Not only the children weep, nor only with pleasure. The great barrage keeps up, the arcadian silence is abolished. Out on the dark sea tonight there would be no way of telling if the sounds were those of battle or celebration and even on the island, as the flames briefly photograph faces streaked with tears and mouths thrown open, it is not really clear. I am suddenly sure it can after all be heard from my hill-top in Kansulay, the concussions crossing the intervening miles of sea as once across the English Channel the summer winds wafted the sounds of slaughter in Picardy and Flanders to the ears of ladies in long gloves and netted hats bending over their beehives in Sussex. Sometimes it seems this century has re-drawn all human boundaries so that now we shall always be within earshot of war, of that battlefield on which we so increasingly live.

Time passes until the dawn is only an hour or two away. The hut is crammed with sleepers. Boys sleep on their sides among the rocks, hands between their drawn-up knees. The women and girls who have done most of the cooking are rolled together beneath a tattered yellow tarpaulin. Drunken artillerymen are slumped over their cold pieces, for the last grain of carbide has gone, the last drop of paraffin, the last trickle of petrol. Nobody knows how much oxygen is left in the cylinder. It is one of the marvels that it appears to be inexhaustible in a world of things which perpetually run out. A ringing silence has descended on Tiwarik which suddenly swims out from under a smokelike cloud of overcast and sails beneath a clear stellate sky. I lie on my back and watch the meteorites end their billion-year dark voyages in evanescent streaks.

And bit by bit across the strait the cocks awake and crow in the deserted village which is Sabay.

11

The catharsis of fireworks springs us forward into the new year as if under a common obligation to forget what we know of all previous new years and their outcome. The Sabayans and I reminisce for days, recalling mental pictures taken by the light of fires and the muzzle-flashes of *kanyon* while avoiding all mention of the mortal passion which had gripped us. The recognition of an unspoken, unspeakable desolation pouring down from the stars and welling up from the ocean is, I think, the basis of our affection for each other, as why might it not be for anybody anywhere.

Going back to spear fishing after a lapse I find my neck muscles aching. It is like 'weaver's neck' from which Second World War fighter pilots suffered in their constant searching for enemy aircraft. In their case it resulted in chafing (it was to prevent this, rather than out of gratuitous dandyism, they wore silk scarves) but muscular cramps afflicted them as well. My own neck muscles bunch and knot as I go hunting fish through alien skies. The combat is unequal, my victories comparatively few, besides which there is the arduousness of working always against the inner oxygen clock. This can produce beautiful effects of heightened detail, of the special kind of noticing one associates with limited time. Whether scared or simply fighting the body's craving to be spared this discomfort I carry back up with me vivid details which have about them the aura of being acquired against the odds, of having been wrested from somewhere obscure. Fright, which occurs quite often, is especially good for freezing indelible images: the grey shark hanging there ten feet away and watching, the moray one did not notice, the banded sea-snake investigating a pair of legs rendered motionless by an act of sheer will.

Much later and many thousands of miles away I will come upon Oliver Lyttelton's *From Peace to War* which has this paragraph about his experiences in the trenches in the First World War:

> Fear and its milder brothers, dread and anticipation, first soften the tablets of memory, so that the impressions which they bring are clearly and deeply cut, and when time cools them off the impressions are fixed like the grooves of a gramophone record, and remain with you as long as your faculties. I have been surprised how accurate my memory has proved about times and places where I was frightened . . .

Turning to Paul Fussell's book again I will find not only this very paragraph quoted but nearby a sentence from Max Plowman's *A Subaltern on the Somme*: 'What a strange emotion all objects stir when we look upon them wondering whether we do so for the last time in this life.' At first sight it might seem merely pretentious to draw a parallel between being caught up in a famous holocaust and doing a bit of fishing, but the mind cares nothing for such scruples when it makes its associations. Fear for one's life echoes straight down a dank well into the soul. The circumstances do not much matter, it is enough to know one may very shortly be dead and that the translation will be violent and painful. Besides, the exactness of Lyttelton's image is too great to be ignored. I have carried with me out of the sea a nearly eidetic memory of a hundred different expeditions, of my comrades and of our victims and of our wounds. I can remember things such as I never can on dry land. Yet while the details can be recalled with clarity the gaze has often passed through them. Undersea terrains are not to be mapped by their details: the land they compose is viewed under strain and at once becomes somewhere else. I scan it with an accurate haste beside which my view on land has a leisurely vagueness.

For the chronological as well as the oxygen clock ticks on. One day infirmity or age will keep me from the sea for ever and it is not fanciful on any sortie to wonder whether I have shared an element with a cuttlefish or squid for the last time. This is Max Plowman's 'strange emotion' which in large part consists of tenderness. I devour the sight of these creatures with a kind of gentle greed, marvelling once again at the language of their skin, at the 'passing cloud' effect as their chromatophores blink and meld to send colours chasing over their bodies, at the violet lightnings of their skirts. I can hardly believe there will come a day when I shall no longer be able to watch them.

My beating heart drives me downwards. Wordsworth showed how hardly possible it is for us to disentangle our landscapes from our childhoods but I wish I knew for certain where it came from, this extravagant desire of mine for something so distant from all the landscapes of my youth and which now makes my middle age look foolish. The feud with my father may well have closed off certain possibilities, but I would like to know why it should be in this subaqueous world – of all the marches of earth – that I should have looked for and found a magnificent and lonely poetry.

When I first returned to Tiwarik (it now feels almost a lifetime since I clapped eyes on it amid careering wavecasts) I remember thinking it could not assume a proper identity until it had acquired a position in the mind. But already I must have been imagining living there because when for lack of a better site my hut was built a little above the strand it caused me to feel disorientated for some time. Instead of its facing Sabay across the strait I must always have imagined it on top of the island somewhere and facing out the other way across the expressive blank ocean. Consequently I experienced a strange twisting sensation as if the island were being rotated against its will from right to left – that is, anticlockwise as seen from above. This persisted for some weeks and was mildly bothersome because it hinted at strain in a pattern I was trying to impose on the island (or it on me).

Less mildly, this phenomenon involved me in a good deal of unnecessary swimming since at night I often lost my way. If one is spear fishing on a moonless night with only a torch, and especially if one is too far away from shore to hear its breakers above the wash of surrounding waters, it is easy to become lost. Then, buoyed up on a swell I would glimpse the yellow lights of Sabay, faint oil lamps nearly drowned, and think I was on the wrong side of Tiwarik because for me my house was really perched above an imaginary beach on the seaward side. Half exhausted by three hours' hunting and towing a catch-line with several kilos of fish, I once arrived beneath the sheer igneous headland standing deep in lurching tons of surf. I was expecting to step out and stroll up a coral beach to my hut where I could smother my catch beneath a layer of salt and sleep until dawn. Instead of which I found I still faced a long swim against a strengthening current.

I am intrigued by this whole process of orientation and Tiwarik is the perfect place for throwing it all into doubt. One day I spend a lazy morning after a night's fishing, marinading and then laying out the catch on the drier. Something far away in my mind is nagging, meanwhile. It is that even to this remotest of remote places I have brought a chore with me for which there is a deadline. It is a literary chore, itself bizarre in the circumstances: to re-read a children's novel I wrote long ago as a preliminary to writing an outline treatment of it for a film script. I have frequently come across this book over the months, down at the bottom of my bag jumbled up with spare torch batteries, lengths of elastic, a copy of James's *Princess Casamassima* (why?) and a treasured cake of Roger & Gallet's 'Vétiver' soap. Now I go and dig it out reluctantly, climb up to the edge of The Field of Guavas and sit in the shade of an *antipolo* tree.

On reading it again I remember little of the story yet at the same time it remains utterly familiar. Suddenly I come upon the sentence: 'To his left he could just make out the huge bulk of the Seneschal's House . . .' and am brought up short. Not by the redundancy of the adjective but by that *left*. Surely I meant right? The sea is on the right together with the house being pounded to pieces by the waves. It must mean that sixteen years ago I had 'approached' the fictitious town of Carisburgh by the wrong direction.

This is very odd. The one consistent thing about one's own writing is the position of the eye. I do not know what governs the way in which one always sees an imagined view – a house, a road, a room – from a particular angle. Maybe there was a time in childhood when the bearings of such things became fixed so that after a holiday, for example, certain kinds of imagined coastline are for ever approached from the same direction, *thus*, the sea always on the right. There is a plausibility about this. It took me a long time to perceive how my fantasies and day-dreams set indoors ('set', of course, being the word in this theatre of audience participation) took place in rooms which, no matter how disguised initially, tended to slide back into archetypes of rooms in the first two houses I can remember and usually into my own bedroom. Not in terms of colour or upholstery but of disposition: the window *here* in relation to the bed; the bed lengthways against the wall rather than with the head against it; the door (representing threat of intrusion) in *that* corner and opening in *this* direction. And thus the writer as the dreamer of narratives calls instinctively upon the same internal compass to orientate imaginary acts.

How then could I have written 'left' when I had to have meant 'right'? The book slips off my lap and I discover I have been gazing out to sea for an unguessable time without registering either it or the distant boat crawling across it. (How swamping the inward view which rises up and drowns the visible world!) I drag myself back to the text and forcing myself to read with more attention now discover what I had missed. The character Martin – and hence the narrating eye – is approaching the house from a different and not wrong direction. It was deliberate. I am relieved, having for a moment been disorientated by not being able to visualise my own story and feeling that peculiar twisting sensation as if something were trying to turn itself round the right way. In the human brain there is no magnetic north and yet all imaginary actions, all dialogues, all ideas feel as though they take up an inner physical direction peculiar to them alone and assigned them as they form. It is the route they take to reach the mind's eye; each route is unique and imparts its own flavour. Later it is easier to recall the flavour of ideas and memories than the originals themselves. I can often not remember an argument but usually the scent left by its trail in my mind, the olfactory echoes lasting vividly long after the words in which the thought was expressed have vanished without trace.

Again the book has slipped off my lap and again I find I am staring at the ocean which now contains no boat at all, not even a faint wake across its directionless expanse. Inner twistings and flavours: maybe this is how it feels to migratory birds and animals, one of whose forbears once went on a summer holiday or winter journey thereby orientating itself so thoroughly that it passed on a new set of directions for ever. Modern science glosses this inaccurately by referring to gravitational fields, stellar patterns, magnetic poles, the position of the sun and so forth, but that is only because modern science as yet knows no way of quantifying the influence of summer holidays on impressionable organisms.

Meanwhile I remember Marisil, Sising and Bini's eldest daughter who once went to stay with relatives on the other side of a town not much more than nine miles from Kansulay. She was unbearably homesick and returned three days later even though she was supposed to have gone to be formally employed as a maid. I asked her how it had struck her, being away from home for the first time in her fifteen years.

'I was always so sad,' she said. 'It's not like here in Kansulay, they haven't got any hills there.' She spoke as if she had been to a foreign country. 'And the sun was in the wrong place.'

What did this mean? I found out her relatives' house was differently aligned. When she sat outside the front and expected the sun to rise as it did at home over the coconuts on the left and set behind the bamboos up on the hill near the place they called Babag it did no such thing. Instead it slouched across the sky in an unexpected direction. In addition to feeling immeasurably touched because she looks so like her mother I felt complete sympathy with her, knowing of the inner wrenching, the sense of bending which she could only describe as homesickness and which really told of an offence against the map in her mind. I imagine I am now at ease with the map of Tiwarik I carry in my own mind. This, however, turns out to be self-delusion, at least when it comes to my own orientation.

My disabuse begins one evening when they come for me as the light is beginning to go: Arman, Intoy and Danding in one boat, Silo, Jhoby and Bokbok in the other. They sit around drinking small nips of *anisado* to warm them for the long night ahead while I change into night-fishing gear: black cotton jogging suit with long sleeves and a pair of dark nylon socks. This is partly a protection against stinging plants and sea-urchins but it also lessens the attraction of my pale flesh to passing sharks. I strap a knife on the outside of my right leg. Ever since a near-disaster some months ago I seldom hunt at night without one. Arman, who played a heroic rôle in that particular drama, also wears a knife, as does Jhoby. Once none of us would have dreamed of taking knives but now we are well past feeling self-conscious and making jokes about looking like Lito Lapid, a Filipino film star of immense popularity whose endless hand-to-hand combat parts have made him a sort of ageing Bruce Lee.

By the hurricane lamp's benign glow we check our equipment: spear guns, elastic bindings, plywood flippers, masks and goggles, torches. At the last moment Arman decides to change the batteries in his torch which takes a minute or two because of the home-made waterproofing. We are all using the same design, ordinary three-battery Chinese flashlights encased in motorcycle inner tube warty with patched repairs. The tyre is cut off with about six inches to spare, doubled back and rolled up on itself like the end of a toothpaste tube before being bound around with elastic. The result is a fat rubber torch, bulbous with air and waterproof to a great depth. A disadvantage is that it takes time to change the batteries and even longer to replace a bulb. Another minor disadvantage I have discovered occurs only at depth. Beyond a hundred and thirty feet or so the water pressure squeezes the rubber flat over the switch making it impossible to turn the torch off. This makes one-handed signalling very difficult. Tonight we will be at such depths, using both the boats' compressors.

I am slightly tense with excitement as I run a file over the tip of my spear. I like fishing before moonrise, which effectively puts an end to it. Tonight the moon is very late and will come up at about 2.30 a.m. When the cycle changes and the moon rises almost at sunset, going down at midnight, it is a different experience. Then one drags oneself from sleep and lowers oneself over the side of a boat into black sea beneath black sky. It is too uncertain whether a dream is ending or has just begun. But now day has conveniently elided with moonless night. I have slept this afternoon, I am rested and alert. At the last moment I bring with me a spare spear and catch-line. Leaving the oil lamp burning low in the hut's doorway I follow the others down to the shingle.

For me this anticipatory moment before a dive is almost the best part. I am fully aware of what may be waiting for us out there in the deeps but on dry land, suited up in black cotton, knife on calf and spear gun in hand, I feel competent. Food will be won from an alien element. Tonight the breeze is onshore, carrying over from the mainland a smell of incense which I recognise as *sahing*, the soft aromatic mess of gums used as a firelighter in charcoal stoves. It intensifies the sense of ritual, of being prepared for a mixture of ordeal and awe. For all that they are born to it I really think my companions are themselves not unaffected. Their movements as we pile equipment into the boats and push off with a hollow grating sigh of keels are practised but not casual. It is – why pretend? – a dangerous business to be conducted far below the upper air with its summer lightnings. Apart from natural hazards there is always the possibility of equipment failure. If the frayed old fan-belt driving the compressor snaps or if the engine breaks down there is a rusty standby tank which will supply two divers with about forty seconds' worth of air. This is not enough to get them up from forty-five metres if they have been there an hour. (Indeed they ought not to have spent more than five minutes at that depth without decompressing later.) At the end of that gasping ascent will be minor haemorrhaging if they are lucky, the bends and aneurisms if not.

But we none of us dwell on such specific disasters. They simply blend into a general latency of threat enough to keep us silent as the boats head out across the sea to the far side of the island, outriggers snubbing the occasional wavelet so that it bursts into grains of phosphorescence and sows our wake with bright pollen. Except when lightning defines the horizon for an instant it is impossible to tell where water and air meet. We forge ahead into the blackness aware of Tiwarik's proximity only because the racket of our engines comes back to us as a hollowness on the right side. The breeze is cool on our faces. We stare out with our private lack of thoughts letting the black air flow through our minds.

Danding and Bokbok cut the engines and in silence we abruptly lose way. We have arrived at the place where the seabed is strewn with huge boulders which over the millennia have been shed from the invisible cliff above. It is a good place to start for the boulders are usually a dormitory for *lapu-lapu*. Then the current can carry us back towards the strait over some of the richer corals. If we are still in the water when it changes we can even work our way partially across the strait to the deepest point of the channel. In this manner we will not have to waste energy swimming against the current, for although it is not as strong far underwater as it is at the surface it still counts, particularly when towing a full catch-line.

The polythene hoses are checked by torchlight and roughly straightened into two coils fore and aft. I will take one and Arman the other. On the other boat Silo and Jhoby are also preparing to dive. A boy in each boat will follow his swimmers by paddling while Bokbok and Danding do their best to keep the engines running and the compressors working. It will be a long cold night for them especially if it rains from the overcast which fits above our heads like a manhole cover. Not a star can be seen, only pinkish–mauve discharges of electricity as from faulty circuitry in the planet's wiring. Now Bokbok has his engine running and Silo and Jhoby are in the water. I watch their torchlights turn from bright white to small green clouds as they head downwards. The torchlights of companions as they dwindle beneath the surface look most like lightning reflected on the top layer of clouds seen from a high-flying aircraft in the clear stratosphere above them: a limitless floor of greyish ground glass on whose underside appear momentary puddles of green light to tell of lone activities below. I yearn to join them.

Now Danding has our own compressor going and Arman and I gird ourselves with the narrow plastic hose: two turns around the waist and a loose hitch allowing enough free tubing for us to take the end in our mouths and leave movement unhindered. The coldly gushing air stinks of oil and the dank yeasts which have taken up residence in the walls of the tube. I bite the end to close off the supply to a mere trickle. Long before the end of the dive our jaws will ache intolerably and we will have to take a bight of the tube between our fingers and pinch it shut. Such are the low-tech recourses for those who make do without refinements like airflow regulators. *Bahala na* . . . Intoy gives me a grave salute with the paddle and a broad grin. He is huddled in the *Jhon-Jhon*'s stern in a plastic raincoat several sizes too big. I wave to him, adjust my mask, signal to Arman and slip over the side. Together we angle downwards towards the boulders and begin our night's work.

Without the constraint of having to keep coming up for air one's search is more thorough, the experience altogether less impressionistic. The submarine landscape settles down into one continuous entity instead of being broken up into small disconnected patches. In just such a way the dispersed streets of an unfamiliar capital combine to form a city. With air-supply I also miss fewer fish. Working without the compressor there is always that moment when, right on the point of surfacing for air, one spots a mullet sheltering beneath a rock and has to decide whether to take a quick shot and maybe miss, maybe get entangled in the corals and have to leave the spear and claw upwards for air; or whether to mark the place mentally, go up and breathe and go back down in the hopes of finding it again. If there is a current the chances of retrieving either mullet or spear are practically nil, as they are if the sea is at all cloudy. Merely turning around on the surface is enough to disorientate me. I find it quite possible to return to the same rock with a fresh lungful but from a different angle and not recognise it. The mullet is lost. But with the compressor inflating my lungs with the reek of oil and mildew I can take my time.

The boulders are truly immense. They lie against one another on a stony, weedless bed. There are no corals here and few plants. Not many fish are to be found here during the day except in the sparkling upper waters. But at night the caves between adjacent boulders provide shelter for quite large fish where they can hang motionlessly in the dark for nine or ten hours. With a plastic air-hose between my teeth I can go into these cave systems, into narrow tunnels whose roofs curve and hang like the skin of a tent, needlessly anxious lest a thousand-ton rock might choose that moment to settle a little more firmly in its sleep, more sensibly wary of a savage stubby eel which might be waiting in a cross-passage. Tonight I find a reasonable haul of surgeon-fish, dark brown and flattish, each weighing a good half-pound. I also find a couple of *samaral*, speckled and rather rectangular fish whose flavour I prize above that of nearly all others in these waters. They are adept at flattening themselves against walls and even roofs to avoid torchlight, whereas if they are surprised on an open seabed they will do the opposite, adroitly angling themselves so as to present only their narrow backs to the beam of light. (The practised spear fisherman holds his torch sideways at arm's length and brings his spear tip to within six inches of the fish from the opposite direction.) Fish like these *samaral* which flatten themselves against rock walls are easy to spear but just as easy to lose unless they are thick enough in the body to engage the barb. Otherwise the spear tip alone goes through them, striking the rock on the far side and allowing the fish to wriggle free before it can be grasped. Grasping a *samaral* is like holding a snake: it must be done with address and decisiveness because its dorsal and ventral spines are agonisingly poisoned. I grip the heads of these ones and pass them back to join the surgeon-fish, hoping they will not drift into the path of one of my kicking feet. (I once shot a *bantol* dead through the top of its head and was proud of getting it safely onto the catch-line since it is a member of the family which includes stonefish and lionfish and is similarly armed with poisoned barbs around its head and back. Half an hour later the current brought the catch-line tangling into my legs. Forgetting the *bantol* I kicked out. The pain was so awful I had to go ashore: it monopolised attention even to the extent that it became possible to forget not to breathe water.)

Now from between some boulders I catch a glimpse of Arman's far-off light and change direction slightly to bring us closer. We have traversed the field of boulders and are at the extreme range of their tumbled trajectories. The seabed is changing as the water deepens. So far we have not been much below thirty feet but now there is a perceptible slope dotted with coral outcrops. This, I know, will remain fairly uniform since we are working our way along its face as we round the island. To our left the boulders, to our right the black gulfs. The slanting horizon ahead raises its metropolitan skyline of turrets and spires, avenues and arcades. At least, it does so in daylight. Now my torch reveals not cathedrals and office-blocks but anatomical details attached to amorphous bulks: tripes, spines and brains; antlers and tusks; wens, polyps, lipomas and sea-cancers. The rocks are encrusted with living corals of all kinds, most of the rocks themselves being dead growths. Plants incline gently to the current. The delicate silver-beige fans of hydroids wave their plumes. They sting worse than nettles and can leave a brown stain on the skin like the aftertrace of a burn. This vegetable mass conceals all sorts of nooks and caverns, fissures and pits which are home or shelter to a vast variety of living creatures only a tiny percentage of which are my own potential prey.

Arman appears from behind an outcrop. His torch-beam catches the brilliant craters of air spilling from his mouth and wobbling upwards. Briefly we light up each other's catch-lines to make sure that tonight's luck is evenly distributed. I used to be quite competitive until it became obvious there was no way I could compete with him over an extended period. Luck might win me a bigger catch than his even on two consecutive nights, but finally he was far the better fisherman and could go out on nights when I hardly found a fish and bag enough to keep his family in food for a couple of days. At this moment, however, we have roughly the same amount. Arman stays where he is while I head off to the right towards deeper water, my own preference, and work parallel with him roughly thirty metres away.

I am examining a coral as tall as I am and shaped like a series of crinkly interleaved ice-cream wafers. The technique with these is to swim above them and shine the torch directly down into the deep fissures; several species like to rest in the crisp folds but tonight there is nothing worth bagging. As I move off my line snags something behind me, tugging the tip of my spear momentarily downwards. Simultaneously, in the water beside the coral and then directly through my legs a torpedo slides. It stops and turns and hangs there not two metres away, sideways on, a five-foot shark. Its mouth is not fully closed and from it trail white strands.

A five-foot shark is no threat to me so although my first reaction is the usual one of freezing shock this passes at once. I have met sharks before during day and night, ones twice the size and on one startling occasion a fifteen-footer. But anything seen underwater appears larger than it is and viewed as a fish this small shark is extremely big. I do not wish to take my torch-beam off him to examine my catchline but assume that, attracted by the blood of my catch, he has just helped himself to the lot. As I watch, his mouth cranks open another inch. There is the whiteness of many teeth but no green nylon. Tentatively I bring my spear-tip round as if to perform a wholly imaginary act and in that instant the shark is gone. I do not even see his tail flick. My light stares through an empty chamber of water where not even a few threads of meat hang to betray his recent occupancy. Half expecting him to be circling nearby, or maybe a larger relative, I nervously shine my beam around before inspecting the catch-line. It appears intact but then I find the first three fish I shot are only half-fish. All of them have been snipped neatly away leaving three heads strung on the end of the line. From one of these hangs a white worm of gut.

Disgruntled at having three decent fish ruined I return to the hunt with the feeling of going back to the beginning again, like on that night long ago when I was a neophyte but shooting quite well, passing a series of fish back down my catch-line and finding things surprisingly easy only to discover that the stop-knot on the end had come unravelled and I was towing an empty line. Now I re-orientate myself with respect to the slope and see somebody's torch on the far side of a mountain range briefly outline its jagged crest with a sad lightning. I assume it is Arman but at that moment I see another flash from deep in the gulf to my right where somebody else is mining his private seam of fish. Strangely enough this evidence of companions down here fills me with reassurance less than it emphasises distance and isolation. I very often hunt alone at night without a compressor and the initial sense of being companionless in unbounded dark is transformed into absorption. One cannot see anything one's torch does not illuminate so moves forever as in a room whose fragmentary and misty walls expand before and close in behind. Tonight those far-off lights in the deep, their dim green winkings like algae, arouse in me the melancholy of infinitudes. There is a beautiful story by Ray Bradbury in which he describes the aftermath of an explosion aboard a spaceship. It consists of radio conversations between the survivors who have been flung outwards in all directions, all of them receding from each other, some heading for deep space, one for the Earth to flare briefly in its atmosphere as a meteorite. Their conversations are necessarily short as one by one they go out of radio range on their individual paths to nowhere. Now in the sea off Tiwarik the abysm of salt atmosphere which covers nearly three-quarters of the planet's face seems to close in on me as the twinkling asteroids of my friends recede. I think I can never catch up with them, not even if I close the distance and work side by side.

We are at about a hundred and twenty feet, to judge from the pressure, the species of fish and occasional plants. Even at midday the light down here is muted to the dimmest blue. The extravagance of foliage swaying in the brightness of the upper water becomes, at this depth, the occasional bank of dark weed whose colour is lost because the lens of water above them filters out practically all red and orange light wavelengths. But the holes in the rocks are full of fish and the increasingly large stretches of sand are not deserts at all. They are alive with shellfish making their purposeful, wavering tracks, with swaying garden eels growing like beds of reeds ready to retract into their holes, with fish drowsing motionlessly just above the seabed while those species which are active at night cruise restlessly above them in the dark. Every so often I turn round completely, flashing the light behind me to surprise anything which has been attracted to the activity and has warily approached. By this method I have already speared (lucky shot) a small barracuda two feet long and viciously toothed and now I turn and am confronted with the large silver platter of a *mabilog*, a roundish fish of the pampano family which tries too late to shy away from the light. It has already turned when my spear takes it from behind through one open gill and going clean out through its mouth. It is too big to thread alive onto the catch-line, its struggles would be a great hindrance, so I kill it by putting a finger and thumb up under its gill-covers and pinching its heart shut. This is a good quick method but it is unfortunately only practicable for certain species. Some fish are too large to allow one's fingertips to meet inside while others have razor edges to their gill-covers.

At this point two immense spurs of rock extend like roots from the island, anchoring Tiwarik to the sound. Between these mountain ranges there is a deep ravine floored with sand. I now fly slowly along this valley as through the skies of Drune itself, studying its floor from a few feet up. I must be at a hundred and fifty feet now for the air from the compressor somewhere far overhead no longer gushes into my mouth but leaks sluggishly. If for any reason I had to quicken my respiration rate I should have to drag the air into my lungs. If I were alone on the machine this would not happen before a hundred and eighty feet but the compressor is old and cannot cope with the two of us much deeper than this. So I drift slowly through the night skies of Drune trailing my mouldy bubbles when suddenly I spot a pair of eyes in the sand. There are all sorts of eyes down here – crabs' eyes, shrimps' eyes, tiny glitters of sentient ruby – but only rays have them that large and closely set in a lump like a cockpit canopy. Now I can make out the faint edge of its buried body, the long tail with what looks for all the world like an old-fashioned black and white quill fishing-float. This quill is the animal's lure, sticking up from the sand, so unignorable that even knowing what it is one is half tempted to pull it up. I am surprised; I had not known *pagi* lay up for the night as deep as this. It will need a careful shot. I want to kill him outright because he is big, about a metre from wingtip to wingtip, and with that surface area he can displace a powerful amount of water if he struggles. Above all I do not wish to engage with his sting. This is a backward-angled thorn on the dorsal surface of the tail nearer its root than its tip, and for this reason appears poorly sited and unmenacing. This is until one has seen a ray's rubberlike flexibility with which it can lash its entire body back on itself and sting a creature immediately in front of its head. It would therefore be a bad mistake to hold a stingray's head thinking that the sting itself was safely down at the other end.

I draw a careful bead between its eyes and fire. The creature explodes in billows of silt which at once obscure it. The nylon line between my fingers snaps tight, goes suddenly limp. I fear the ray has shaken loose the barb and escaped with a headache but the line tautens as I gain a few feet of altitude and there, arising from the spreading cloud below, is the great grey diamond of my prey, showing flashes of white underside as its wingtips curl like the rim of a galvanised bowler hat. Soon the spastic curling changes to regular waves rippling fore-to-aft as if the messages of its dying brain had been reduced to a basic sine-wave pattern. Much relieved I swim off a few metres to a patch of undisturbed sand and settle the ray on the bottom. I lean my weight on the spear and drive its tip right through the fish. This produces no further effect so keeping one hand on the end of the spear I flatten myself to one side, knife in the other hand, and with a strong slash at arm's length cut through its tail just in front of the sting and slice backwards, carving off the gleaming white thorn which even in this lost wilderness I push point downwards into the sand out of sheer habit.

The only problem with this prize is its weight and resistance in the water but it can't be helped. It is not worth going up yet. I have lost all sense of time. Now and again I think to see torch-flashes like migraine warnings from somewhere ahead, off to one side, even above me. I picture the four of us each hanging at unequal heights in this dense void at the end of a plastic umbilicus while far overhead the two boats keep pace in silence. By now they will have rounded the island and be heading out towards the mainland. Down here at the bottom the sea's arcades extend on all sides, infinite in their possibility. A cuttlefish floats in the water beside me in that hunched posture they adopt in readiness for flight; the head up and the body angled slightly down almost as a horse's head sits on its neck. The large intelligent eyes with their crumpled pupils watch me thoughtfully and it sets up its 'passing cloud' defence, hoping to disconcert me with the shimmers of colour crawling over its skin. I nod to it down there, grateful my companions can't see me failing to shoot a good-sized *bagulan*. All at once I know too well that sound of the spear going through its crisp bony plate like a nail through styrofoam, the sight of the explosion of ink.

I feel as though I can go on for ever down here letting my light play over this prodigious landscape. I am sure that with a bit of practice I would even be able to survive without breathing like those fabled yogis who bury themselves for months. What a difference between lying in a premature grave staring up at a wooden lid and moving in these blissful ranges. The only thing is I am gradually becoming aware of a change in the sea: it is beginning to smell rather, and it takes me a moment or two to identify the smell as being not unlike hot flux. Maybe somebody is soldering down here. Also, somewhere a long way off, my head has begun to ache. It is no problem, though. It is all a matter (I tell myself) of keeping one's head. *If* . . . Now that takes me back to my second school where Rudyard Kipling's poem was framed and hung above the dining hall door. *If you can keep your head* . . . What makes me think of that down here? The weirdest thing. I find myself reflecting further on the whole ethic of that particular school, with its treatment of literature as either morally uplifting or punishment (*Sweet Auburn* . . .) and its dotty militarism. Why, one had only to look at the names of the dormitories. What were they, taken in order from the end of the corridor? Haig, Kitchener, Beatty, rather than Owen, Sassoon, Rosenberg . . . Rosenberg? *Isaac* Rosenberg? You must be joking. What about that first school in Sussex, though, what were its dormitories called? Wellington, Marlborough . . . More dead warriors, the whole playing-fields-of-Eton ethos.

Somewhere my body shoots a two-kilo grouper, by itself worth forty pesos in the market at Malubog tomorrow, while my brain struggles to be fair. No, Wellington and Marlborough were followed by Oundle so they must have been referring to public schools. Collectively they represented a much more realistic aspiration for the baby scholars sleeping in them. Who on earth would want to be Haig? 'If you can keep your head,' though. What a deeply foolish poem by an often good writer and how typical that our headmaster – like many others of his ilk, no doubt – should have thought it worth hanging up to inspire his little grey-shorted troops. My mind jumps to the South Vietnam–Cambodian border in 1971, to the so-called Parrot's Beak and the province of Svay Rieng whose territory Congress had repeatedly been assured no American soldier had ever violated. I am reading the flak-jacket of a black US Marine. Carefully written in large magic-marker lettering it says: *If you can keep your head when all around are losing theirs they probably know something you don't, fuckhead.* How I wish I had known that in 1953.

Is that a shark or a submarine my light picks up? It is neither. I swim through the space where it wasn't. The concussions of my heart reach me through the water. As if from afar on a warm summer night the crowd cheers in the Roman Colosseum, a constant roar, a million mandibles applauding. Thumbs down: throw him to the sharks. Good old shark, the raptor of the deep.

Raptor of the deep? My brain is trying to tell my mind something but my body gets in the way, shooting a sea-snake in the head. Always shooting things, my body. Why? It's silly; you can't eat sea-snakes, any fool knows that. I make a mental note to punish my body for that later but it seems a bit preoccupied at present with the smell of soldering and an ache in its head. 'If you can keep your head', indeed. That's exactly what *not* to do. One should make every effort to lose one's head for good and all and give oneself up to the rapture. Only look at it . . . I shine my torch around. What I see brings the run of tears to my eyes. They trickle down inside my mask and make the sides of my nose itch as I contemplate the sublime otherness of this place: the solemn architecture of Drune softened by the bunches of coloured weeds disposed with consummate artistry at exactly the right points to gladden the spirits. From a million windows wink a million eyes. Motes and beams dance luminously in the streets, hang their fragile violet banners in the air, float diaphanous buntings which glow in the dark and disappear at the flash of a torch like insubstantial green phlegms. I am in it at last, in it and of it, the underlying real. Another quotation floats out from behind a rock in letters of fire, this one by William Burroughs, a writer whose greatness brings further tears to my eyes. 'A psychotic is a guy who has just found out what's going on.' Right. *Right.* Exactly. Only the truly mad understand the underlying real. Perfect wisdom for flak-jackets.

Now the entire picture is becoming brighter. The colours are coming out of their shells, stretching and glowing. De Chirico himself sits on a tussock of concrete moss and designs it all. He is a little bald Italian with half-moon spectacles and something inside wonders whether he really looked like that but it hardly matters because there he is, pulling from his mouth a string of words which glow nacreously like the pearls I can see they are: 'Schopenhauer and Nietzsche were the first to teach the deep significance of the senselessness of life, and to show how this senselessness could be transformed into art.' There is a pause. Then he brings out a final triumphant sentence which glitters and stings the eye: 'The dreadful void they discovered is the very soulless and untroubled beauty of matter.' The truth of this overwhelms me. It cannot be denied. Is not the proof all around me? Soulless and untroubled beauty is here in abundance. Gratefully I offer de Chirico the mouthpiece of my hookah for a puff but it turns out I am myself inside the hookah because the smoke comes out of the end as bubbles, which is wrong. The smoke must be *outside*. Sadly I replace the tube and de Chirico vanishes.

Far off a light beckons.

I swim towards it and the arcades ascend obligingly, taking me with them. I am sure I am no longer swimming though. It is far more like the progress in a dream, an effortless gliding through the black press of fathoms. I realise why this is. In reality water is not solid at all but layered like flaky pastry. Providing one finds one of the horizontal seams between its strata one can shoot through as if expressed between sheets of oiled rubber. More than ever I am sure I could manage down here without breathing but I am doing so well with my effortless gliding I decide to wait for next time before acquiring another new skill. One thing at a time, this is of the essence. Meanwhile my practised hunter's body is spearing and spearing, killing and killing until the catch-line is more like a sheet anchor I am towing, a dead weight which retards even my sliding progress.

A light closes on me. I flash my own at it. A terrifying insect face with huge beetle eyes stares back, mouth parts extruding a bubbling proboscis. Its name is Arman and it reaches out a pale claw to touch my shoulder before making a downward jabbing gesture. I grin at it and water rushes into my mouth. I had forgotten there was water out there. I swallow it and follow Arman the beetle. An eternity scuds by in which my body begins to pass back messages. Out of the incoherent weight of there being *something* I disentangle one or two definites: I am cold, I am immensely tired, my jaw aches, my head aches, the forearm holding the spear gun aches. We are heading down, steadily down and down. As we do so my body is strangely lightening while an oppressive melancholy grows. I am losing something, there is a loss, something recedes. Almost vertically downwards now, deeper and deeper until my head bursts with a roar against the bottom. I wonder what we are doing here but rest for a while in pain. Then a light blazes nearby and, flashing my own in reply, I see Arman the beetle approach with a headache. He reaches out a limb and gently plucks out my own proboscis. This time water does not gush into my mouth but rinses in and out. His voice reaches me. I can hear him perfectly but cannot understand the words.

'Enough,' he is saying. '*Ay*, very cold. Also my head aches.'

As if reminded, his headache leaps across and settles on top of the one already in my own skull. His light splits into many parts, his voice into others. In a sickish lurch the universe rights itself and drains away leaving me in my proper mind but with a raging head lolling in the black water next to a boat. The engine's throb is silent. Intoy is standing up in the prow coiling in Arman's air-hose, Danding in the stern does the same for mine. A tug at my waist reminds me and I unloop it, weakly, put out a hand and clutch at the bamboo outrigger.

'My head aches too,' I say, but with difficulty because my mouth is misshapen, the teeth on one side no longer meeting as they used to and the tongue blundering in so unfamiliar a cavity.

'Maybe the wind carried some exhaust into the compressor. *Monoksyde. Ay*, very bad.' He laughs. 'I think maybe I get a little crazy down there.'

'Me too.' I thought it was nitrogen rather than monoxide which made that happen. 'Christ, my head.' I vomit into the sea, voiding what feels like half a gallon of hot saline over my upper arms and chest as I cling to the rocking wood.

'Do you know what time it is?' Arman is asking. 'Four hours we are down there. Very long.'

'Where are we?'

'Guess where. No? Sabay.'

'*Sabay?*'

'Right. We've crossed right over. Look there.'

A mile away across the strait, so faint and lost in the night as to be all but out of sight, glows the hurricane lamp I left burning back on Tiwarik.

Somehow I heave myself on board. I am still not able to rid myself of a memory which goes on insisting I was heading downwards when I surfaced, that this upper air, this night is in the wrong place, that the entire universe has been stood on its head. *Tiwarik*. We inspect the haul by the light of our now dim torches. My own catch-line says it all. First the three mangled fish, then a dozen weighing about a pound each, the ray, a splendid grouper. Thereafter my catch becomes more and more bizarre.

'You're going to eat this?' Danding indicates the sea-snake.

'Well . . .' The evidence is that my head had indeed been lost down there. The snake is followed by a small sea-cucumber, a selection of insignificant aquarium fish and finally some carefully threaded bunches of weed. The last item is a lump of abraded red coral which has a hole in it large enough to admit the fluke of my spear. Arman and Danding laugh. They have seen such things before.

'Don't worry,' Arman says. 'We should have come up earlier. Never mind, you've got some *huli*. That's a good forty-peso fish you've got there.' He pokes the grouper with a toe. 'Maybe fifty if there's not much else in the market.'

Suddenly I realise what I am crouching over. Lying along the bottom of the boat, intermittently visible between thwarts and decking, is a great grey corpse. A shark.

'Arman?' I cry. 'You didn't . . .?'

But he had. He explains he noticed this five-footer which was obviously interested in his catch and momentarily being presented with the creature's soft gill-slits a mere metre away had fired his spear from behind and slightly downwards into the gill, the only possible point of entry into that tough hide. Immediately the shark had rolled in the water instead of darting away and tearing itself free had spun and wrapped the spear around itself like a wire collar. Evidently its own struggles had driven the point into some vital organ for thereafter it had rapidly become feebler enabling Arman to tow it up. He had continued the dive with my spare spear. It was a truly astonishing feat of strength and nerve; the insides of both forearms were raw as if sandpapered by that thrashing hide. I give my own account of the shark which mutilated my catch and show the evidence. It is almost certainly the same animal. 'We'll soon know,' says Danding. 'When we cut it open we will find the missing halves of your fish.' The other boat with our three companions is long gone. Danding ferries me back to Tiwarik on my insistence: I need to be by myself. On the way Intoy praises me extravagantly for my ray, putting his finger into its mean little slit of a mouth. I think he feels I need consoling in the face of Arman's amazing triumph and for that I am grateful. I bequeath him and Danding my entire catch except for a couple of fish for my own breakfast. I am full of residues: of disorientation, of headache, of being so outrageously bested by Arman. Of course it was competitive, how could it not have been? Left alone I stare sleeplessly up at the thatch and reflect on the underwater journey we have made, on the barricades of reason I crossed. I have no real idea where I am. Endless black water is still flowing around and through me.

In the morning my headache has more or less gone but I am sluggish and subdued as if not merely my body had been flattened beneath the incalculable tonnage separating the place where I sit from the distant village of Sabay. For an entire morning the world seems oddly two-dimensional while somewhere inside there persists that conviction of the world's being inverted. I am sure I was heading downwards when I came up. It takes many hours for this certainty to fade during which time the landscape fattens out again and things gradually take on depth. I am re-oriented.

In the afternoon I walk to the top of the bluff overlooking the beach and sit in the sun like an invalid or the survivor of a bad accident made thoughtful. The island feels warm and reassuring beneath my back but then it turns scornful of my stupidity. Your element is the air, it says, blowing its grasses across my face. Your element is the sun which falls in brilliant crimson on your closed eyelids. You may carry them safely with you beneath the sea as long as you don't surrender them to the compressor. You relied so much on mechanical assistance you lost touch with your proper element and equally lost touch with the sea. Instead of heightened awareness you experienced mere hallucination. You may extend the limits of your landscape to take you beneath the sea but only if you go down unassisted. Lungfuls of air, a hut on an island. That is all. That is enough.

Why bother? I ask the island in return. Why the undergoing of extremes to see a few things a little differently? What need of such harshness?

No answer. The grasses continue to brush my face, the sun to fall on my shut eyes. Far off below the sea crumbles and crumbles away at the shingle.

12

To live alone on a coral-fringed island in the South China Sea might stand for some Europeans as a consummate antithesis to their own lives, almost as a romantic ideal. In fact the notion of a 'paradise island' has long since stopped being an aesthetic judgement and has become instead a tourist industry description, a travel brochure category like 'handicrafts capital' or 'cultural Mecca' or 'popular resort': if that is what enough people call it then that is what it is. Obligatory, then, for a paradise island in these parts are white sand, coconut palms, ice for the drinks, a beach shop selling sun lotion, barbecues and disco music at nightfall.

Tiwarik is not a paradise island. It has only discomfort to offer. Its single white beach is a shifting bank of sharp coral rubble. The drinking water arrives sun-hot from the mainland, tasting of plastic jerrycan and brackish from the well there. The flies are often bad. The shingle bank is used as a restaurant and lavatory by passing fishermen and the remains of their improvised meals provide the island's insect life as well as the hermit crabs with cheer and sustenance. The *cogon* fields are home to two species of snake. Large ragged centipedes are common. Often they can be seen through the slats of the floor making their way across the earth beneath the hut. Sometimes they climb up at night. Once I was woken by one lying across my forehead; it bit me savagely when I brushed it off. I cut that one vengefully in half and in the morning the two halves still preserved a semblance of life. Intoy tells me you have to bury them separately otherwise they will crawl together and join back up again. I tell him this is a simple matter to test but all subsequent observations do nothing to discourage his belief.

It would therefore be a rare person who could incorporate

Tiwarik's painful reality into his dream of alternative living. The ruse which might be employed in Manila of choosing not to see what one looks at would hardly be open to him here, that trick performed by the tourist busloads as they pass. On Tiwarik this person would also be immune to the terminal lassitude of tropical provinces which afflicts so many Westerners, turning them to drink and despondency and indefinitely postponing the writing of soulful letters home. He would on the contrary be filled with a sense of urgency, aware always that he is seeing and doing things just in time.

For occasionally on Tiwarik the detonations of dynamite fishers lose their free-enterprise innocence and acquire menace. I hear them as not merely an assault on a pocket of food but as part of the increasing barrage sustained against the natural world under the often specious guise of feeding the massing mouths of humanity. At such times my aversion to meat seems likely to extend to fish and for a while I hate this whole bloodletting process by which I have come to know and watch the sea. But a camera is no substitute for a hunter's spear: it gets in the way of the eye. Therein lies an irony.

At other times the explosions jar the balance at a deeper level, hinting at threat and unease. They suggest a different kind of encroachment, the very blatancy of their echoes drawing attention to their unlawfulness. One day Arman will look back and be amazed at the freedom he had to go about his daily life with bombs and poison. Sooner or later political control will come. It will come to me, too. The very oddness of my presence and lack of any plausible cover story draws attention to me as effectively as dynamite. In a world besotted by control – and hence phobic about its lack – the days of the stranger who can spend his time alone on an island may be numbered.

Already I can look back and see that many of the things I did in my twenties are virtually impossible today. I once worked a passage from Manaus to Recife aboard a German tramp steamer, the *Hilde Mittmann*, scrubbing down the engine-room walls in exchange for food and a bunk. At night I sat in the forepeak or walked the deck while the pilot, taken on in mid-river one afternoon and conversant with the ever-changing sandbars and shoals of the Amazon, took us close enough into the bank to send showers of seeds and leaves bursting in through portholes and jalousies to lie on the bunks. It was on one of those nights that the ship's wireless officer, a gruff, square lady who shared her cabin with an ape, left her door open for a breath of air and was desolated by the sight of her companion's hairy backside flashing skyward as he clutched at a passing branch and regained his freedom. In Belém I took spells of duty in the hold as Brazilian stevedores unloaded sacks of pepper. Beside me, visibly to hand, was the Captain's revolver (unloaded) as a deterrent to theft. The rich oily smell of hot peppercorns still evokes the pungent memory of those days.

Similarly, I worked a passage from Singapore to Labuan Island and on to Sarawak aboard a freighter. On Labuan I went to the cottage hospital – a cool thatched building with a verandah all round it in whose shade pregnant women chatted as butterflies drifted in and out – to have a deep splinter removed from my foot. The young Malaysian doctor sent to deal with me turned out to have been trained at St Stephen's, Fulham Road at the time when I had been working there and we recognised one another on sight. A few nights later I was standing at the ship's rail staring out past a natural gas burn-off flare in mid-ocean towards the unseen coast of Borneo, tired after a day spent re-stacking sacks of copra in the hold. The world suddenly seemed blissfully full of adventure and possibility, my passage through it an intent drift in the course of which it was entirely to be expected that one would bump into fragments of a previous life in London on tiny tropical islands. By day I leaned over the side during breaks from work and watched the flying fish burst like pheasants, late and at unexpected angles, from under the ship's forefoot and skim away across the aquamarine. It was hypnotic, the blinding white scud of foam sliding across the vision and vanishing astern. Tears of pleasure rose to my eyes. I had found a vocation as wanderer and seafarer.

Nowadays, I think, such casual journeyings have become more difficult. Not only has the world's merchant

navy changed its habits since containerisation but se-
curity and union regulations lay down strict guidelines for
crewing. Throughout this century the wide-open world
which people were once remarkably free to wander if they
had the time and inclination (little money was needed) has
shrunk and shrunk. Air travel has become nearly obligatory: there is often no alternative. The lemming habits of
tourists do, it is true, help define the areas of the world the
rest of us may avoid; but governments and even local
expectations can sometimes make it hard to escape being
treated like a tourist who has merely had the misfortune to
become separated from his party.

I am thankful to have been alive in an age when it was still
just possible to be footloose without having to join either
package tours to Seven Asian Cities or marijuana trails to
Khatmandu. Meanwhile the explosions which lift little
exclamation marks in the straits off Tiwarik remind me of
lawlessness but also of the massing infantry of control
which societies are so anxious to deploy and which on all
sides is poised to rush in and occupy the remaining hinter-
lands. For the special wildness of Tiwarik will be
thoroughly and finally dispersed the day silence falls and it
is designated an official nature reserve or a scuba-diving
resort.

'After-comers cannot guess the beauty been,' Hopkins
wrote of the cutting down of the poplars at Binsey, firmly in
the English literary tradition which associates landscape
with loss. But now from a very un-English landscape and
with the sensation of hearing great sawings, bulldozings
and demolitions borne on the wind from somewhere over
the horizon, I pass on that disheartening thought to my
bereft counterpart in fifty years' time as he contemplates
beds of dead corals beneath a sea as empty of fish as the
summer lanes of England will be of butterflies. It will
always be too late for each generation to see all the previous
generation saw.

Sooner or later I shall have to visit England, see people.

Such trips fill me with mixed pleasure and dread. There is that imperceptibly widening gulf between oneself and family and friends, the crack of black water opening up as between a departing ship and the quay. This is an absurd perspective, of course. Such things are relative, neither the ship nor quay stands still. But with the passing of each lump of time it becomes apparent that we are bound on gently divergent courses. It is a melancholy fact. I am attuned to another climate, other sounds, different smells. In particular I am attuned to a different speed. The last time I was in London I was bemused and stunned by it. I stood on kerbsides unable to remember where I was going, what I was supposed to be doing, who I was. There were too many clothes on my body, my shoes pinched, the air was cold and stank of fumes. After the lively silences of Kansulay and Tiwarik the battering traffic blotted me out. It seemed there was no space left in which to think, in which to move. I must have looked like any hick or bumpkin forlorn in the great metropolis, a city I had once known quite well and even on occasion liked for its quiet backwaters, its libraries and abandoned wharves. Now the sea felt immeasurably far away and it was in any case the wrong sea: freezing green–grey masses of water trawled for great numb cod rather than the basking gulfs, the individual prey stalked like lovers through coralline waters.

In rhetorical moments I say: 'I don't know how on earth people can live in England.' What I actually mean, of course, is that I no longer know of any way in which I could. I have lost the knowledge of how to get by in a predominantly urban society. I am no longer intrigued enough by its arcana, blandished enough by its pleasures, consoled enough by its facilities. Provided the climate is warm I don't mind a leaky roof, washing dishes in the sea, fetching water on my shoulder. They are neither pleasures nor hardships, simply the minimal terms on which one lives in a way one chooses in a landscape of one's choice.

Thirty-five years ago I would look wistfully at the milk-float arriving outside the school kitchens. It had come of its own accord from another world, a world beyond the gates where people were free to do as they wanted. That world was not so much the territory of adults as the location of an unstructured freedom of choice. There, people could get up and leave rooms without asking permission; they could legitimately find themselves in a shop at ten o'clock in the morning; get on a bus, go to the cinema; they weren't forced to say prayers or write letters. Nowadays when I am in England the sense of once again being captive in an institution grows on me. I strain as if to catch the faintest signs of life seven thousand miles away, the light and freedom for which I yearn. I panic. Perhaps I may never escape the uniform shopping malls, the fast-food bars, the sheer civic determination of it all. Some unsuspected law or sudden edict will prevent my leaving so that for the rest of my life I shall have to languish in dullness, overeaten, overmedicated, overinsured, overanxious. As the red buses hiss past in the rain and the double glazing shudders to the harmonics of their engines I ache and ache for the sea, to go back to work deep in the fish-mines. I long for the forest where the *komokons* call and the great bats fly, for lost companions.

One summer day, many years ago in Oxford, I had sat at luncheon with Robert Graves, then Poetry Professor. The great man had dried shaving soap in his right ear and three days' silver stubble. The ordeal of Encaenia was over, his year's duty done. I imagine he itched to shed his borrowed finery and get back to Majorca. He asked me what I wanted to do or be and my reply irritated him.

'But it seems to me you *are* a poet,' he said dismissively, as if certain things might be taken for granted while I ought at least to have come up with a more amusing suggestion. All right for him; I secretly burned with pleasure for a long time. It was the only compliment of my life whose manner of payment made it almost credible.

Years later Arman helps me back on board the *Jhon-Jhon* after three hours' fishing. Our haul is not by any means spectacular, his better than mine but not by much. I scarcely give it a thought, it is a workaday morning's food-gathering. As Intoy starts the engine and heads the boat for Tiwarik to drop me off Arman says, staring at his home village's distant shoreline:

'You know, if you had been born in Sabay you would have been as good as anyone and a lot better than most. But starting when you were, what? Forty . . .?'

He makes my belated change of profession sound a sad error rather than a bizarre affectation. The compliment overwhelms me. I am so pleased I can hardly bear myself. One might remain a poet for life without writing much more than the odd sonnet. But to be a hunter one had to hunt: one had to go down and get food and come back up, time and time again.

'Look at us,' says Arman, meaning the people of Sabay. 'How old am I? Twenty-eight next birthday. And the others? Hardly any of them twenty-five, most twenty, twenty-one. The people here don't usually go on spear fishing much beyond thirty, you notice. It's too hard, it's a young man's business. They go on to dynamite, hook-and-line, nets, fish-traps.'

'I know. I've left it too late.'

'To become the best, of course. You'll never be that. That's why I said you ought to have been born here. Plenty of boys born here, *ay*, they don't want to fish, they're frightened or they don't like the sea so they plant rice and hunt *baboy damu* instead. But the ones who do want to fish are watching and learning for fifteen years.'

There is no catching up, of course. Defensively I say to the scudding water:

'Well, old Inso is still spear fishing and he's fifty-six.'

'Surely. There are several men around here even older than him who still take their *panà* out. And they're good, not just because they're so experienced but like you they've got something which keeps them good even when their wind's going and they've no longer any stomach for tackling the big eels. They love it. That's what makes the difference. Ha, I've watched you so many times. I've seen you go down straight past a *bantol* or a ray hidden in the sand and I wonder if you've gone blind. But I think you just like being down there. I think often you are not so interested in killing fish.'

Arman drops me off on the shingle and heads back home to cook up fertiliser. Even though I have irrevocably mis-spent my life, even though I have wasted my chances of

doing something really well, I climb up to my hut full of
self-pleasure. It is deeply satisfying for love to be found out.

But it is nothing to carry back to England. A passion for
the blue glinting flakes of micro-organisms borne along in
the tropical drift, a passion for insignificant molluscs, for
the colour of a weed, for the single eye in a crevice, is
rendered dumb in London's uproar. It sounds silly, too,
when expressed over a dinner-table sandwiched between
gossip from Academe and scandals in Bohemia. All of a
sudden a love which has sustained me for isolate months is
unconvincing, jejune. If one had wanted to study a fish's eye
one should have been a marine biologist. Had one intended
to talk about the Philippines one ought at least to have read
the right books. Instead I make the mistake of trying to
describe what it is to be a hunter. It is disastrous, the very
word has the wrong sound: Hemingwayesque, fading-
macho, anti-conservationist. Mine is a world away from
such stuff, from trophies, record tarpon and barracuda,
from high-powered boats with 'fighting chairs' bolted to the
deck. But once the images have been set loose they are
beyond recalling. When I crossly demolish the aura of
Caribbean playgrounds I am left with that of native chic or
– far worse – of a pelagic Richard Jefferies. Having
explained myself badly I become ratty, withdrawn. I scowl
from a sofa and sip coffee. I myself begin to wonder whether
I might not just have returned from a choppy passage
through a 'mid-life crisis', a concept which was aired over
dinner.

Yet all the time the sea moves in me. It inhabits me like a
massive angel in this landlocked city. Only, I cannot say it
aloud. As if it were an eccentric belief, an embarrassing
perversion, I hide my secret although not so well it could
never be inferred. There are many things worse than being
thought perverted and one is to be pitied for having no love
of any kind.

Thus the irony of having made an exhilarating discovery
is that one must fall silent on a sofa in a city. The discovery
itself is simple enough but is such an insult to the twentieth
century it does appear perverse: the wish to keep the sun's

time, to listen to the wind. I like to watch day break and night fall although I still have little interest in sunrises or sunsets. But unless I live with an eye, an ear and a nose to that slow, complex cycle I am cut off from a source of intelligence. This being said I readily acknowledge how badly I would fare without work, without writing, without something to counteract the tendency towards rural idiocy. Maybe only mystics can live in caves, eating mist and drinking rain and excreting holy laughter. Others like myself are much too amused by doing things in the sun, brief as it is.

I only wish there were a way of transmitting a message back through time to my former self as he sat whiling away a French lesson in June 1953, although I am not sure what that message would be. How could I reply to the one he sent me, dense child, ignorant of what he was doing and yet getting it right? Disdainfully rejecting his father's demand that he should admire sunsets and views he drew his answer, saying plainly: *There is no such thing as landscape: write your own.* Probably the only message I could send him is: *Keep this exercise book; one day it'll surprise you.* So maybe I have sent it after all and maybe he did receive it. I can't imagine how else I could successfully have kept the book's existence a secret from myself for thirty years unless I was acting on my own instructions.

From its cap of wild forest to its coral roots Tiwarik is entire. But on certain cloudless days it can be that each of its extremities dissolves into blue, its bounds become endless. Instead of remaining a cartographer's outline the island expands like a drop of intense colour let fall on a sheet of wet paper. It is as though I might walk or swim indefinitely without crossing my own track and without ever leaving the place. Its air draws memories out, absolves them, opens wide on all sorts of happy possibilities.

We might not imagine a more re-creational task than drawing our lands, like certain Filipinos wistfully mapping Manila to themselves, as having the largesse of desire and with the spaciousness of the future. Beneath each map are visible the traces of previous sketches, outgrown essays. The re-drawings, imagination itself, are endless. Proto-cities, proto-islands, they accrete upon their predecessors' foundations, become our own patina. Only after an unknown length of time there is no desire left and expectation ceases. Then a new strange wind blows up and like the echoes of clouds on a glassy sea the many outlines tremble and waver, erase themselves, are blown away. The space they leave is filled at once with energy and playfulness.

It is shortly after sunrise. Pallid day is coming on behind marbling clouds. The boat, its paint weathered away, rocks with its nose on the shore, ashy beneath callow flukes of light. Intoy and I are cleaning our night's catch on the coral shingle. He seems disinclined to go home, which given our catch he certainly should: six large blue and green parrotfish, a decent squid and several small octopus, surgeon-fish and much else besides including a *kamansi*. This last is a porcupine fish, one of the *Diodontidae*. It is still alive. Its sad, ugly face is tacked ridiculously onto one side of its inflated football-sized body. At the opposite end a minute tail wiggles as an absurd appendage. Far out on either edge tiny fins whir spasmodically.

As we clean the other fish the *kamansi* lolls impotently on the edge of the violet sea to which it will never return. Its defensive hydraulic system is leaking water slowly through my spear holes but periodically and with pathetic wet pantings it tries to pump itself up to its original iron hardness. It sounds like what it is: a sucking chest wound. Its bulging black expressionless eyes suddenly catch a ray of the strengthening light and I glimpse the shadowed gold of its retinas. I am filled with pity for the creature, with the utmost remorse for what I have done to it. Whatever the respect of the hunter for his prey, whatever access the hunt may give him to a hidden and accurate world, however much he kills only to eat, there are times when he feels the force with which he jars up against that dilemma which everybody alike faces, even if they think their hands are spotlessly clean of blood. It is the same dilemma of which Barry Lopez wrote after the Eskimos he knew had hunted whale and walrus, 'how to live a moral and compassionate existence when one is fully aware of the blood, the horror inherent in all life, when one finds darkness not only in one's own culture but within oneself.' This is not a religious darkness, not the soul's night, nothing as mere as depression. It is the great rage, the value-free savagery every mortal carries within him, even the gentlest and most reflective of men. Denying it is useless: it declares itself obliquely in dreams, in patterns of speech, in unconscious acts. Too studied a gentleness comes to look like ignorance; later it is its own form of aggression.

I kill the *kamansi* with difficulty, needing to lean on my knife to get its point to penetrate the creature's hide and then its skull. Sawing away at its skin eventually releases the water and the whole fish deflates into a flaccid thorny sac with pop-eyes and a toad's mouth. As I do this and as Intoy busily guts and de-scales beside me the sun rises above the horizon and the clouds begin to disperse. The sea changes from a featureless waste into a luminous landscape whose shallow hills are tinged with reds and greens and among whose slopes a small school of dolphins now frolics. Their polished backs rise over and over, dorsal sails flashing in the light as if they were parts of mysterious wheels trundling beneath the surface. The entire scene is of the profoundest tranquillity and sentience, the grazing flock moving calmly off to other pastures far out in what men are pleased to call featureless wastes. For all I know these magnificent animals are following submarine ley-lines as plain and familiar to them as are the paths through water-meadows to any herd of Jerseys.

Intoy glances up at them with interest. '*Lumba*,' he says. '*Masarap 'yon.*' I disagree: they are not in the least delicious. Their dark, oily meat reminds any English war-baby of the whale steaks which used to be sold as a substitute for ordinary meat in the late Forties and early Fifties and which ended up as dogs' meat before being banned altogether. (The exact opposite, in fact, of coley: a fish I still think of as cheap catfood but which has now become a quite expensive human dish.) In any case I won't eat dolphin and regret it when the fishermen of Sabay catch one and redden the sea with its thick mammalian blood.

The place where we have been cleaning the catch now looks like the scene of some mass interrogation: dark smears and splashes and, littering the shingle, great blue and green scales like wrenched-out toenails. From the nearby trees the birds begin their songs. Arcadia.

'Why not take this lot over so it will catch the jeep?' I ask. There must be seven or eight kilos of fish, more than enough to make worthwhile sending it to the market in Malubog.

But he seems strangely reluctant and I suddenly realise I do not understand the pattern of Intoy's life at all. I have been looking at it – as at those of his friends and colleagues – as a simple sequence of economic propositions: *fishing, fish, selling, money, fishing* and so on while attributing to myself rich complexities of motivation. Of the life below his life I know next to nothing. There is no reason to suspect it resembles its surface aspect to the least degree.

'If somebody comes,' he says. It is clear he does not want to go over to Sabay or that he wishes to stay on Tiwarik or both. We pull his *bangka* out of the tide's reach and carry our cleaned haul up to the hut. Some of it we pack with salt, some of it we marinade for drying later, much of it we cook and eat for we are both ravenously hungry. Then Intoy falls asleep on the floor, on his back with his knees drawn up and sagging apart like a baby. I clean our tackle, sharpen a knife, eventually drowse off in the shade of the fish-dryer which is ill advised since within minutes I am covered in ants.

Later that morning another boat arrives so we send back much of our catch for relatives and friends. Intoy is restless like a bored urban teenager wanting diversion. He tells me of his plans to go to Manila, stay with distant cousins and get a job. It is of no significance to him that he is only fourteen.

'I can't stay here all my life. I don't want to be just a fisherman. I want to see things, do things.'

The sadness with which his words fill me is so familiar it leaves me with nothing to say but raise practical objections.

'Who will your companion be?'

His elder brother, of course. He also wants to go.

'What work will you do?'

Oh, anything . . .

What to me is a desperate gangland of pavement vendors, beggars, prostitutes, scullions, grease-monkeys, casual labourers, exploited labour, loiterers in cardboard shacks, endless victims, is to him a fabled city, a whirligig of opportunities. I see him as a dishwasher in a Chinese-run eating house, on his feet sixteen hours a day, paid a pittance, sleeping up under the stifling roof according to a rota system, his hunter's reflexes dulling. I see his body marked with the tattooed letters and devices of the gangs, the eye and hand once so marvellously attuned growing into disharmony, becoming separate.

Could I loan him the fare to Manila? he asks as we walk slowly up through The Field of Crabs. The new *cogon* is shooting from the burnt clumps: the land is predominantly green again, the volcanic soil visible only here and there. In another month or two the remains of the fire, like those of the crabs themselves, will be buried beneath a fresh meadow. I tell him not to be disingenuous. As there is no question of his going alone and equally no possibility of his brother's having the money, he actually needs two fares not one. Well yes, he sort of does. I say it's a lot of money and promise to think about it, which is me being disingenuous: their combined fare will be rather under six pounds, not a sum which needs much deliberating over even in a life as ill run as my own. The truth is, of course, I don't want to lose him. I don't want the break-up of the familiar gang, the loss of mates, the vanishing of companions. Only I am permitted to go away. He is as cheered by my vague reply as if I had pressed the notes into his hand so maybe this has been yet another opportunity for me to mis-read him. Anyone might prefer re-assurance to a loan.

We have walked high up to the far side of the island, squeezing between the clifftop and an edge of the forest where it has run down lopsidedly like ill-applied icing on a little cake. And here I set eyes on a tree as for the first time. I must have seen it before yet I have never noticed it. It is a mature tree of a species I do not recognise with a thick gnarled trunk, growing right on the edge of a precipice which drops sheer two hundred feet to the sea beneath. The water at the bottom is shades of azure, light in the shallows with the clumps of coral as clear as the whorls and crenellations buried in the depths of a paperweight. From this height the other world cannot conceal itself. Drune is there with its mountains and forests, its peasants and predators.

'*Pakoy*,' says Intoy, pointing, all at once the hunter rather than the would-be migrant. The portly fish makes its way slowly across the face of Drune like a stately dirigible and heads for the deep where it grows hazy and disappears.

What is unusual about this tree is that it has a stout branch about twelve feet up forming a precise right-angle to the trunk and running exactly parallel to the cliff edge. The rest of the tree is somewhat haywire and ill defined. It is as if all its design and energy were expressed by the one perfect branch, the remainder having been left to grow as best it could.

Both Intoy and I stare speculatively at the branch. Down below in Drune the peasants lower their mattocks and stare up with open mouths. It is clear what we are going to do.

We go back to the hut where I have some good rope. Intoy finds a hardwood thwart in his *bangka*. He carves notches in it as we walk back up. Once at the tree he climbs gracefully, walks along the branch above that fearful drop, secures two ropes with double knots. The ropes dangle down. I tie on the seat, adjust the height, check it all, lose courage. The swing hangs on the edge of space.

Intoy is consumed with pleasure, utterly distracted. The dream of Manila is in abeyance. Intrepid country boy, he slides down the ropes onto the seat. For someone accustomed to shinning up fifty feet of slippery palm trunk in the rain to fetch down a few pints of *tuba* this is playing. It is all playing. Directly beneath the seat is a surface of flat rock but a yard in front it slopes straight off into the drop. Intoy pushes off. Within a few swings his trajectory takes him out over the chasm, far above the skies of Drune. At last he makes me take my turn. It is stomach-lurching, exhilarating, the highest swing in the world. It is a masterpiece of our joint imagination. The world beneath the world tilts and drifts between my legs. I stare up at the bough instead as I swing, expecting to see a knot unravelling, a rope's end parting from the branch. There is no such thing. The knots stand out black and bunched against the sky but the sky itself wheels crazily and I lose my sense of up and down. I cling to the ropes; the swing slows.

Intoy leaps back on. There on the edge of the world he soars off and comes back with a rush. His hair streams and changes direction at the tops of his arc. His yellow T-shirt flutters, is pressed close to his slender back, flattened across his chest and stomach. He cries like a bird, like an oriole in its swoopings. Flashing brown and gold he stares excitedly into the middle nowhere which comes and goes, comes and goes.

I watch the flying boy.

For a while after Intoy left I had neither heart nor stomach for our swing. News reached me that he and his brother were delivering ice in Caloocan. One empty afternoon I walked The Field of Crabs through whose growing mane a wind ran. Suddenly I was reminded of the South Downs, of grasses bending their sheened blades under a bald sky. I should not really have been surprised to come upon myself, a nine-year-old stooping among the tufts, scowling privately in his search for cartridges. He might straighten up on catching sight of me, the pockets of his shorts lumpy with grenade fins, a smear of mud on one cheek, not a becoming child. Seeing only some boring man in middle age he would move away and return to his hunt while I smile nervously and carry on up towards the crown of the island.

I stand beneath the tree. Somebody in the intervening time has been up and cut down the swing; it was good stout rope. One of the severed knots is still lying trapped in a crevice. Of the seat there is no sign. I am neither surprised nor unsurprised. It seems not to matter very much. I lie on the edge of the cliff with my chin in my fists and gaze out over the middle nowhere which, if I have one, I suppose must be my home.

The huge chasm at my face is full of light. There is nothing which is not suffused with it. It is a downpour from the sky, an upwelling from the sea. Far out on the ocean's surface are the tiny pencil marks of fishing boats. I will know many of the invisible figures who wait there wearing straw hats against the sun, their faces wound with cloths against the glare. Many I will not know; they will be from away up the coast. Others, where a minute tatter of white sail shows among the dancing glitter, are probably from the dim bulks on the horizon, far islands, other worlds. We are connected by water, made inseparable by light.

It is at the last a motionless place on the very edge of motion, where the watcher himself dissolves into the movement and clarity. It is in just such a place Filipino archaeologists have sometimes come upon a single skull in a niche overlooking the sea, resting in a delicate Celadon-ware bowl of pale green cloudy glaze.

And so with his half-relationships in half-lived-in places the footloose citizen of no abiding city wanders and wonders his days away. His life is bereft, satisfactory, privileged. Nothing very much comes of it, but of what might very much have come? It seems like no alternative, but how else could it otherwise have been? The sun burnishes a bamboo hut into a gold pavilion. Its wickers creak. It is a basket slung beneath some radiant balloon where a dreamer might look down and gaze between the slats of its floor at brilliant strips of passing lands. At each dawn it is set down afresh, jarring new blond dust from termite holes, pale cones of powder on its ledges telling of inner depredations. In early afternoon when the sun lifts its blazing foot from the thatch and leans instead its dazzle against the upper walls, brilliances sift down to fall upon the dreamer's face. I do not really know him. He is not the friend. He may wish to kill me with his love of deeps and inchoate things. It is the face of a man beginning to grow old though sometimes he reminds me of a distant child. Once he looked for cellars and now he has

walked a field of freshly baked crabs. He will not live for
ever.

But what is this love of his? Why this romping with the
elements, the frisking with light, the bathing in fire, the
scuffing up of earth? The playing with water? Will he not
tire of it? Might he not weary even of the place beyond
place? I sit outside my hut and watch the massive wrinkles
crawl across the straits as night falls. A dog barks in Sabay;
the moon slides up one side of the sky. It is The Moon: round,
perfect, immemorial. It tells the hunter that tonight his task
will be in vain. It awakes the dreamer to set about the
proper business of dreaming his land.

Like The Moon, Tiwarik is an act of the imagination. It is
not its grasses my feet have trodden nor its little coastline I
have so lovingly followed, and neither does it retain any
trace of me. There is another island locally known as
Tiwarik but it is only an exact facsimile, a fly-spit on the
map of the objective planet which we agree to inhabit. That
particular Tiwarik is indeed pocked by the post-holes of my
hut, the earth slope nearby where I stood and gazed
seawards while cleaning my teeth splotched white as with
the droppings of some exotic bird of passage until the next
rains. On that Tiwarik, also, there is a hanging tree on top of
a cliff with a bough whose bark will be faintly scarred by
ropes, just as there is fresh grassland where recently there
was a fire.

Yet even though it is a facsimile this solid island still has
magical properties. Somehow in its inverting lens it alter-
nately conceals or reveals the other Tiwarik whose image
was seen entire thirty years before and which then disappeared into the shadow-play of the mind, fragmented,
mocking, celestial, naive, to emerge once more as from a
prism at an unexpected angle but miraculously whole.
Whatever weird instrument, whatever bent telescope con-
nects that time with this, I am left amazed. The conviction
I have of the appositeness, of the inevitability that once
having been glimpsed Tiwarik was destined to re-appear is

impossible to reconcile with the arbitrariness of existence. What if I had died in the meantime? It might so easily and unremarkably have happened. *I was waiting for Tiwarik.* The man of bones at the door with his black cowl and unrusting scythe has perhaps already concealed a yawn and nodded equably. This year, next year, some time; it is all the same. Nothing to him the desperate appointments of sublunary lovers.

Experiences of great intensity – an especial dream, a period of concentrated work, a sudden absorption, maybe a love-affair – have in common that they are unusually real while they last. Yet it is precisely this quality which so easily vanishes. Afterwards, how unreal it all suddenly seems! We lost ourselves in that dazzling fugue whose importance to us we do not doubt and yet which now is so imaginary. Time which seemed not measurable, so endless, suddenly lapses back into the diurnal and leaves behind it disquiet and longing for a lost intensity. We observe there is no rapture which will not later seem chimerical, no vision or intellectual fervour which will not come to feel more vaporous than that waking sleep, the dull discourse of ordinary days. It becomes a toss-up as to which is the more delusional, the higher reality or the lower. For everything shares a common insignificance in this vain pursuit, this hapless devoir of taking an accurate stock of how things are before they cease to be.

Yet there does remain a knowledge, like the pleasurable stiffness in muscles after a previous day's unaccustomed exercise, to prove that something occurred. Something did after all take place to tax the muscles of the mind. For an unmeasurable time one went somewhere extraordinary and loved extraordinary things. One has been a traveller; and it is not a traveller's feet which ache.

Glossary

Author's Note

The inclusion of Tagalog and Pilipino words is largely of nouns for which there is no single or simple English equivalent and which would otherwise call for a laborious explanation in mid-paragraph. A good example is the word *yamas*, grated coconut from which two lots of coconut milk (and hence most of the oil) have been squeezed for use in cooking and which is then given to pigs and chickens. A few Tagalog words, *cogon*, for example, occur throughout the text spelled with a 'c'. In Tagalog the letter 'c' does not exist and 'k' is used instead, taking its place in the alphabetical order. However, certain words are often spelled with a 'c' even in the Philippines and since they are commonly recognised by Westerners I leave them in this less authentic version. I have also left a few other words of Spanish origin such as 'barrio' in their original form.

ABAKA: abaca, Manila hemp
AMPALAYÁ: a bitter cucumber (*Momordica balsamina*). Like many other bitter foods (endive, dark chocolate, coffee, grapefruit) it is delicious. In this province it is also called 'marigoso' partly from the Filipino habit of reversing the order of letters and syllables – for the Spanish knew it as 'amargoso' – but no doubt also from some pious confusion
ANISADO: a perfectly acceptable *anise*-flavoured spirit
ANTING-ANTING: amulet, fetish, lucky charm
ANTIPOLO: a quite useful timber tree, *Artocarpus incisa*
BABOY DAMU: wild pig
BAKLÂ: an effeminate man, hence homosexual
BAHALA NA: a nearly untranslatable phrase so frequently

used it has claims to be the national motto. In the present context it expresses something like 'with any luck' or 'trust in fate' or 'it's in the lap of the gods'

BANGKA: a long, narrow boat with outriggers. It is the basic boat design of the archipelago and comes in sizes ranging from single-seater to thirty-metre inter-island craft

BANTAY: a guard or watchman. *'Bantay salakay'* is a favourite adage, meaning 'the guard invades' and embodying the same irony as the rhetorical Latin question *Quis custodiet ipsos custodes?*

BANTOL: the venomous stone-fish, although the word is often used indiscriminately for the other camouflaged members of the same family (*Scorpaenidae*)

BARANGGAY: effectively a village, the smallest administrative unit. Historically the name derives from that of the long-boats in which the Malay settlers arrived in the Philippines. At that time such a boat-load would typically have comprised a headman and his extended family. Even today it is possible to find *baranggays* which are still virtually single-family villages despite the effacing by countless outside marriages of the original family name. The office of *baranggay* captain is elective and carries distinct local status as well as the power to settle disputes and right minor wrongs (*baranggay* justice). It thus represents a great temptation to unscrupulous politicians to 'job in' their own supporters in *baranggay* elections on the grounds that he who controls the *baranggay* captains allegedly controls the country at grass-roots level. President Marcos's KBL party was in effective administrative control of a majority of the country's *baranggays* until his downfall in 1986, so in the event this seems not to have helped him much. In any case the psychological significance of the *baranggay* as a historical and self-sufficient unit persists strongly. The word is often misspelled *'barangay'* even in the Philippines. See also the following entry

BARKADA: deriving from the Spanish word for boat-load or crew, this concept has great significance for Filipinos and its meaning varies according to context. At its most innocuous it can describe one's workmates, one's circle of friends, one's drinking companions, which groups can command intense loyalty. In less savoury circumstances it means gang, from the merely criminal down to the political

BARRIO: see following

BARYO: district or subdivision of a municipality. Generally a larger unit than a *baranggay*

BAYANIHAN: the principle of doing one's bit for a community project. Filipinos often cite this as evidence of a boundlessly altruistic national spirit. Not surprisingly the motives for someone giving his labour free range from neighbourly love to respect for majority public opinion

BAYATI: the fruit of a bush which I have not been able to identify. The fruit is cooked, pounded while still hot and can then be mixed with the meat of hermit crabs to make a poisonous fish-bait

BIBINGKA: sweet, flat, circular cakes of rice flour and coconut, properly leavened with fermenting *tuba* (q.v.) and most improperly with baking powder

BISLAD: sliced, salted and dried fish (syn. *daing*, q.v.)

BOLO: large knife, machete

BONAK: a name used indiscriminately to describe several species of coral-eating parrotfishes (family *Scaridae*)

BUKAYO: a sweetmeat made of grated coconut and sugar. The nearest English equivalent would be coconut ice.

BULAKBOL: truant

CALAMANSI: (see *kalamansî*)

CALESA: (see *kalesa*)

COGON: (see *kugon*)

KALAMANSÎ: a small, acid citrus fruit. It is round and no bigger than a marble

KALESA: a two-wheeled high trap with a roof

KAMOTENG-KAHOY: cassava, manioc

'KANO: *Amerikano*. Virtually any white Westerner

KAWAWA: pitiful. Hence '*ay, kawawa!*' can mean (according to the amount of irony in the speaker's tone) anything from a sympathetic 'Poor sod!' to an entirely unconvincing 'Oh, poor darling!'

KAYURAN: a grater or rasp

KBL: *Kilusang Bagong Lipunan* (New Society Movement). The political organisation created by President Marcos as the main vehicle for his own support

KOMOKON: a species of small dove

KUGON: long coarse grass (*Imperata cylindrica*) much used for thatching

DAING: see *bislad*

DUHAT: the Java plum tree (*Syzygium cumini*) or its fruit. Also known as *lumboy*

ESQ: Extra Smooth Quality. This is the slogan on Tanduay Distillery's rum and has become the name for the drink. See also *lapad*

HULI: catch. It can refer to animals of all variety, including fish, taken with any sort of snare, trap or device. *May huli mo?* addressed to an angler is the equivalent of 'Any luck?'

LAPAD: lit. 'broad'. As a noun it almost invariably refers to the flat 375ml bottles of ESQ which are commonly used as containers/units of measure for kerosene, cooking oil, fish sauce, vinegar, spices and a hundred other things

LAPU-LAPU: generic name for fish of the grouper (*Serranidae*) family

LUMBOY: see *duhat*

MALUNGKOT: there is no single English equivalent for this word since it means both 'sad' and 'lonely'

MANITIS: commonly, the Indian goat-fish but can describe several other members of the *Mullidae*

MERYENDA: an afternoon snack often taken for elevenses as well for good measure

NINONG: a godfather or a sponsor at a wedding, confirmation or baptism

NIPA: leaves of the *nipa* palm (*Nypa fruticans*) used for thatching

NITO: thin, whippy vines whose tough outer layer can be stripped and used for plaiting, binding and decorative handicrafts

NIYUBAK: a heavy, doughlike mush made of pounded

bananas, grated coconut and sugar. Many children appear to like it

NPA: New People's Army

PAKIUSAP: near enough the word for 'please' but used in the present context in its modern idiomatic sense of a favour done for any one of a dozen possible reasons. *Pakiusap* is a rather weaker version of *palakasan*, which is definitely augmenting somebody's personal power or fortune (and which has lately come to mean 'cronyism'). *Pakiusap* is somewhat the equivalent of the Italian *appoggio* and is considered perfectly proper – indeed sometimes a duty – except when the favour sought is unethical but granted for the sake of *pakikisama* or frank nepotism

PANÀ: bow and arrow, hence spear gun

PASALUBONG: a gift expected of anyone arriving after a journey, typically brought by people returning from a stay in Manila or by *balikbayan*, migrants returning from abroad

PETRON: the Philippines' national brand of petrol

PORMA: shuttering

PULUTAN: snacks served with drink

SAHING: the 'white pitch' obtained from the *sahing* tree, otherwise known as the *pili*-nut tree (*Canarium luzonicum*)

SAMARAL: any of several varieties of rabbit-fish (*Siganidae*)

SAMPAGITA: the Philippines' National Flower (*Nyctanthes sambac*)

SARI-SARI: lit. a mixture or variety. *Sari-sari* or general stores are the basic shop of the Philippine provinces

SAYANG: as an adjective it means 'wasted' or 'lost'; as an interjection, 'What a pity!'

SULIRAP: panels of woven palm fronds used for roofing and walling houses. Each frond, split lengthwise down the centre of its midrib, provides two panels. In this province a common variant is '*surilap*'

SUMAN: a delicacy made of slightly sweetened glutinous rice bound about with a leaf into the form of a sausage

SUPERWHEEL: ubiquitous brand of blue detergent soap sold by the flat bar

TALISAY: a large and shady species of tree (*Terminalia catappa*)

TAPAHAN: a dryer or smoker

TUBA: the fermented juice/sap of the palm tree. It is drunk throughout the Philippines and surely qualifies as the National Drink. The juice is retrieved morning and evening. When it is still a few hours old it is generally quite sweet, but fermentation is continuous and the *tuba* gets progressively stronger in alcohol and more acidic. After eight or ten hours it is virtually undrinkable and, left to itself, gradually turns into *suka* or vinegar. Since there is no grape wine in the Philippines *tuba* vinegar is the only variety available although *kalamansî* juice and tamarinds can also be used for sourness in cooking

TUBLI: (root of a) vine which I cannot identify and which, pounded, is used for stunning fish. It is most commonly used for squirting into undersea holes where there are milling shoals of *sumbilang*, the catfish (*Plotosus anguillaris*) which is defended by venomous dorsal and pectoral fin spines

TUKO: the gecko

TUYUAN: a device or a place for drying firewood or fish

YAMAS: the residue after the milk has been rinsed and squeezed out of grated coconut, used for animal feed. True coconut milk, *gata*, is extensively used in Asian cuisine and has nothing whatever to do with the dank water found in the middle of the nut, to which the English refer as 'milk'. No Pinoy (Filipino) would thank you for a glass of this rancid, elderly liquid which comes from the antique nuts with leathery flesh exported to Europe. Such are prime copra nuts, not eaters. They have nothing in common with young 'eating' coconuts, *buko* (hence *bukayo*), with their sweet, clear water and thin skin of slippery milky flesh beginning to form on the inside of the nut like the white hardening in the shell of a gently boiling egg

Notes

1. (p. 10) For a sidelight on the relation between poison and love I cannot resist quoting Francis Huxley's brilliant and playful book about Alice in Wonderland, *The Raven and the Writing Desk*. Speaking of *treacle* as deriving from *theriac*, an antidote against snake poison, he writes:

> For *theriac* only came to mean 'medicine' because it originally meant 'snake-venom', the medicine being nothing less than a homeopathic dose of more snake-venom to cure the original poison. *Venom*, however, comes from the opposite direction, from *venenum*, a love philtre straight from Venus herself; just as *poison* comes from '(love-) potion'. To show the two movements involved we can express this simply as a proportion: Love turns to poison as poison turns to antidote . . .
>
> (pp. 105–6)

Ignoring the wholly illusory etymological similarity between the French words *poison* and *poisson* as a red herring, it is still interesting that I was once told of a cure for an unwanted *tiwarik* spell. This was that within nine days the true lovers should perform an act of copulation so brief it might last only a single stroke, followed by immediate withdrawal. This now seems to make sense for two reasons, the more pragmatic being that if the couple were not already married such an event should under all social convention result in marriage, which would presumably put the jealous spell-caster for ever on the wrong side of the pale of hope. But a further reason would be that it obeys the homeopathic principle, *viz.*, that a small dose of fish can be counteracted by an even smaller (even though the species itself might be larger). Untreated, though, *tiwarik*'s venereal poison becomes incurable after nine days. Why nine, though? This remains a mystery, but one quite easily elucidated if we bear in mind the importance of (ecclesiastical) Latin in Filipino superstitious beliefs and spells. Treated topsy-turvily, as befits anything to do with *tiwarik*, the word *novem* re-arranges itself comfortably as *venom*. It will be objected that Tagalog speakers of Spanish times would not have known the English word 'venom'. This is too pedestrian a quibble to argue about. Instead the objector should go straight on and ponder the significance of nine as the product of the magical three multiplied by itself which appears in all sorts of Tagalog spells and incantations.

2. (p. 89) Independent as people like Sising are they still live within a money economy. Generally speaking, Sising's income in hard cash comes from collecting and selling *tuba*, selling the occasional piglet or chicken he can keep from the clutches of the Widow Soriano, selling his labour for things such as *lokad*, or copra-making.

At the time of writing this (July 1986) the exchange rates, with rare convenience, are more or less US$1 = 20 pesos, £1 = 30 pesos. At these prices, then, his eleven *tuba*-producing palms cost him 17p each per month. Each must be climbed twice daily in all weathers and at all seasons. The amount of *tuba* a tree produces depends on the season as well as on the tree's individual quality: July is a bad time whereas in February yields are higher. Sising is currently earning about 27p a day from his trees, which works out at a clear profit of some £6.25 a month.

Once a month, maybe even twice, he will work on making copra. This is an exhausting process which usually lasts three days, depending on the number and dispersion of the coco-palms. In recent years the price of copra – and hence the rate of pay of Sising's labour, which is directly related – has been falling steadily. This is partly due to a weakening international market for commodities like coconut oil and partly to mismanagement under the Marcos administration of Cocofed, the Coconut Producers' Federation, the net result of which is a situation of near-despair in a thousand places like Kansulay whose income, daily life and even culture centre largely around the coco-palm. The buying price of copra here is now down to around 3p a kilo and scarcely a centavo appears to have been ploughed back into the industry by its monopolistic representative body to induce landowners like the Sorianos to plant new, higher-yielding stock or encourage more efficient production. This is not merely a cause for lament: it is a cause for bitter anger amongst those like Sising who understand perfectly what has happened and who understand also that their three days' backbreaking labour will earn them a total of 84p. A few representative prices will indicate how far this sum will go. In this province a kilo of rice, the staple belly-filler, now costs 19p. The price of fish fluctuates wildly according to season, to whether the market has been flooded by a bumper catch or starved by a typhoon or adverse current. Insofar as there is a 'standard' fish here it is the *tulingan*, a member of the tuna family about the size of a mackerel which is caught practically the year round. In the past month the price of *tulingan* has veered between a low of 10p per kilo to 75p. It at once becomes apparent that for the inland-dwellers or non-fishermen of Kansulay many days are fishless. Eggs, depending on size, sell for about 5p each. A *lapad* of coconut oil costs 12p, one of vegetable cooking oil 14p. A *lapad* of paraffin costs 9p, one of ESQ rum 29p. The cheapest cigarettes are sold in paper rolls of thirty with a charming blurred picture of a Twenties Spanish-style couple on the wrapper. They are called *Magkaibigan* (Friends) and cost 5p. Otherwise cigarettes range upwards to 20p for twenty by which price they are all in the Virginia-tobacco-and-menthol bracket. Above that are American brands made under licence. Here twenty Marlboro cost 25p, twenty Camels 26p.

A thin cake of detergent soap, which is one segment of a three-cake bar ('Ajax', 'Mr Clean', 'Superwheel' etc.) costs 9p. Bini, like most of the other inhabitants of Kansulay, does her washing in the stream. Her cake of soap might be stretched to last a week. A quarter-kilo of brown sugar costs her 5p, white 9p. Finally, a box of matches is 2p but the village shop quite frequently runs out of supplies and it is then one sees people with burning sticks hurrying along, swinging them into curlicues and arabesques of aromatic smoke to keep them alive.

3. (p. 130) Where Malacañang was concerned even Nick Joaquin, writing in August 1968 – i.e. some thirty months after the Marcoses moved in – was oddly unwary in his essay 'Art in the Palace' which described Imelda Marcos's ever-growing collection of *objets*. Those were the early days of the Marcoses when it was perhaps easier to accept Imelda at her own valuation as a humble aesthete and patroness eager to support Filipino artists and preserve the nation's cultural heritage. But it should not have been easier at all, not for a wily old bird like Joaquin, a travelled and sceptical journalist who is quite capable of philippics when on the subject of his own countrymen's failings (as in his essay 'A Heritage of Smallness'). He ought surely to have detected the country-girl made good, the small-town Cleopatra speaking in the voice of the First Lady. His ears heard her homiletic and he evidently believed them:

'As the President said, a government is like building a house. And he told me he would build the structure, I was to take care of the refinements, the trimmings, the details – like curtains, for instance. What kind of people will live in the house? Cultured people, good people. So then the President said: "That is the house I would like to put up."'
The model could well be Malacañang as Mrs Marcos has transformed it – into a treasure-house of art and artifact. When she shows you around it she is sharing with you the rewards of a connoisseur, and that joy of walking in beauty brims over into amused commentary . . .

If this lyrical description of the House Beautiful full of good and cultured people is at variance with the final reality it ought to have surprised nobody, least of all Joaquin who maybe has a little more Carlyle in him than he would care to admit. Inasmuch as the world will ever remember Imelda Marcos it will recall the palace of Malacañang the Filipino crowds filed through eighteen years later: the video pornography, the three thousand pairs of shoes, the crates of scent.

And yet . . . Even as the Filipinos ascribe all their ills to those two decades of Marcos rule the unpalatable suspicion remains that the Marcoses were not alien monsters visited on their people by an uncaring fate but entirely typical of a certain aspect of the national character. Everything that ruthless dyad did and were in their guise as First Couple is to be seen on a smaller scale and scattered throughout their country. The vulgarity, the racketeering, the self-praise, the political chicanery, that special contempt for the law which only lawyers acquire and above all the endless clawing-in of wealth and more wealth: all these are to be glimpsed in microcosm in the courts of certain provincial governors, mayors, landowners, judges, professionals and military men.

The only thing which need be added as a codicil to such an accusation is that nobody writing from the depths of Margaret Thatcher's Britain – from that self-righteous slough of entropy, greed and anti-intellectualism – is in any position to score points about moral mediocrity and national character flaws. He can only observe that like any country, and for reasons of whatever sad permutation of culture and pathology, the Philippines and Britain have both had the governments they deserved. This being said, it of course remains true that it was American interference in their political system which effectively prevented the Filipino people from getting rid of their President earlier.

4. (p. 138) A paragraph in David Joel Steinberg's 1982 book *The Philippines* gives a certain perspective to this sort of event:

Ferdinand Marcos has publicised the *anting-anting* he received from Gregorio Aglipay [the founder of Aglipayanism, the movement which broke with the Church of Rome at the turn of the century]. This talisman is a sliver of magical wood bequeathed across the generations, and it gives the owner supernatural powers. Aglipay, according to the Marcos official biography, inserted it in Marcos's back just before the Bataan campaign in 1942. It protected Marcos, gave him magical powers, and confirmed him as both a man of supernatural power and someone graced in the peasants' spiritual tradition. This link, one that Marcos has been keen to foster, suggests that the magical, local tradition is not so exotic or isolated a phenomenon as is often claimed. If the *anting-anting* is quaint superstition, it is also good politics.

(p. 73)

Mr Steinberg might have added that in the Philippines the credence commonly attached to such magic vastly exceeds that accorded official biographies.

5. (p. 144) It is, of course, the job of tourist brochures to sell the countries they describe to potential customers. They are thus written entirely from the reader's viewpoint. There is a kind of political journalism which, incredibly, tries to sell the *author*. It relies not on an intimate knowledge of a country but on the imagined purity of the literary eye. The argument seems to be that real knowledge hinders the imagination which alone can transmute the base metal of some scrubby, crisis-torn little country into nuggets of writerly gold. When this kind of journalist turns his attention to a country the reader happens to know and love his writing produces anguish and anger, not least among the politically literate and serious natives of that country who actually go through the nasty business of poverty and persecution and dying young so that the writer may bear off his holiday snaps in triumph. In the case of the Philippines such a writer has recently been demolished by Benedict Anderson in his savage and funny essay 'James Fenton's Slideshow'.

6. (p. 154) The incomes of the people of Sabay tend to be somewhat higher than those in Kansulay. This reflects the fact that fishing is more lucrative than copra-making or, indeed, working the land in general. I estimate that in Kansulay 80 per cent of the villagers' work-hours are spent in land-based activities and only 20 per cent either fishing or combing the foreshore at low tide for edible shells, crabs, small octopus etc. In Sabay it is the reverse, 70 per cent of

time being spent in fishing activities and only 30 per cent on the land.

Where ordinary fishing is concerned an average 35 per cent of a man's catch goes to feed his family whether as immediate food or as *daing*. The other 65 per cent he sells at the fluctuating market rate.

A spear-fisherman of Arman's skill with access to a compressor can earn an average of £2.60 each time he goes out, even after deducting a kilo of fish for family consumption. The family which has one or more skilled fishermen among its members can often make as much as £33 a month, depending on the season. Arman is thus a significantly higher earner than Sising, although his outlay is greater. Fishing equipment is generally more complicated, more expensive and demands far more maintenance. In addition there are considerable fuel costs for running both *bangka* and compressor.

Even higher incomes may be achieved by collecting aquarium fish. If a fisherman specialises in this form of *similya* and works at it full-time his earnings may average as much as £45 a month. On the other hand, a family man's annual income of £540 is not, in today's world, riches beyond the dreams of avarice.

7. (p. 199) The commonest proprietary remedies are Cortal (aspirin), Biogesic and Neozep; at Sabay a glass sweet-jar holds these separate from the other pills. Spear-fishermen often have recourse to Sinutabs because of the pressure-induced congestion. Indeed, decongestants in general are much used all over the Philippines since TB and respiratory diseases are so prevalent. I have always assumed this accounted for the great popularity of mentholated cigarettes and sweets, which are everywhere on sale.

I have already alluded to the belief in Sabay that cigarette-smoking can help keep a fisherman warm. Levels of ignorance in health matters are such that few people seem to think smoking is harmful, and this in the face of daily personal evidence of its effects on diving performance and respiratory impairment. I presume the great exertion and expansion of lung capacity – surely the ultimate in aerobics – which this life-style requires tend to counteract the immediate effects of smoking which would be so much more in evidence were the Sabayans more sedentary.

All the same, it is a lowering business to come from the West, where at long last a real awareness of the dangers of tobacco is becoming widespread, to a country where the sway of the tobacco companies is still virtually unchallenged. It is like going back twenty years to start all over again. In the West the international tobacco companies have been more or less forced to acknowledge the scientific evidence of the injurious nature of their product. That they should continue to promote smoking by the most unscrupulous and unregulated advertising and sales gimmicks in the less aware underdeveloped countries of the world where they can still get away with it is, to say the least, unedifying.

8. (p. 199) There are still many societies in the world where fatness is considered desirable to the extent that it is seen as physical evidence of a decent standard of living. It is thus taken to be the polar opposite of the thin-ness of malnourishment. In more sophisticated urban circles of the Philippines slimming and weight control are gradually being accepted as part of the modern aesthetic of good looks and good health. But in the remoter provinces the gauntness of sheer want is still prevalent enough for its opposite to be uncritically welcomed. There the phrase *'mataba na!'* ('you've become fat'), which would send many a Westerner into a downward spiral of mortification, is undoubtedly a compliment.

References

The following are the books and authors I have quoted or to which I have referred.

The epigraphs at the beginning are:

Charles R. C. Sheppard, *A Natural History of the Coral Reef*, Blandford Books, 1983
Barry Lopez, *Arctic Dreams*, Macmillan, 1986
Chiang Yee, *The Silent Traveller*, Country Life Ltd, London, 1937

(p. 3) John Clare, 'Salters Tree'
(p. 44) Paul Fussell, *The Great War and Modern Memory*, Oxford University Press, 1979
(p. 45) Oliver Goldsmith, 'The Deserted Village'
(p. 75) Wilfred Owen, 'Miners'
(p. 93) Michael Herr, *Dispatches*, Pan, 1978, p. 168
(p. 102) Henry Ward Beecher, *Eyes and Ears*, New York, 1862
(p. 129) Nick Joaquin, 'Calle Azcárraga', *Language of the Street*, National Book Store, Manila, 1980, p. 97
(p. 168) Geoffrey Winthrop Young, 'I have not lost the magic of long days', *Collected Poems*, Methuen, 1936
(p. 174) Rachel Carson, *Silent Spring*, 1962
(p. 177) Rainer Maria Rilke, *Sonnets to Orpheus*
(p. 183) 'O time too swift . . .' is from the sixteenth-century lyric 'His golden locks time hath to silver turned' by George Peele. Gerald Finzi set this poem in 'Farewell to Arms'
(p. 185) Cao Xueqin, *The Story of the Stone*, trans. David Hawkes, Penguin Classics, 1978, vol. 1, p. 167
(p. 224) Oliver Lyttelton, *From Peace to War*, p. 152
Max Plowman, *A Subaltern on the Somme*, p. 36

Both the above are quoted in Fussell, *op. cit.*, p. 327

(p. 236) Ray Bradbury, 'Kaleidoscope', *Thrilling Wonder Stories*, © 1949 Standard Magazines

(p. 241) William Burroughs. I cannot trace this exact quotation. Presumably it is my intoxicated version of a more tentative epigram which appears in *Friends – 1970*: 'A paranoid is a man who knows a little of what's going on.'

De Chirico's observations were quoted in Walter Hess, *Dokumente zum Verständnis der modernen Malerei*, Hamburg, 1958, p. 122

(p. 250) Gerard Manley Hopkins, 'Binsey Poplars'

(p. 257) Lopez, *op. cit.*, p. 413

(p. 273) Francis Huxley, *The Raven and the Writing Desk*, Thames & Hudson, 1976, pp. 105–6

(p. 276) Nick Joaquin, 'Art in the Palace', *Doveglion and Other Cameos*, National Book Store, Manila, 1977, p. 11

(p. 277) David Joel Steinberg, *The Philippines*, Westview Press, Colorado, 1982, p. 73

(p. 278) Benedict Anderson, *New Left Review* 158, July/August 1986